WAYS OF SEEING

WAYS OF SEEING. COLLECTION OF MUZEUM SZTUKI IN ŁÓDŹ

READER

CONTENTS

Introduction

INTRODUCTION

In Karol Hiller's article "New Seeing" from 1934, which features in the present volume, the author chides some artists for their reluctance to reflect on their own work:

> Much of what we know on the subject has been worked out by painters throughout the years, but due to their aversion to writing, entire sections of the visual culture of the past remain unavailable to the broader public and unassimilated into mainstream knowledge. With such access, we would have a much clearer picture of a given era, derived from specific properties of shapes, colors, and contours, revealing propensities deeper and more entrenched than the thought processes accompanying the development of specific social views.

Hiller is pointing to the essential link between the choices made by artists, and ideas and transformations in the sociopolitical realm. The call he put out might also seem paradoxical, given that the epoch in which he was working sometimes saw a flourishing of artists' attempts at theory. To apply this reflection to works at the Muzeum Sztuki in Łódź, an indisputable symbol of these undertakings is the influence on a generation of artists exerted by the theory of Katarzyna Kobro and Władysław Strzemiński, as set down in their books *Composing Space/ Calculating Space-Time Rhythms*, and *Theory of Seeing*.

The *Ways of Seeing: Collection of Muzeum Sztuki in Łódź* exhibition focuses on issues tied to visual perception. The artists' works have been grouped into thematic sections that explore seeing as a function of the body and a facet of perception, as well as a sociopolitical construct which affects how we apprehend the world. These aspects of making art are expressed both in the works themselves and the theoretical texts.

The multi-voiced nature of this exhibition is reinforced by the present anthology of texts on perception. This book could be of assistance in visiting the exhibition, offering a look at the broader context of the individual artists' work. It could also be a travel companion while exploring the various sections of the exhibition, whose structure is reflected in the book.

Yet it can also be read quite apart from the Muzeum Sztuki collection and the experience of visiting the exhibition. This anthology then becomes a composition of texts written in a wide variety of poetics, but pointing to methodological choices that were central to the art, becoming, as it were, a cross-section of "auto-theory." The polyphony of artists' voices contained here includes manifestos, poems, and essays, as well as extracts from diaries, letters, and critical texts.

We were also determined to show that the Muzeum Sztuki in Łódź collection is not just an array of objects, but above all, a gathering of individual creative approaches. The Muzeum Sztuki is an institution that has learned a great deal from the artists whose work is gathered in its collection; this relationship has built its identity and path of development for nearly a hundred years. As such, in this latest presentation the key was to create a space where our visitors can hear the artists' voices as well.

Daniel Muzyczuk
Natalia Słaboń

CHAPTER

IT DEPENDS THE POINT VIEW

I

ALL ON OF

Władysław Strzemiński

17

WŁADYSŁAW STRZEMIŃSKI
(1893, MINSK – 1952, ŁÓDŹ)

A painter, art theorist, teacher, and a key figure of the Polish avant-garde. The creator of Unism and the author of the landmark *Theory of Seeing*, in which he developed a concept of historically changing visual perception. In the present text, Strzemiński analyzes the development of "visual content," a concept to describe historical and individual changes in ways of seeing. Tracing various stages in the development of perception, from local colors to the Cubist interpenetration of forms, he arrives at a vision of the abstract picture as a system structuring visual data. Perception emerges as a dynamic, culturally determined function, evolving and analyzable through the picture's form.

Władysław Strzemiński, [untitled], *Forma*, no. 2 (1934) 17–18, in: *Władysław Strzemiński. Pisma*, ed. Zofia Baranowicz (Wrocław–Warsaw–Krakow–Gdańsk: Instytut Sztuki, Polska Akademia Nauk, Zakład Narodowy Imienia Ossolińskich, Wydawnictwo Polskiej Akademii Nauk, 1975), 185–86.

[COMMENTARY ON A PAINTING][1]

The content of our vision, that is to say, the quantity of visual impressions of which we are conscious, does not remain static, but develops throughout the course of known human history. Every individual undergoes this same process in their development from infancy to full adult capacity, halting, for the most part, at one of the stages already known from the history of painting.

A relatively early type of visual content consists in the perception of isolated objects, each rendered in its own local color and demarcated by the impassable boundary of the contour. This type prevailed during the Gothic and Early Renaissance periods, when it had its heyday.

An expansion of the preceding visual content was the observation of the play of shadow upon the curvatures of objects, and the effacement by shadow of the previously rigid contours.

A further step was the realisation that the color of one object influences the color of another; that owing to the mutual influence of colors in nature, there exists a chromatic harmony of nature as a whole (Impressionism, the nineteenth century).

Now, through Cubism, we have come to know that it is not only colors that exert a mutual influence, but shapes as well. As our gaze shifts from one object to another, our retina retains a trace of the preceding object, combining its form with the form of the next. This enables the composition of a picture with a vastly expanded rhythmic scale. Form is no longer a property of isolated units in nature. We see not a series of separate objects, but a vision of the painterly continuity of the world and the mutual influence of every formal element upon all others. In this mutual interpenetration, similar visual elements vanish, and only contrasting features remain, forging a continuity of matter and form.

An abstract painting is the conscious ordering and purification of the compositional methods that arise from the foundation of a given visual content. By virtue of this s y s t e m i c p u r p o s e, it attains a greater clarity and uniformity than is possible in direct contact with the complexity and randomness of nature. To be sure, for those who consider randomness and richness to be synonymous, the abstract painting is an impoverishment of painting, as it fails to offer the mostly unforeseen complication and surprise. Its aim is to organise within a system the data yielded by our visual content.

It is self-evident that each subsequent abstract painting has a justification for its existence only insofar as it presents new findings in relation to the painting that preceded it. An abstract painting, therefore, should be painted only when the artist has something to articulate within it.

This, I believe, justifies the creation not only of abstract paintings, but also—alongside them—of paintings that arise from contact with nature, treating them as a restful or experimental phase.

For the painting reproduced here, the point of departure was nature: a woollen glove, a box of cigarette tubes, and a packet of tobacco lying upon a table in a room. To integrate these objects with the general plane of the picture, I reduced their forms to elements that could be apprehended as flat components: lines, planes of color, and planes of texture (the glove). The mutual interaction between the forms of these objects finds its expression in the effacement of similar elements and the emergence of contrasting ones (for instance, the textural, dissolving patch of the glove beside the almost geometric linearity of the box of cigarette tubes). The more contrasting elements are drawn from nature, the greater the overall formal tension of the painting. Yet what absorbed me most in this painting was the rhythm produced by the impact of the color patches, a rhythm born of their chromatic force.

Translated by Łukasz Mojsak

1 The commentary concerns the painting *Still Life*, 1928, oil, 38 × 46 cm, Muzeum Sztuki in Łódź, inv. no. 224 (currently: MS/SN/M/177). – Ed.

WŁADYSŁAW STRZEMIŃSKI, *Still Life*,
oil on canvas, 38 × 46 cm, 1928

Nancy Holt

25

NANCY HOLT
(1938, WORCESTER – 2014, NEW YORK)

An American visual artist associated with the land art movement, she made experimental films and installations. She is known for her works exploring the relationships between place, light, and perception. She consistently undermined traditional ways of perceiving space, pointing out the link between point of view and surroundings. In her "The Dialectics of Locator with Spotlight and Sunlight" (1972), Holt looks at an installation juxtaposing artificial and natural light, which works as a tool for splitting perception. Describing contrasts—static and changing light, inside and outside, flatness and depth—the artist shows how optical conditions modify the experience of space and seeing.

Nancy Holt, "The Dialectics of Locator with Spotlight and Sunlight," in *Nancy Holt: Sightlines*, ed. Alena J. Williams (Berkeley: University of California Press, 2011), 240.

THE DIALECTICS OF LOCATOR WITH SPOTLIGHT AND SUNLIGHT

1. Artificial Light vs. Natural Light.

2. Stasis vs. Change: The light intensity of the spotlight remains constant while the sunlight grows brighter or dimmer depending on the time of day and the weather, eventually ending in darkness after sunset when only a dark hole in the window and an oval of light on the wall remain.

3. Two-Dimensional Perspective vs. Three-Dimensional Perspective: Looking through the locator one way, vision dead-ends on the wall, the oval of light cast by the spotlight becoming a circle of light. Looking the other way, the window frame bar, which is visually off-center frontally, bisects the circle of vision. The white bricks of the adjacent building seem to lose depth and approach the window bar and the viewer, resulting in a change of depth perception.

4. Indoor vs. Outdoor: Light is pressing against an interior wall, while light floods through a hole open to the outside world. Vision is being directed against the gallery wall and is being led outside the gallery space.

Maria Jarema

29

MARIA JAREMA
(1908, STARY SAMBOR – 1958, KRAKOW)

A sculptor, painter, set designer, and writer, a founding member of the Krakow Group. In her notes on Piet Mondrian, Jarema saw her work as a radical and deeply practical project: the abstract as *pure visuality* was meant not only to structure the picture, but also to give balance to everyday life. Mondrian's layouts of horizontals and verticals, expressing the tension and harmony of oppositions, were a model for a new construct—not aesthetic, but existential. Jarema treats art not as a form of contemplation, but as an experiment changing the conditions of life: the structured composition is meant to reflect and shape the order of the world. In this sense, the abstract is not an escape, it is an emancipation.

Maria Jarema, “Plastyka par Piet Mondrian. Notatki,” in *Maria Jarema, Wymyślić sztukę na nowo*, ed. Agnieszka Dauksza (Gdańsk: słowo/obraz terytoria, 2022), 99–103.

THE PLASTIC ARTS PAR PIET MONDRIAN: NOTES

Unconsciously, every artist has always been governed more by the beauty of line and color and their interplay, than by the subject they represented. With their own media, the artist has always striven to express energy, a richness of vitality. Consciously, they mostly pursued the form of objects. Consciously, they sought to render objects and emotions through natural form and technique.

And yet, subconsciously, they were creating flat planes, intensifying the tension between lines, ennobling the color. Thus, over the centuries, the culture of painting progressed towards a complete distillation of pure form from its particular representation.

Today, art stands liberated from all that has hindered it from being truly plastic. This liberation is of profound significance, for the aim of art has always been to transmit individual expression and to register the general condition of life wherever possible.

Every artistic expression is subject to its own laws, and these correspond to the fundamental law of art and of life: equilibrium. It is these laws that determine the degree to which equilibrium can be realized and the extent to which disequilibrium can be overcome. This becomes evident when one compares the forms of artistic expression of the past with those of today. Both have, using all means, perpetually sought to express equilibrium and have striven to forge a method of general (universal) expression. The drive for equilibrium and the drive for disequilibrium are ceaselessly simultaneous (and contradictory). This very contradiction reveals that culture itself strives towards equilibrium. The evolution of culture is contingent upon our liberation from the oppression of the tragic. In nature, complete liberation from the tragic is impossible. In life, equilibrium will forever remain extremely relative.

Nevertheless, the individual who cultivates a sense of equilibrium within their own dualism (duality) will form, in life as in art, balanced relations of ever-increasing perfection. The social and economic life of our era already demonstrates a striving towards a precise equilibrium. Material life shall not be eternally condemned to the tragic. Neither shall our spiritual life be forever oppressed by the burdens of material existence. Knowledge increasingly secures our physical well-being. As technology develops, the wealth of materials serving human needs constantly expands. Human life, for all its dependence on material (matter), will not remain forever threatened by a (disordered) nature. Equilibrium will be achieved in all purely plastic creation; through an equivalence of relations and of plastic means, humans can construct a new reality. After a centuries-long culture of the defined form, art has established a new type of plastic expression: one found in the pure, lucid realisation of a free and universal rhythm – a rhythm once distorted and hidden within the individual cadence of the defined form. The path to creating a new plastic form across all the arts, this form of free (liberated) rhythm, was prepared by various movements, but above all by Cubism, Futurism, and Dadaism. Art cries out for liberation from the defined form, for such form is an impediment to the articulation (expression) of pure rhythm. Pure art, without in the least ignoring our individual nature or seeking to remove the "human mark" from the work, is the union of the individual element with the universal. The liberated rhythm is composed of these two aspects of life held in equilibrium. From this, it follows that art, creating pure plastic means, must arrive at a precise equilibrium born of absolute contradiction. And thus, the opposition of the vertical and the horizontal becomes equilibrium.

Through abstraction, art has deepened form and color, elevating the curved line to its maximum tension: the straight line. By using the opposition of the right angle, a constant relation of the universal-individual duality has established unity.

The varied proportions of the duality born from the opposition of the straight line establish a rhythm that, while constantly changing through the proportion of its measures, is simultaneously constant through the stability of those proportions. Where the defined form is eliminated, the liberated rhythm is the plastic expression. The defined form is always anecdotal; it is descriptive.

So long as emphasis in the work of art is placed upon this form, the individual expression prevails. It may be argued, of course, that the descriptive element is of little hindrance when the universal expression is sufficiently potent. And indeed, many artworks of our time and of the past seem to support this view. But why use a form that can only diminish the purely plastic expression? In truth, everything depends on the epoch we live in.

The form in artworks of the past does not irk us. Yet in our own time, every manifestation, in life as in plastic expression, reveals a desire for liberation. The defined form thus becomes an impediment. And yet, an unconscious desire for the tragic, much like the sheer weight of tradition, compels the use of such forms. Our material environment/architecture, objects of utility, which can be freed from the expression of traditional forms with greater ease, often demands a more complex plastic expression. A current tendency seeks to reject aesthetic feelings. And yet such feelings are fundamental to all creation because of the liberation they offer from the demands of utility.

A new aesthetic for our material environment, one that so profoundly influences our inner being, can be constructed (built) on the principles of pure plastic arts. In the future, the realization of pure plastic arts in tangible reality will supersede the work of art. But for this to occur, we must orient ourselves towards a universalist conception of life and break free from the pressure of nature. Then we shall no longer need paintings and sculptures, for we will live within an environment of art made real. If we accept true human life to be the ceaseless joy of discovering and creating a concrete equilibrium, then equilibrium itself becomes life's most fundamental element. All abstract forms of life's expression, including science and philosophy, and all the abstract creations of art, can be seen as equivalent means in this pursuit of equilibrium.

Translated by Łukasz Mojsak

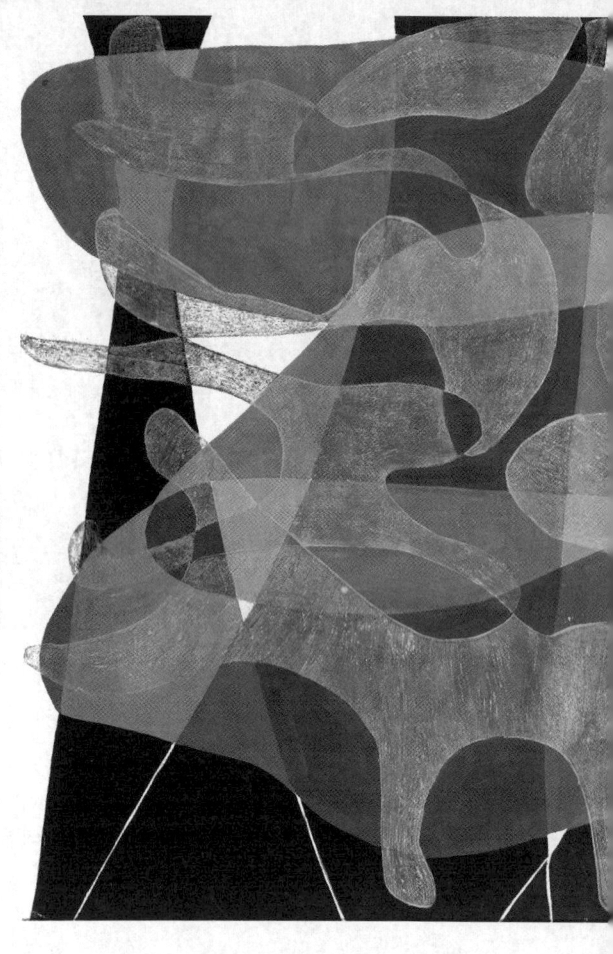

MARIA JAREMA, *Penetrations I*,
tempera on paper on canvas, 75 × 97 cm, 1957

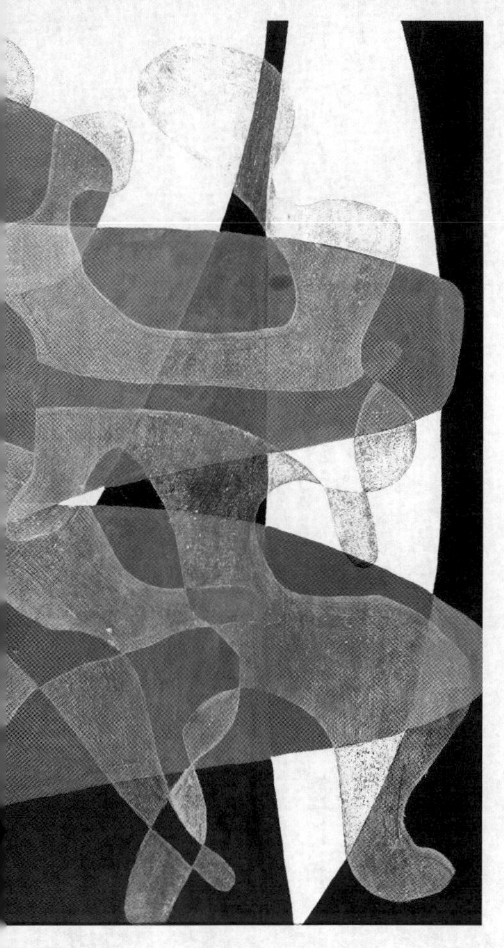

Krzysztof Wodiczko

39

KRZYSZTOF WODICZKO
(B. 1943, WARSAW)

An artist, designer, and theorist, known for his media interventions and work that straddles art, technology, and politics. In his text on the work *Personal Instrument*, Wodiczko describes a device designed at the Experimental Studio of Polish Radio as a tool to modify the experience of the world. The *Personal Instrument*—equipped with directional microphones and headphones—allows the user to selectively "amplify" certain sounds in their surroundings, thus taking active control over the field of perception. Wodiczko treats *Personal Instrument* as a critical apparatus, unmasking the illusion of neutral perception and showing that listening, like seeing, is always an act of choice and elimination.

Krzysztof Wodiczko, *Critical Vehicles: Writings, Projects, Interviews* (Cambridge: The MIT Press, 1999), 141–43.

MARIA MORZUCH:[1] I would like to make a connection between your work from 1969 titled *Personal Instrument* (presently in the collection of Muzeum Sztuki in Łódź) and your recent public projections. Despite the fact that your early "equipment" in its direct physicality (as the body, the photo cells, and sound filters) differed from later public projections which engage the larger socio-political sphere, can one see both projects as an examination of the problem of communication and silence, speaking and being mute?

KRZYSZTOF WODICZKO: Since 1969 all of my works, from the *Personal Instrument* to the present projects, refer to the socio-political sphere. The *Personal Instrument's* silence is haunted by its public voice. Mysterious private play with public sound is its socio-political statement. By its very name, the *Personal Instrumen*t suggests its close association with private rather than public space. The private character of this instrument is made visible, however, only through its use of public space, on which it depends in two ways: first, as an acoustically active environment (it needs the sounds of the city to process), and second, as a socially active environment (it needs passersby who would observe its performance and imagine how it works).

The *Personal Instrument*'s private character (privacy) is thus submerged in the public character (publicity) of this space, and this determines its social character (communality). The *Personal Instrument* is a public-private exaltation of the citizen's freedom. It is an art of private countercensorship.

The street presentation of the *Personal Instrument* in use was an attempt to create a public monument to a private human being in a monumental public space, in "state socialism" of the early 1970s, during the epoch of Gierek's[2] liberal technocratic autocracy (comparable in some ways to Franco's[3] late rule in Spain). It was a metaphoric articulation of the boundaries of freedom and of the ways of practicing it, as well as of the individual Polish citizen's reserves of power in relation to the use of public space.

The *Personal Instrument* was the point of departure for all my public projects; it was my first attempt to metaphorically define the situation of a human being as "citizen" in a totally controlled environment. It was also my first test run for tactics of speaking through public space under conditions of the practical deprivation of speech rights. Operating in space that was completely politicized by the state, I abandoned direct speech and proposed instead a technique of indirect but *public* speaking through half-silence/half-truth; a grotesque exaltation of virtuosity in creative listening. My current works (the public projections, the homeless vehicles, and the immigrant instruments) are a continuing investigation of the strategies of communicating through public space, but this time under the conditions of a nonautocratic yet troubling capitalistic system.

Since the days of the French Revolution, the public space of capitalist democracies has been intended to function as a space of communication (a space for the exercise of communicative rights). The Declaration of the Rights of Man and of the Citizen (France, 1789) assured communicative rights as a fundamental human right. And the active practicing of this right was recognized as the only means of spreading and reinforcing it. Public speech was considered a primary civic responsibility. Democracy and freedom are therefore everyday practices. Rather than something given or guaranteed, as a gift from "good authorities," they should be understood as an obligation to communicate through space, to insert one's original voice, to voice one's own opinion, to share a public discourse.

It is my opinion that art is an alternative act of speech and an important ingredient of the practice of democracy. Active and critical art helps democracy to preserve its life.

Under the conditions of life in existing public space, democracy as the practice of making oneself heard (instead of passively listening to someone else's voice) is possible almost everywhere, including Poland. However, communicating one's own critical voice through the kind of public space that exists today is a truly difficult political, cultural, and aesthetic undertaking. Poland must learn how to do it "from scratch," just as I was forced to learn it after my departure from Poland in 1977. To make the passage from "speaking through silence" (critical listening) to "speaking through voice" (critical speech), despite and often against the presence of great orators who are speaking too much already and who do not intend to stop speaking, is the real task of the artistic speech act. How is one to speak in or through a space jammed with powerful voices? How is one to treat such a crowded space as an instrument of democracy when this instrument is not in our hands and when public space is barricaded and sealed off by the colossal bodies of the great speakers (demagogues), ringing with the choirs of advertisements, and occupied by armies of heroic memorials?

The strategy of public art, as an art that is critical and not official, is the object of my socio-aesthetic investigations and experiments. while public space is both their terrain and their stake. Today, art is one of the voices in the complex discourse of power and freedom taking place within the space of the city. To be silent in such a city would mean to give a sign of agreement and a seal of approval to the disappearance of public space and consequently the disappearance of democracy. Without disturbing voices, such public space would become in the end a private space for the rulers, who would consequently be its owners. It would become a totalitarian work of art, created by real-estate magnates, drug lords, landlords, and city politicians corrupted and coopted by the present-day corporate and industrial action groups.

The public space in Poland would then become a capitalist extension of Stalinism, a stage for a life in the nightmare of "capitalist realism" as the only and official response to the demand for public art. The *Personal Instrument* would once more become the only critical option permitted. And then once more a proletarian revolution, and again a battle for the return of a democratic public space? I would not like this scenario to have to happen again.

1 Maria Morzuch – art historian, curator at the Muzeum Sztuki in Łódź in the years 1979-2020; she co-created the institution and devoted her entire professional career to it. – Ed.

2 Edward Gierek (1913-2001) – Polish politician, First Secretary of the Central Committee of the Polish United Workers' Party in the years 1970-1980. – Ed.

3 Francisco Franco (1892-1975) – Spanish general and military dictator. – Ed.

Józef Robakowski

47

JÓZEF ROBAKOWSKI (B. 1939, POZNAŃ)

A multimedia artist, creator of experimental films, performer, art theorist, and teacher, associated with the Łódź Workshop of the Film Form. He explores the capabilities of mechanical media, especially film and video, in recording, processing, and organizing perception. In his "The Case for 'Pure Film', Once Again" (1971), he posits liberating film from the dominance of plot, words, and semantic logic in favor of experiments with rhythm, perception of light, afterimages, and the structure of the image. He treats the film medium as a tool for intensifying physiological sensations, not illustrating stories. Here the stress falls on the tension between the abstract, physical quality of the image and verbal "literary custom," of which film must radically purge itself if it is to regain its identity.

Józef Robakowski, "Jeszcze raz o 'czysty film'," *Polska*, no. 10 (1971) [Warsaw] and *Robotnik Sztuki*, no. 4 (1972) [Elbląg]

THE CASE FOR "PURE FILM", ONCE AGAIN

I believe that film is the most perfect form of expression. Consequently, I regard all other activities—in the realms of art theory, the visual arts, photography, poetry, psychological tests, and the organisation of events and interventions—as essential supplements for perfecting cinematic vision.

My current work is focused on eliminating from film the elements characteristic of literary expression. I am aware that this strategy restricts my freedom of action, erects artificial barriers, and pushes the medium to the peripheries of genre specificity. However, I believe—or rather, I am convinced—that through various investigations, experiments, and concepts, I will succeed in liberating film from the burden of habits inherited from literature, habits that are uncritically and almost universally accepted by filmmakers and audiences alike. The long-standing marriage of literature and film has led to an obvious impasse, resulting in a manifestation that is excessively illustrative, stripped of any power to act abstractly upon the viewer's imagination. By employing the word as an element of sequential (narrative) storytelling governed by a semantic layer, literature continues to act abstractly on the recipient's imagination through mental representation.

Employing the physically existing photographic image, film acts directly and concretely. Its abstraction is achieved only in the stages of editing, special laboratory processing (all kinds of technical distortions, visual manipulations, etc.), and sound design.

My current work in the Workshop of the Film Form at the Łódź Film School affords me the possibility of conducting practically unlimited trials and experiments to investigate the limits of how my films are perceived by others. My films thus become tests of various kinds, through which I seek to determine to what extent it is currently possible to subvert the habits of perception of a literary kind. In this research, often undertaken as a team, we seek an answer to the question: what laws govern non-literary film? Even while still at the university in Toruń, I attempted to create—using purely abstract film images combined with sound—certain gradations of mood (emotional states) driven primarily by rhythm as a dramaturgical device, as in my films *Swan Lake* and *Suite* (in collaboration with A. Mikołajczyk). Today, my work involves, among other things, objective registration of reality by the film camera (*After Man*, in collaboration with R. Meissner and T. Junak), for I consider the film camera to be the machine that most faithfully records reality.

In another experiment, I deliberately abandon registration—which is, in any case, illusory—to make a film without a camera (*Test*). The film is created solely by rhythmically controlling the emission of the beam of light from a film projector's optical system. Varying the intensity of the white beam induces a physiologically fascinating phenomenon known as the afterimage. In the short film *Market Square* (made in collaboration with T. Junak and R. Meissner), I seek to disrupt real cinematic time by using time-lapse photography to mechanically condense images that capture reality with a degree of objectivity. The day-long recording of the market square was conducted from 7 AM to 4 PM at a rate of two frames every five seconds. For many viewers, the resulting extract from a normal recording process gives the impression of a continuous documentation of the event. In *Collage*, I juxtapose freely arranged film material with radio broadcasts recorded on a magnetic tape that was usually activated at random during each projection. This method produced the effect of a "fluid dramaturgy". The essence of the recently completed *Composition* lies in shattering the melodic continuity of a classical organ piece with a color image (red), resulting in a rhythmic and temporary "suspension" of the melody and a new equilibrium between sound and image.

My recent piece, *Recording*—created during the 1st Cleansing of Art event in Warsaw by making some 200 film portraits of random people—pointed to the fundamental difference between the cinematic and the photographic record. It also became apparent that classical dramaturgy in film can be replaced by the rhythm-controlled variability of recorded phenomena. I undertake all these attempts, both theoretical and practical, with the aim of discovering and understanding the specific characteristics of film, for I believe that—just as it has occurred in music, poetry, ballet, painting, and architecture—this discipline must be "cleansed" of the unnecessary ballast of literature.

Literary thinking characteristic of the nineteenth century distorted the cinematic phenomenon, stripping it of its essential properties from its very inception. This is why I often return to the prehistory of cinema, for it is there that one can still find many paths prematurely abandoned by filmmakers who were unconsciously beholden to literary film.

The achievements to date of "pure cinema" prove that plot and anecdote are now archaic means of cinematic expression, and that, as a consequence, the functions of the actor, the word, editing, image, sound, and color are also changing...

By bringing contemporary knowledge, art theory, and our existing technical achievements and experience into the battle for "pure cinema", we have a great chance of success.

Translated by Łukasz Mojsak

Joanna Rajkowska

53

JOANNA RAJKOWSKA
(B. 1968, BYDGOSZCZ)

A visual artist and creator of performative projects, both in the public and symbolic spaces. “Walls That Look” (2025) is a multifaceted essay on *Rosa’s Passage*, a monumental installation that is a mirror mosaic inspired by a picture of her daughter’s iris. Rajkowska concentrates on the physicality of seeing, speaking of perception as a material, corporeal process limited by disease. The installation works like an eye touched by illness—a camera that captures and also warps the image, taking away the viewer’s control over what they see, making them part of the space of observation.

"I can see you moving your head. I can see, but I can't focus on what I'm seeing. It's like I can see it, but... I can't."
"So it's as if the eye is seeing, but you aren't?"
"Yes."

Conversation with Rosa,[1] 28 June 2025

"I am not interested in images that hold no power over me."

From a conversation with curator Marcin Romeyko, National Museum in Warsaw, 2024

"The relationship of a work to the body—of a work that truly exists, in a real space—is crucial for me. It's difficult to speak of a project and its impact on the public sphere if it doesn't exist, if everyone is merely imagining what such a project might look like....Everything else is of great importance, but not for the life of the city itself, which, in its very substance—evolving, ageing, fluid—remains unchanged."

From a conversation with curator Dorota Grobelna about the unrealized project *Minaret*, Poznań, April 2011

WALLS THAT LOOK

1.
FLEXNER-WINTERSTEINER ROSETTES

Rosa's Passage comprises 800 m2 of mirror mosaic covering the walls of the courtyard annexes of the former Hotel Polski, a nineteenth-century building in Łódź at 3 Piotrkowska Street. Thousands of shards, pieces, and splinters of mirror are arranged into Flexner-Wintersteiner rosettes, the characteristic formation of a retinoblastoma tumour—a cancer of the retina that affects young children. In essence, the seemingly abstract mosaic of *Rosa's Passage* is the surface of a retinoblastoma, magnified many times over. This is not a healthy retina—the light-sensitive membrane at the back of the eye—but its cancerous form, after the eruption of a tumour from the *macula lutea*: the very spot responsible for sharp, precise vision. It is here that we find the greatest density of photoreceptors responsible for distinguishing color and perceiving the finest detail.

2.
THE FESTIVAL OF TREES AND A REACTION TO LIGHT

The story of this project begins in 2012, with the festival of Tu BiShvat (The Festival of Trees). For the occasion, the Jewish Community Center in Warsaw invited me to lead a workshop on my palm tree project, *Greetings from Jerusalem Avenue*, as part of their Bezalel educational programme. We were living in Berlin at the time, and the Warsaw workshop meant undertaking an exhausting journey with our nine-month-old daughter Róża. During the workshop, my daughter developed a high fever. Although its cause was a harmless rotavirus, a paediatrician at the Warsaw Children's Hospital insisted on examining her thoroughly, suspecting a far more serious problem. Our last night in the hospital was dramatic, with Róża covered in a web of tiny cables and sensors, surrounded by monitors. I remember the scene at six o'clock in the morning. An ambulance sliding silently through the still-sleeping, grey city. And us, after a sleepless night, in a state of unbearable anxiety.

The diagnosis, delivered immediately at the Children's Memorial Health Institute in Warsaw: retinoblastoma, a form of cancer that had affected both eyes, already advanced. And in the next breath: chemotherapy, a return to Berlin, and then a move to London. Ahead of us lay three years of cycles of chemotherapy, followed by laser photocoagulation to burn away the tumours and cryotherapy to freeze them at three-week intervals. Every single time, Róża was put under general anaesthetic. That period, from 2012 to 2015, was marked by ceaseless anxiety and intense contemplation of the diseased eye: its system of light-receptive cells and their complex process of healing. How was the chemo affecting the tumours? How was it shrinking them? Would they disappear entirely, or would dead, cancerous tissue be left behind in Róża's eyes? And what of the retina itself, ravaged by tumours and plowed through by surgery? Would it regenerate? And finally, the most important question: would our child be able to see, and if so, how? From the Royal London Hospital, where her treatment was conducted, we would receive RetCam images of the fundi of her eyes. We examined them with a mixture of terror and fascination. Every regression of the cancer was a miracle. We felt boundless joy, knowing that Róża would see. The desperate fight to save even the smallest fragment of healthy retina and the maculae narrowed our contemplation of vision (that is the interaction of light, eye, and brain) to an analysis of the process of light reception. It became a meditation on the retina itself: on its photoreceptors, equipped with cones and rods, with their extraordinary ability to transform light into neural impulses, and to create a primary, diminished, and inverted image upon its surface.

This is what became the essence of *Rosa's Passage*: the retina after a tumour's eruption, still responding to light–torn, but healing; beautiful. Those 800 m2 of mosaic represent three years of a parallel struggle: for the retinas in Róża's eyes and for the creation of a project that tells the story of what was unfolding inside them.

3.
A JOURNEY TO THE INTERIOR OF THE EYE

Rosa's Passage was conceived as a journey to the interior of the eye; an image so absorbing and disorienting to the viewer's optical organ that it renders any integral perception impossible. The viewer was meant to fall victim to their own inability to visually apprehend the work in its entirety. Even when they remain seemingly motionless, the slightest millimeter of bodily movement triggers a cascade of visual changes. The image transmitted, or rather released, by the *Passage* is dynamic, relative, and mutable. From any given viewpoint, it is unrepeatable, atomized, fragmentary, and incomplete. Inducing a sense of the limits of one's own physical perception, as one is blinded by glints of reflected light, concentrated to the point of pain, was a strategy intended to arrest the viewer at the level of the sheer physicality of the visual process. *Rosa's Passage* was thus designed to push the very act of seeing to its own borders, revealing its limitations and impossibilities.

4.
DOMINION OVER THE IMAGE AND COMPLICITY IN THE DISEASE

The walls, covered with the light-sensitive tissue of the mosaic, cause the viewer to become part of a three-dimensional image. The spectrum of its visual impact is

360 degrees. The *Passage* is, quite literally, a passageway; anyone moving through it is "absorbed" by the reactive mosaics and becomes, literally, part of them. They are tracked, deformed, and dematerialized. In effect, *Rosa's Passage* assumes dominion over the viewer.

Crucially, this is an image with no defined borders. Any attempt to confine it within a geometric frame causes it to die. That is why this project resists a single, iconic photographic representation, and proves difficult to capture in any static visual equivalent.

The traditional Western relationship between the viewer and the image—one in which the viewer maintains control, analyzing the image while remaining external to it—is here inverted. Control over the image is seized by the building's wall, covered as it is with a light-sensitive mosaic. It is the mosaic that "creates" and atomizes our own image. The reflections, replicated *ad infinitum* by an effect of convergence, create an illusion of this image's immateriality. One of the most insightful comments I have heard was about the dematerialization of the subject upon entering *Rosa's Passage*, and its rematerialization upon exit.

This inversion of control and consent to surrender power to the image provides the foundation for many of my projects, from *Greetings from Jerusalem Avenue* to *Rhizopolis*. The dematerialization and atomization of the image, however, take this a step further. My dream that the viewer should not remain external to the image is brought here to its ultimate conclusion: the destruction of the subject through its own fragmentation and deformation. It is as if the reactive, light-sensitive mosaic that covers the walls not only seized and deformed the image of the subject, but also shared its very disease of vision. The experience of the *Passage* means complicity in this disease, the result of which is a transformation of the apparatus and, consequently, of the way of seeing.

5.
THE PHYSICALITY OF THE EYE VERSUS THE "CONCEPTUAL EYE"

Rosa's Passage has an affinity with Władysław Strzemiński's afterimages—not as "an attempt to go beyond visibility" (as analysed by Andrzej Turowski[2]), which in my view it is not, but because it stems, much like his solar canvases, from a fascination with the possibilities and the limitations of the human retina.

I do not believe that afterimages of the sun are a "radical utopia of the Modernist vision of light". I would argue, in fact, that they have very little in common with the Modernist faith in infinite human potential. Przyboś, in his introduction to *Theory of Vision*, rightly states that Strzemiński "painted not a view of the sun, but its afterimage". Afterimages are records of physiological processes and the natural limitations of our human vision—an exceptionally honest depiction of the real experience of confronting the limits of physical perception. This is neither the "conceptual eye" nor the "supreme faculty of consciousness". It is not so much an act of being dazzled as it is a moment of fleeting blindness. When we gaze intensely at a source of light, the photosensitive cells (the cones and rods) in the retina become fatigued. This renders them inactive, and we begin to see an image in complementary colors (yellow, for instance, becomes its blue afterimage). It is therefore a kind of lingering mirage that persists after the light stimulus has ceased; in medical terms, a successive contrast.

Strzemiński was a man with disabilities. In World War I, he lost an arm and a leg, as well as his sight in one eye. People living with disabilities are acutely conscious of the limits of their capabilities.

Rosa's Passage deliberately remains within the borders drawn by illness and makes no attempt to transcend the possibilities of an atomized retina. Instead of "reaching the absolute of vision at the cost of transgressing visibility", what we find here is a radical acceptance of the limits of sight, a sharing of the illness, and the entirely new mode of perception that comes with it: seeing through eyes that are regenerating after the destruction of the very area crucial for sharp vision. In place of a "radical utopia of the Modernist vision of light", *Rosa's Passage* takes us on a dystopian journey into an image of light that is fragmentary, deformed, inconsistent, and incomplete. The physicality of the eye and a profound concern for the body with its susceptibility to illness supplant the concept of the absolute of vision and faith in a transgression of corporeal limits. In place of the "conceptual eye", the Passage sees with a real eye, and a diseased one.

And as such, it is an anti-Modernist manifesto.

6.
INCARNATION OF THE PROCESS OF SEEING

In May 1951, when Władysław Strzemiński collapsed in the street in Łódź, Jerzy Nowosielski was already based in the city. A painter, but above all a mystic and theologian, Nowosielski was just beginning what would become a twelve-year adventure in Łódź. Nowosielski proposed an understanding of the image profoundly different from that of Strzemiński. His vision was shaped by the practice of "writing" Orthodox icons, which he had studied in Lviv. Icons are not created within the canon of representation; they do not re-present, they incarnate their painted subject. The intensity of this being is overwhelming. The power that an icon holds over the viewer is also of an entirely different order. If we relinquish analytical control, we become part of the image, part of an eschatological narrative. Nowosielski introduced the practice of incorporating everyday human life into painting. His Łódź landscapes from this period are among the most extraordinary images of the city ever created. In a sense, they are afterimages of streets and buildings, imprinted upon the tissue of Nowosielski's eschatological sensibility.

His thinking about the image gravitated not only towards religious traditions, with their vast legacy of the dispute over the image's ontology, but also—and through the power of his vision—intensified what is, in my opinion, the most fascinating area of Polish art: the zone of mutual influence between the Western tradition of representation and the Eastern tradition of incarnation. This vital, fundamentally important area, so central to our cultural identity, is an interweaving of two modes of the image's existence. How does an image exist as a being, situated on the axis of the dispute over depiction? How does a quasi-religious fear of the image's power transform the canon of representation? Are Strzemiński's afterimages the incarnation of his fleeting blindness, or rather a visual equivalent, a kind of substitute for the "fatigued" spots on his retina? Is *Rosa's Passage* a representation of a fragmented retina, or is it an actual, light-sensitive, architectural tissue?

I believe that the *Passage*—a multiple, elusive, limitless image that assumes dominion over the viewer and operates with a considerable emotional charge (my own critical fear for Róża's eyes and her sight)—is not a representation. It is the incarnation of the process of seeing through diseased eyes—through Róża's eyes. And as an incarnation, it is a translation of the Eastern tradition of imaging the absolute to the level of corporeality and mortality in its most existential dimension: the fear of a mother trying to imagine how her child, afflicted with cancer of the eyes, truly sees.

Translated by Łukasz Mojsak

1 Rosa is the author's daughter. In this text, she is referred to as Róża, the Polish name she was given as a child.

2 I refer here to Andrzej Turowski's text and a passage quoted within it from Julian Przyboś's *Na oko – Strzemiński. Wykłady i seminaria* [By Eye: Strzemiński's Lectures and Seminars]: Strzemiński. Wykłady i seminaria [By Eye: Strzemiński's Lectures and Seminars]:

"It was in Turner's works that the perceptual process of blinding became a subject of study, and with it began a cerebral approach to the sun as a painterly subject. The eye was directly confronted with the sun: it merged with it, forming an inseparable whole. Looking at the sun was blinding, and there was nothing to see in it but seeing itself, and seeing itself is nothing but a series of afterimage-like, blinding illuminations. A spectacle of visibility. The idea of afterimages returned in Strzemiński's work almost a hundred years later. Its best expression was the series of so-called solar paintings, which implemented the radical utopia of the Modernist vision of light. Strzemiński painted the sun. These paintings are like perturbations of colors, like unset explosions, continuing in a mad rush—wrote Julian Przyboś about them in his introduction to Strzemiński's *Theory of Seeing*. He painted not a view of the sun, but its afterimage, rendering the color of the interior of an eye that had looked into the sun. In this way, Przyboś added, he rendered the dream of painters rational. In Strzemiński's paradoxical work, looking into the sun was, as with Turner, a desire to reach the absolute of vision at the cost of transgressing visibility, in the blinding of the eye by light. In this sense, too, Strzemiński revealed himself to be the last heir to Platonic heliocentrism, and equally, to a Modernism that bound the invisible Idea to the supreme authority of consciousness. Of the conceptual eye, gazing into its own effulgence."

CHAPTER

STARS THINGS

II

ABOVE

Suzanne Treister

67

SUZANNE TREISTER
(B. 1958, LONDON)

A British multimedia artist whose work combines speculative art, the history of technology, cybernetics, and mysticism. Since the 1990s, she has been developing her own strategy of "exploring power systems" by creating alternative histories and fictional characters, exploring the fringes of science, occultism, and technology. Her work has complex visual and textual narratives, often in the form of diagrams, prints, web sites, or archives. "Networks in Reverse" (2013) is a dystopian tale that resembles a hypertext, mapping an alternate history of the Internet—from ARPANET to the fall of the Internet and corporate data structures.

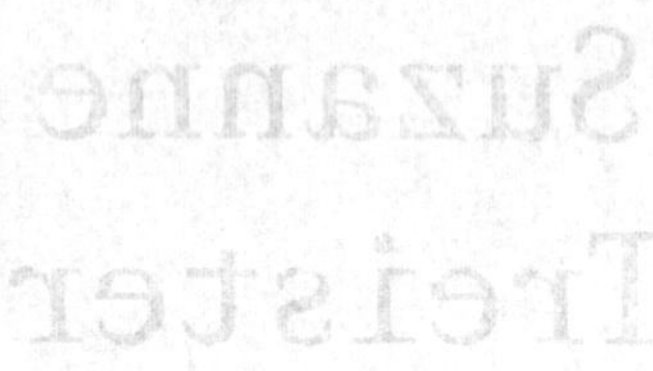

Suzanne Treister, "Networks in Reverse. From the Interplanetary Internet via the ARPANET to the Last Pre-Internet Moment," *Networks*, ed. Lars Bang Larsen (Cambridge, London: The MIT Press, 2014).

NETWORKS IN REVERSE

From the Interplanetary Internet via the ARPANET to the Last Pre-Internet Moment

Vinton G. Cerf, U.S. Internet pioneer, Google's Chief Internet Evangelist and creator of the Interplanetary Internet, was pacing around his lab at the Jet Propulsion Laboratory (JPL) in California. Concerned that the Interplanetary Internet had been incurring large delays and errors in communication due to the increasing distances involved, he scratched at his grey beard as he read the latest bulletin from *The Daily Tech* on the screen of his console.

'NASA Plans Hack-proof "Interplanetary Internet" for Use in Mars, Moon Missions. Architectures should be cost effective, extensible and sustainable in a flat and/or decreasing budget environment' http://www.dailytech.com/NASA+Plans+Hackproof+Interplanetary+Internet+for+Use+in+Mars+Moon+Missions/article30102.htm

Over the following months signal degradation set in across the IPN network and as a result the U.S. Defense Advanced Research Projects Agency (DARPA) held a conference to resolve the issue. The following day they released the news that they were pulling funding from the IPN project.

Subsequently all space probes and satellites which had served as Net gateways, conveying data packets to and from Earth and among themselves were retasked.

Vint Cerf's dream of a collaborative, stable backbone of satellites serving as IPN's nucleus was eradicated.

With funding freed up from interplanetary communications, DARPA now had more than adequate finance for its DARWARS military simulation game training project. In their own words: "Continuous online, mission-level training. Cognitive training systems that include elements of human-tutor interactions and the emotional involvement of computer games coupled with the feedback of Combat Training Center learning. Using the example of commercial, persistent, massive multiplayer online games, the program will link these new training approaches with existing Service and Joint training systems into a self-sustaining architecture, allowing continuous on-demand training anywhere, anytime, for everyone."

DARWARS' primary architecture developer was the military subcontractor Bolt, Beranek and Newman (BBN) Technologies, who had led a wide range of research and development projects including the U.S. military's 'Boomerang' mobile shooter detection system; quantum information processing; 'Natural Communication with Avatars Through Speech and Gesture' technology; and the standardisation effort for Internet security architecture (IPsec).

After several years in operation and many round table discussions DARWARS was decommissioned by the US Government. The decision had no tangible effect on the average person in the street. The territorial network for civilians was still the Intercloud, the interconnected global Cloud of Clouds, an extension of the Internet network of networks, one global interconnected database. Housed in multiple data warehouses across the globe the Intercloud facilitated access to all 'available' data, no matter which Cloud corporation you happened to subscribe to for your data storage, network communications and apps.

Led by a broad coalition of industry practitioners, corporations, associations and other key stakeholders, including the U.S. Department of Defense, eBay, Google, Amazon and assorted telephone companies, security analytics professionals and arms manufacturers, the concept of a Cloud Security Alliance (CSA) was born at the Information Systems Security Association (ISSA) CISO Forum in Las Vegas. The CSA was a non-profit organisation formed to promote the use of best practices for providing security assurance within Cloud Computing, and provide education on the uses of Cloud Computing to help secure all other forms of computing.

When, despite best efforts, secure transmission between individual data warehouses became increasingly problematic, the architectures of the Cloud and the Intercloud were gradually abandoned. For the time being, however, Internet governance bodies remained in place.

Governance that shaped uses of the Internet had been overseen by several, for the most part, U.S.-controlled entities. United Nations World Summits on the Information Society were held where the U.S. Department of Commerce had made it clear that it intended to retain control of the Internet's root servers indefinitely.

The Internet Corporation for Assigned Names and Numbers (ICANN) was a U.S. non-profit corporation founded by Jon Postel in California which controlled and managed the Internet's Infrastructure. Vinton Cerf was chairman of the board of ICANN during the first decade.

The Internet Assigned Numbers Authority (IANA) was the body that oversaw global IP address allocation, autonomous system number allocation, root zone management in the Domain Name System (DNS), media types, and other Internet Protocol-related symbols and numbers. IANA was operated by ICANN. Prior to the establishment of ICANN for this purpose, IANA was administered primarily by Jon Postel at the Information Sciences Institute of the University of Southern California, under a contract USC/ISI had with the United States Department of Defense, until ICANN was created to assume the responsibility under a United States Department of Commerce contract.

The Internet Society (ISOC) was an international, nonprofit organization founded to provide direction in Internet related standards, education, and policy. It stated that its mission was "to assure the open development, evolution and use of the Internet for the benefit of all people throughout the world". Vint Cerf, Bob Kahn and Lyman Chapin released a document, announcing ISOC, which explained the rationale for establishing the Internet Society. ISOC had offices near Washington, DC, USA, and in Geneva, Switzerland. It had a membership base comprising more than 80 organisational and more than 28,000 individual members. Members also formed "chapters" based on either common geographical location or special interests. There were more than 90 chapters around the world.

ISOC conducted a great range of activities under three main categories, namely standards, public policy, and education. Under the standards category, ISOC supported and promoted the work of the standards settings bodies for which it was the organisational home: the Internet Engineering Task Force (IETF), the Internet Architecture Board (IAB), the Internet Engineering Steering Group (IESG), and the Internet Research Task Force (IRTF). ISOC also sought to promote understanding and appreciation of the Internet model of open, transparent processes and consensus-based decision making.

One of the most powerful commercial online players, Google Inc., the American multinational public corporation, was heavily invested in Internet search, cloud computing, and advertising technologies. After many years of successful enterprise, a series of failed lawsuits caused Google to descend slowly into liquidation. One by one Google systematically scaled down its operations, closing its acquisitions, internal sectors and online applications formerly known as Google Earth, Google Chrome, Gmail, Google Street View, Google Books, its video -sharing site YouTube, Google files on worldwide Genetic data, and finally its algorithmic personally targeted advertising services for third party websites. All other online corporations and multinationals eventually followed suit. The satellite which had provided Google with high-resolution imagery for Google Earth was returned to Vandenberg Air Force Base on the same day as Google deleted the entire known Web from its database. The company's unofficial slogan, coined by Google engineer Paul Buchheit, "Don't be evil" was relegated to history books, chipped mugs and T shirts.

As a consequence of this cyber cataclysm, all corporate owned social and professional networking sites, e.g. Facebook, Bebo, Twitter, MySpace, LinkedIn, Nexopia, Bebo, Hyves, StudiVZ, iWiW, Tuenti, Tagged, XING, Badoo, Skyrock, Orkut and Hi5, Friendster, Mixi, Multiply, Wretch, Cyworld, simultaneously shut down and millions of gigabytes of user data became dead code in abandoned data warehouses.

The Googleplex site at Mountain View, California slowly fell into disrepair, developing the look of an ex-world's fair ground and inevitably becoming a tourist attraction which was soon served by a retro-hippy bus tour company from San Francisco. Nearby the National Science Foundation (NSF), together with DARPA and NASA, were winding up the Digital Library Initiative, refusing a grant application to Stanford University, with the result that two graduate students, Larry Page and Sergey Brin abandoned developing a search engine using the links between Web pages as a ranking method.

Due to closure of all web-based economies and loss of a cooperative backdoor entry for Governments and the CIA, the U.S. National Security Agency's PRISM, TIA and other such data surveillance projects were abandoned, the U.S. Cyber Command program was decommissioned and funds were no longer available for the numerous Internet governance bodies.

What had become known as Net War or Info War and its associated terrorist and anonymous networks, networked revolution, the activities of civil society activists and hacktivists gradually ceased to function. Likewise, swarming attacks, info leaking, attacks on financial, transport, power and food supply systems, spying on and subversion of industrial systems, awareness raising, evasion of government censors and monitors, collective action organising and decentralised network structures began to dwindle to a halt in the digital realm.

Online grassroots networks disappeared one after the other. Nettime, a discussion mailing list for networked cultures, politics and tactics, was abolished by Geert Lovink; The WELL was abandoned by Stewart Brand and Larry Brilliant, and the so called 'new media' festivals and conferences which had sought, encouraged and represented the engagement of artists, writers and theorists in new technologies and the politics of the Net, became redundant. Evangelical Net communities living in disparate and often marginalised parts of the globe, who had come together through listservs and euphoric fantasies for the potential of an Internet-based global change for the better, for empowerment and border free communication for the politically disenfranchised and the war torn, became disillusioned.

Pretty soon Vint Cerf closed down the Internet Society, and the US National Science Foundation closed the Internet to commercial use. Months later the text-based virtual space 'Lambdamoo' finally went offline and The Advanced Research Projects Agency Network (ARPANET), a U.S. Department of Defense funded project which had pioneered the early Internet, resumed its operations.

At CERN in Geneva Tim Berners Lee disabled communications between all HTTP clients and servers via the Internet and dismantled the World Wide Web.

At around the same time Jon Postel, Paul Mockapetris and Craig Partridge redesigned the Domain Name System (DNS), removing all domain names ending in .edu .gov .com .mil .org .net and .int.

The DCA combined MILNET with ARPANET where at the time there were 68 nodes on ARPANET, and 45 on MILNET, the military network and Vint Cerf replaced Barry Leiner at DARPA managing the Internet.

Leonard Kleinrock held the key mathematical background to packet switching and an ARPANET network was re-established between Kleinrock's lab at UCLA and Douglas Engelbart's lab at SRI and the initial 4-node network was reconnected with UC Santa Barbara and the University of Utah.

Vinton G. Cerf went on to work in Kleinrock's data packet networking group at UCLA that connected the first 2 nodes of ARPANET, then went back to work at IBM before returning to Stanford.

Robert Elliot Kahn, who had invented Transmission Control Protocol (TCP) and Internet Protocol (IP) with Vint Cerf and written, 'Host to IMP Spec. 1822' at BBN which detailed the interface between ARPANET host computers and the Interface Message Processors, returned via MIT to his position at the American Telephone and Telegraph Company, AT&T.

Lawrence Roberts, the first Information Processing Technologies Office (IPTO) chief scientist, began design of ARPANET, upon becoming Director of IPTO.

Robert W. Taylor who had conceived of and directed funding for ARPANET and who with J. C. R. Licklider had written, 'The Computer as a Communication Device', the paper which led to the creation of ARPANET, returned from his new role as Director of IPTO at ARPA to work for NASA. Taylor decided to leave ARPA after congress pushed for it to focus its work towards advancing military missions during the Vietnam War, because his mission was for the technology to be available to all.

Ivan Sutherland took over as head of IPTO at ARPA and was shortly replaced by J. C. R. Licklider. Licklider, known for his work in Artificial Intelligence and cybernetics, dissuaded Sutherland, Taylor and Roberts from developing the Internet.

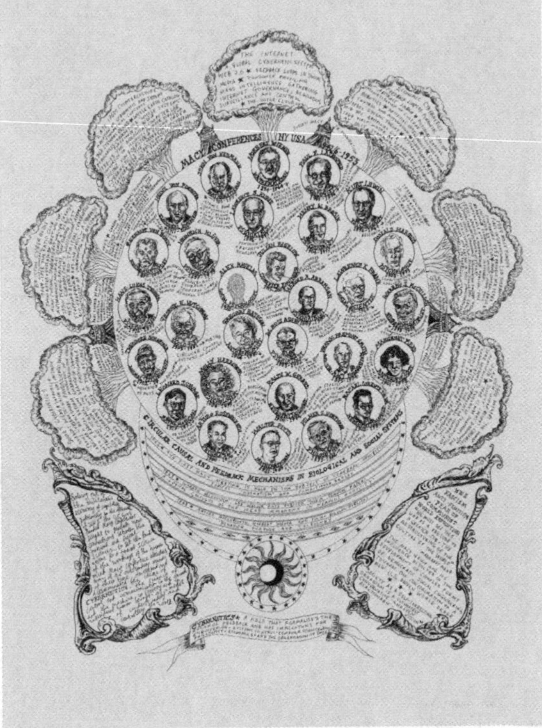

SUZANNE TREISTER, *HEXEN 2.0/Diagrams/From National Socialism via Cybernetics and the Macy Conferences to Neototalitarianism*, paper, 42 × 29.7 cm, 2009–2011

Liam Gillick

LIAM GILLICK
(B. 1964, AYLESBURY)

A British artist, essayist, and theorist, associated with "relational aesthetics" and the critical analysis of cultural institutions. His practice combines text, architecture, printmaking, and spatial design, treating art as a tool for producing knowledge and designing alternate social structures. In an essay from 2011, Gillick analyzes the paradoxes of abstract art as a process—an attempt to grasp what is, by definition, ephemeral. The abstract does not lead to an ideal form, but to a series of "substitute objects" which are traces of failures and tools of critical reflection. Abstract art becomes an epistemological space: it produces knowledge of contemporary processes of concretization, both in aesthetics and in economics.

Liam Gillick, "Abstract," On Curating 2011, no. 20, https://www.on-curating.org/issue-20-reader/abstract.html [accessed: 20.08.2025].

ABSTRACT

By making the abstract concrete, art no longer retains any abstract quality, it merely announces a constant striving for a state of abstraction and in turn produces more abstraction to pursue. It is this failure of the abstract that lures and hypnotises—forcing itself onto artists and demanding repeated attention. The abstract draws artists towards itself as a semi-autonomous zone just out of reach. It produces the illusion of a series of havens and places that might reduce the contingent everyday to a sequence of distant inconveniences. It is the concretisation of the abstract into a series of failed forms that lures the artist into repeated attempts to "create" the abstract—fully aware that this very act produces things that are the representation of impossibilities. In the current context this means that the abstract is a realm of denial and deferment—a continual reminder to various publics that varied acts of art have taken place and the authors were probably artists.

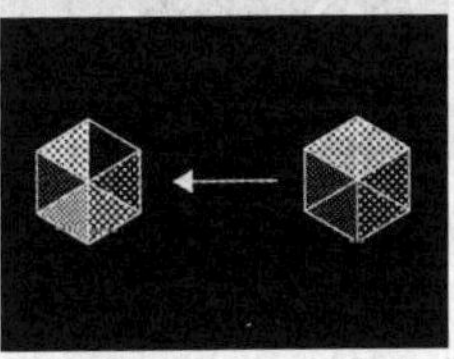

The creation of an art of the abstract is a tautology. It cannot be verified independently. We have to accept that the concretisation of the abstract is a record of itself. It points towards something that cannot be turned into an object. But there—in front of us—is this non-existence. Even further, this non-existence in concrete form can take up a lot of space, supposedly pure colour and variegated form. The grander the failed representation of the abstract becomes the more striking the presence of failure—at the heart of which is a very human attempt to capture an unobtainable state of things and relationships to the unknowable. The abstract in art is a process of destruction—taking that which cannot be represented and forcing it into an incomplete set of objects and images which exist as a parallel lexicon that form a shattered mirror to that which cannot be represented. There is nothing abstract about art that is the result of this destructive desire to create an abstraction. It is a process of bringing down to earth that which continues to remain elusive. It is this search that connects the desire to create abstraction with utopias and is at the heart of its neo-romantic ideology. It is the basis of the symbolic politics of abstraction and its parallel course as marker of hope and ultimate failure. It is the process of attempting to reproduce the abstract that causes the truly abstract to retain its place just out of reach.

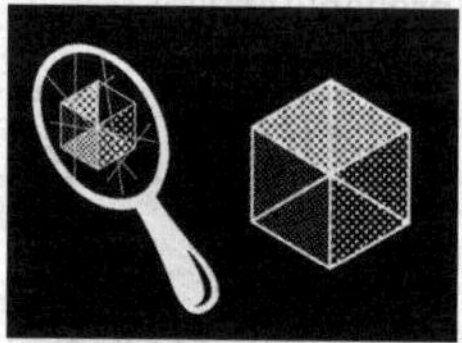

The abstract therefore—in the current aesthetic regime—always finds form as a relational backdrop to other activities, terrains and interactions. By destroying the abstract via making it concrete, the ambient and the temporary are heightened and become an enduring associative abstraction that replaces the lack in the artwork. The abstraction that is produced by abstract art is not a reflection of the abstraction at the start of the process. The making of a concrete structure produces further abstraction—the art object in this case is merely a marker or waypoint towards new abstraction. Tackling the job of producing something concrete through a process of abstraction neither reproduces abstraction nor does it provide us with anything truly autonomous. It produces a lack and points towards further potentially endless processes of abstraction. It is this potential endlessness—that remains productive while reproducing itself—that is the key to the lure of abstract art. The procedure of producing abstract art does not fill the world with lots of abstraction—despite appearances to the contrary—instead it populates the space of art with an excess of pointers that in turn direct attention towards previously unaccounted for abstractions. This is at the heart of the lure of the abstract—this explains why artists keep returning to the elusive zone. Abstraction is not the contrary of representation—a recognition of which is the key to understanding the complete failure of Gerhard Richter's[1] work for example—rather abstraction in art is the contrary of the abstract in the same way that representation is the contrary of the real.

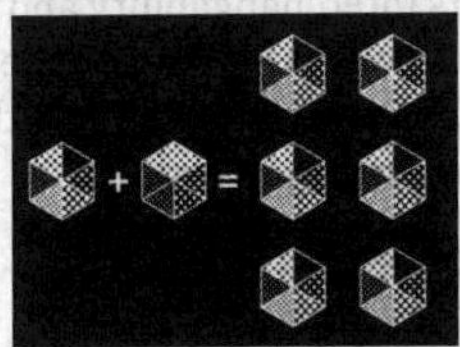

Concrete structure in this case also lacks. It does not hold a functional role within the culture beyond its failure to be an abstraction. The concrete structure becomes a marker that signifies art and points to all other art as structures that contain excessive subjectivities. Abstraction in this case has little to do with minimalism or formalism. Yet it can easily become either of these things with just a slight tweak in any direction. The intention to create a minimal or reductive gesture, object or environment requires a suppression of abstraction towards the deployment of materials that may or may not be in balance or sync with their objectness. This is not the same as the creation of an abstract artwork. The desire to develop a minimalist practice is a denial of the abstract and an attempt to concretise the concrete. Through this process there is the demonstration of a desire to ignore and go past the failure of abstraction. It is through minimalistic gestures that artists attempted to cut out abstraction's failure of transformation and invited us instead to focus on what we imagine is a material fact or set of facts about a material within a given context. The emergence of an identifiable minimalist practice more than forty years ago, while attempting to avoid the problem of abstraction, failed to truly trouble the problem of abstraction. Minimalism highlighted evasion. The minimal created a series of half-facts all of which continued to allude to the abstract of art. This explains the spiritualisation of the minimal in the contemporary context, its interchangability and absorption into the aesthetic of the wellness centre and the kitchen and the association of truth to materials with truthy relationships to cosmic, pick-and-mix spirituality.

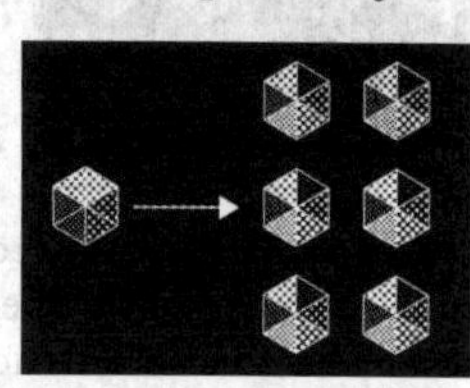

The failure at the heart of the abstract is its enduring critical potential. The demonstration of the concrete brings down metaphors, allusions and other tools that can be deployed for multiple ends to a set of knowable facts. Any attempt to represent through art will always deploy a degree of artifice—this is not a moral judgment, just a state of things. The failed abstract reproduces itself. It does not point to anything other than its own concrete form. Its concrete presence replaces the attempt to pin down the abstract and becomes a replacement object that only represents the potential of the abstract. This process of looking at replacement objects is one of the most provocative aspects of some art in the twentieth century. The presence of replacement objects as key markers within the trajectory of twentieth century modernism is what provokes confused and sublime responses. It is not the forms themselves that have this essential quality. The search for ever more "true" abstraction merely created and continues to create more replacement objects that scatter the globe as reminders of the failure of the concrete in relation to the abstract. This replacement function explains why the concrete in relation to the abstract is so vulnerable to being deployed for ends other than the progressive and neo-transcendental. The earlier concretisation of the abstraction of corporate identity via the creation of logos and smooth minimal spaces can be viewed in parallel to the failure of the abstract in the late modern period—particularly in the US.

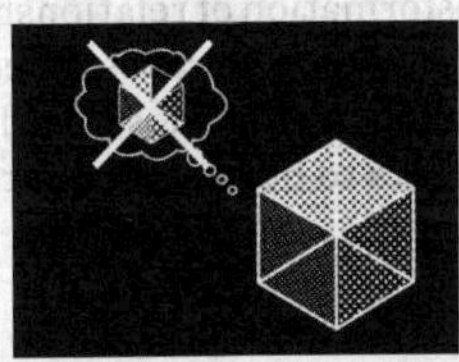

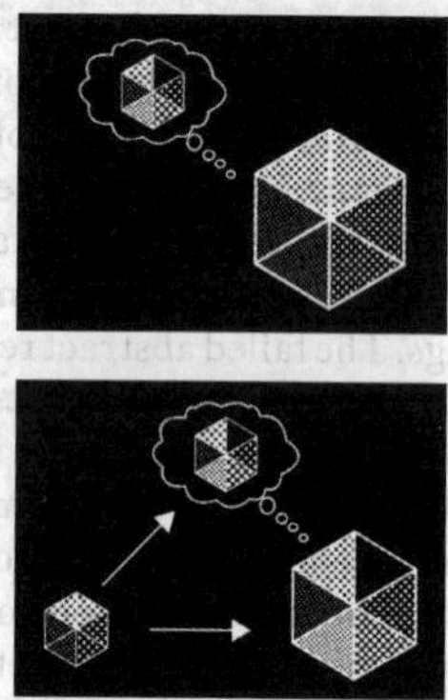

So the endurance of abstraction is rooted in this desire to keep showing the impossibility and elusiveness of the abstract. At the same time it reveals the processes of manipulation that take place within unaccountable realms of capital—the continual attempt to concretise abstract relationships and therefore render them into a parallel form that can be more easily exchanged. Where in the past the concrete was created from the abstract of the corporate now these processes of concretisation have moved into every realm of the "personal". The abstract art produced alongside such a period is a necessity. Forming a sequence of test sites to verify and enable us to remain vigilant about the processes of concretisation that take place around us in the service of capital. The transformation of relationships into objects via a mature sensitivity to a process of concretisation is tested and tracked when the most vivid current artists deploy what appears to be abstract but is in fact a conscious deployment of evasive markers.

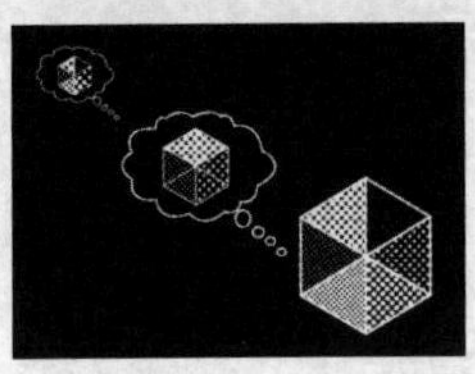

1 Gerhard Richter (1932) – German artist, painter. – Ed.

Jankel Adler

91

JANKEL ADLER
(1895, TUSZYN – 1949, ALDBOURNE)

A painter, printmaker, and teacher of Jewish descent, involved with Łódź's Jung Idysz group and the German avant-garde of the 1920s and '30s. In the 1930s, he collaborated with Paul Klee in Düsseldorf, sharing a studio with him, but also a passion for formal experiments and the spiritual dimension of art. Adler pays tribute to Klee as an artist who treated the creative process as an examination of reality. He began each piece by contemplating the material: the texture of the canvas, its weave, thickness, transparency. He learned the "language of dead material," allowing him to speak through the picture. As Adler writes, Klee's pictures "stretch onto the other side of the canvas" and teach the viewer to look not just with their eyes, but with their entire body.

Jankel Adler, "Memories of Paul Klee," *Horizon: A Review of Literature and Art*, no. 34 (1942): 264–67.

MEMORIES OF PAUL KLEE
(Born December 1879, died 29th June 1940)

In the year 1931 Klee and I were often together. We had studios on the same floor in the old academy at Dusseldorf. We agreed about a certain knock on his door, one rap with the single knuckle and one flat-hand blow. Too many visitors disturbed him. For years he had been interested in my technical experiments. He himself took days to prepare small canvases. Later he glued them to pieces of plywood or cardboard in the same way as the old painters of Sienna. The picture began with the start of the preparation of the canvas and finished with the completion of the frame. So that it is not "of art" but a complete object, an object which makes you richer.

He used to gaze for a long time at his prepared canvas before he began the drawing. The canvas resembled an old piece of Coptic cloth. The warp and the woof acquired an importance of design which the weaver had never imagined. The canvas being thicker or more open in its weaving was of essential significance to his life. It became of great importance to his aims. To the weaver it was dead. Klee would listen to the speaking of his dead thing. He was able to catch a new language with his eyes in this way. Many years after its weaving the canvas was brought alive.

I have never seen a man who had such creative quiet. It radiated from him as from the sun. His face was that of a man who knows about day and night, sky and sea and air. He did not speak about these things. He had no tongue to tell of them. Our language is too little to say these things. And so he had to find a sign, a colour, or a form.

Klee's studio was a spacious room, Spartan and simple. But I do not say empty. Often, when I went in, I did not say "Good morning," and I was greeted by the smell of cooking celery. He was making soup on a spirit stove. One whole wall was a window. From the window you could see the Academy gardens. There was a gnarled and dusty criss-cross of branches, of crippled grey boughs which took away the view from the outside. Between the branches there were little spaces through which we could see the elevated street going up to the Rhine bridge towards Obercassel. On the other side straight across the street could be seen a little hill which the people called Napoleonsberg. There were strange trees taken from foreign countries which had grown up and closed the horizon.

I have often seen Klee's window from the street, with his pale oval face, like a large egg, and his open eyes pressed to the window-pane. From the street he looked like a spirit. Perhaps he was trying to decipher the language of the branches across his windows.

Much sculpture and drawings of the Aztecs has disappeared, destroyed by the Spanish Jesuits; on Easter Island there are knots on strings made in a language; these great figures have about them a timeless atmosphere. That is a beginning. Sometimes I think that Klee in his pictures comes near an unravelling, an explanation of such things. For Klee's voice has not so much to do with the service of island faiths or with visions guided by the climate of those places. His concern is more with the human soul. It is more real for him to be near the first word, the element of making known. And to be the after-word of the people who follow in the future.

Klee, when beginning a picture, had the excitement of a Columbus moving to the discovery of a new continent. He had a frightened presentiment, just a vague sense of the right course. But when the picture was fixed and still he saw that he had come the true way, he was happy. Klee, too, set out to discover a new land.

In his Munich days, at the end of summer, Klee used to sit in the late afternoon in his studio with the graphic artist Kubin.[1] In the window the sky was a soft violet. On a table near the window there was a pot with water, which Klee used for his watercolours. He watched the water's reflection of the sky in the pot. To do this he lay on the table, which began to shudder under his nervous weight. Kubin was watching Klee the whole time. After a while he came over near to him. He put his arms round him. Klee said, "I am not very comfortable—I am not like this—I have nothing to do with this." Kubin leaned over with his mouth to Klee's ear, and whispered very tenderly, "swindler." "Today I laugh about it," said Klee, "but that day I did not laugh." For me this resembles the revolt of the sailors on Columbus's voyage of discovery.

Klee has the courage to walk this clean-swept platform of the twentieth century and not to continue in the shades of Renaissance standards. He did not try to make a new shadow. He made a survey of this place for others who will come.

Now is the time for statement, to make that which is not a slave to optical comparison, which is no more a fragment. We must make a picture which is a complete manifestation of being.

Picasso, the great innovator of the twentieth century, has knocked on the door of every painter's studio in the world. The richness of his form gives a totality from which to build the scaffolding of new painting.

Klee made the background which reflects the intricate moving of our different lives. Here in the quivering of a leaf he experiences the violence of a thunderstorm. Sometimes it would seem that his pictures extend to the other side of the canvas. We connect with his pictures not only with our eyes, but our whole skin becomes a sensitive surface of eyes. We become the awareness of the barometer. Our sensibilities have been buried by the waste products of this life. Klee takes those crippled senses back to the air and the light.

The functional idea in architecture must come from the new building. But alone there is no movement to progress. The road finishes. For its realization it is necessary for architecture to go coupled with the painting and plastic of today.

Malewicz in Russia, Mondrian in Holland, and Nicholson in England preached balance in painting. This has a didactic value. But it is more the scholastic of painting than the expressed value. They are not yet pictures but necessary scholastic examples.

Of all the countries at this time perhaps in Britain there is a chance of retaining the spiritual power of this heritage from Klee and Picasso. This realization has to do with this country's future for living and seems the only reason for its secure and continuing peace.

1 Alfred Kubin (1877–1959) – Austrian graphic artist, painter, illustrator, author of the novel *The Other Side*. – Ed.

CHAPTER

III

SPATIAL COMPOSITION

Dan Graham

101

DAN GRAHAM
(1942, URBANA – 2022, NEW YORK)

An American conceptual artist, critic, and architect of social spaces, whose work combined performance, film, architecture, media theory, and sculpture. He is especially known for his glass pavilion designs, which he approached as a tool for analyzing spatial, social, and perceptual relationships. In "Essay on Video, Architecture, and Television" (1979), he analyzes contemporary visual media as shaping social imaginings of space. His thoughts on architecture and glass facades reveal social asymmetries and the illusion of transparency. His piece shows a space to be a system of signs, and architecture to be a social code, which can be reorganized through an art intervention.

Dan Graham, *Video, Architecture, Television: Writings on Video and Video Works 1970-1978*, ed. Benjamin H. D. Buchloh (New York: The Press of Nova Scotia College of Art and Design, 1979), 62–76.

ESSAY ON VIDEO, ARCHITECTURE, AND TELEVISION

FILM AND VIDEO: VIDEO AS PRESENT-TIME

Video is a present-time medium. Its image can be simultaneous with its perception by/of its audience (it can be the image of its audience perceiving). The space/time it presents is continuous, unbroken, and congruent with that of the real time which is the shared time of its perceivers and their individual and collective real environments. This is unlike film, which is, necessarily, an edited re-presentation of the past of another reality/an other's reality for separate contemplation by unconnected individuals. Film is discontinuous, its language constructed, in fact, from syntactical and temporal disjunctions (for example, montage). Film is a reflection of a reality external to the spectator's body; the spectator's body is out of the frame. In a live-video-situation, the spectator may be included within the frame at one moment, or be out of the frame at another moment. Film constructs a "reality" separate and incongruent with the viewing situation; video feeds back indigenous data in the immediate, present-time environment or connects parallel time/space continua. Film is contemplative and "distanced"; it detaches the viewer from present reality and makes him a spectator.

CENTRALIZATION/DECENTRALIZATION OF INFORMATION

The distribution of both films and broadcast television represents an asymmetrical imposition of information by capital. Film is a consumption product, as is broadcast television, which, in the interest of advertisers of products, installs a terminal in the home and controls access to information. The concentration of power through capital is also facilitated through the mythology contained in the storylines of programs and advertisements, and through withholding or controlling the availability of information.[1] The centralized production facilities of film or broadcast TV exploit the saleable (product) aspects of culture at the expense of the existential. A cable system, by contrast, presents the possibility of becoming two-way and decentralized. Individuals, families and the local, extant cultural system could be given potential self-determination and control. Local cable television could feed back the immediate environment.

ADDENDUM:

TV gains much of its effect from the fact that it appears to depict a world which is immediately and fully present.

The viewer assumes that the TV image is both immediate and contiguous (as to time) with the shared social time and parallel "real world" of its perceivers – even when this may not be the case. This physical immediacy produces in the viewer a sense of psychological intimacy, where people on TV and events appear to directly address him or her.

THE ARCHITECTURAL CODE/ THE VIDEO CODE

An architectural code both reflects and directs the social order. In the not too distant future one can envisage that this code will be modified and in part supplanted by a new code, that of television. As cable television images displayed on wall-size monitors connect and mediate between rooms, families, social classes, "public"/"private" domains, connecting architecturally (and socially) bounded regions, they take on an architectural (and social) function. Video in architecture will function semiotically speaking as window and as mirror simultaneously, but will subvert the effects and functions of both. Windows in architecture mediate separated spatial units and frame a conventional perspective of one unit's relation to the other; mirrors in architecture define, self-reflectively, spatial enclosure and ego enclosure.

Architecture defines certain cultural and psychological boundaries; video may intercede to replace or rearrange some of these boundaries. Cable television, being reciprocally two-way, can interpenetrate social orders not previously linked; its initial use may tend to deconstruct and redefine existing social hierarchies.

"PUBLIC"/"PRIVATE" CODES

Public versus private can be dependent upon architectural conventions. By social convention, a window mediates between private (inside) and public (outside) space. The interior seen defines or is defined by the publicly accepted notion of privacy. An architectural division, the "house," separates the "private" person from the "public" person and sanctions certain kinds of behavior for each. The *meaning* of privacy, beyond its mere distinguishability from publicness, is more complexly connected to other social rules. For example: a private home limits access to members of one family; a bathroom within that house is private as it allows usage by only one person at a time (whereas a toilet in a public space is public as it allows multiple access, but is gender restricted); the individual bedroom of a child or adult member of the family may be considered to be private at certain times. Moral sanctions are attached to violation of these codes. There are areas which reflect transitional social change. The taping of private conversations for public law enforcement is one area of unresolved claims between private (including interpretation of the term "private") rights and public rights to justice or knowledge. The widespread use of video surveillance cameras involves similar "moral"/legal issues. The use of video would have social-psychological implications for the family structure: for instance, children being continuously observed through the use of a video camera by their parents "lose" their "right" to be different in private, that is, to have separate "public" and "private" identities.

CONVENTIONS OF THE GLASS WINDOW

The glass window, like the Renaissance painting, creates a picture plane that places the world at a measured distance for the viewer on either side. The world, held at a distance, frames a conventional view which is defined by the specific size, shape, and direction of orientation of the opening of the window frame. A view from one space into the other space, by what is allowed to be seen, defines one space's socially (pre-)conceived "view" of the other. What someone on one side of the window can see of the other space, and what can be seen of them as part of their space by a viewer on the other side (and, *vice versa*, for someone occupying that other side), is conventionalized by the social/architectural code. A view from one side, as opposed to a view from the other side, may be symmetrical, appear symmetrical but not be, or be clearly asymmetrical. The "picture-window" appears to be symmetrical in the length of time allowed a person on either side to stare, but actually is not. An employer's view of his employees' work space through one-way glass, as opposed to the employees' view of their employer's office, is asymmetrical, expressing inequalities of power.

THE MIRROR IMAGE/THE VIDEO IMAGE

A mirror's image optically responds to a human observer's movements, varying as a function of his position. As the observer approaches, the mirror opens up a wider and deeper view of the room-environment and magnifies the image of the perceiver. By contrast, a video image on a monitor does not shift in perspective with a viewer's shift in position. The mirror's image connects subjectivity with the perceiver's time-space axis. Optically, mirrors are designed to be seen frontally.[2] A video monitor's projected image of a spectator observing it depends on that spectator's relation to the position of the camera, but not on his relation to the monitor. A view of the perceiver can be transmitted from the camera instantaneously or time-delayed over a distance to a monitor which may be near or far from the perceiver's (viewing) position in space or time. Unlike the flat visuality of Renaissance painting, in the video image geometrical surfaces are lost to ambiguously modeled contours and to a translucent depth. Mirrors in enclosures exteriorize all objects within the interior space, so that they appear on the mirror as frontal surface planes. In rectilinear enclosures, mirrors create illusory perspective boxes. The symmetry of mirrors tends to conceal or cancel the passage of time, so that the overall architectural form appears to transcend time, while the interior area of the architecture, inhabited by human movements, process and gradual change, is emptied of significance. As the image in the mirror is perceived as a static instant, place (time and space) becomes illusorily eternal. The world seen on video, by contrast, is in temporal flux and connected subjectively (because it can be identified with) to experienced duration.

ADDENDUM:

The child sees itself formed as an image in the same way as an Other, beside which it identifies. The child's "ego" is formed by an identification with its likeness: that other human being who is in the mirror and the reflection of its body, which is dissimilar to its subjective experience, but is identified with it. In the mirror-image, its "ego" seems to be located in two places simultaneously, outside itself (in the world of other objects and looking back at the child), and within itself (looking out at the image of itself). The child falsely imagines his body image to be a unified and complete entity, identified with the image of Otherness.

MIRRORS AND "SELF"

Mirrors are metaphors for the Western concept of the "self." In his theory of the "mirror phase," Jacques Lacan has posited that a developing child first discovers his "self" by a mirror-like identification with the image of an Other. When the mother holds the child up to the mirror, the child views his body-image reflected in the mirror as an objectified and complete form, at a time when it is subjectively experienced as incomplete and uncoordinated. The child identifies itself with an image of an Other, or an image which is outside its body sensations, but, in terms of social reality, must be taken to be its identity.

VIDEO FEEDBACK

The video feedback of "self"-image, by adding temporality to self-perception, connects "self"-perception to physiological brain processes. This removes self-perception from the viewing of a detached, static image; video feedback contradicts the mirror model of the perceiving "self." Through the use of videotape feedback, the performer and the audience, the perceiver and his process of perception, are linked, or co-identified. Psychological premises of "privacy" (as against publicness) which would derive from the mirror-model, depend on an assumed split between observed behavior and supposedly unobservable, interior *intention*. However, if a perceiver views his behavior on a five to eight second delay[3] via videotape (so that his responses are part of and influence his perception), "private" mental intention and external behavior are experienced as one. The difference between intention and actual behavior is fed back on the monitor and immediately influences the observer's future intentions and behavior. By linking perception of exterior behavior and its interior, mental perception, an observer's "self," like a topological Möbius strip, can be apparently without "inside" or "outside." Video feedback time is the immediate present, without relation to past and hypothetical future states – a continuous topological or feedback loop forward or backward between just-past or immediate future. Instead of self-perception being a series of fixed "perspectives" for a detached ego, observing past actions with the intent of locating "objective truth" about its essence, video feedback encloses the perceiver in what appears to be (only) what is subjectively present. While the mirror alienates the "self," video encloses the "self" within its perception of its own functioning, giving a person the feeling of a perceptible control over his responses through the feedback mechanism.

THE GLASS DIVIDER, LIGHT AND SOCIAL DIVISION

Window glass alienates "subject" from "object." From behind glass, the spectator's view is "objective," while the observed's subject(ivity) is concealed. [4]The observer on the outside of the glass cannot be part of an interior group's "intersubjective" framework. Being mirror-reflective[5] glass reflects the mirror-image of an observer, as well as the particular inside or outside world behind him, into the image of the space into which he is looking. Abstractly, this reflectiveness of glass allows it to be a sign signifying, at the same time, the nature of the opposition between the two spaces and their common mediation. The glass in the window through its reflectiveness unites, and by its physical impenetrability separates inside and outside. Due to its reflective qualities, illumination within or without the space that the glass divides, produces either complex reflections, non-reflective transparency, or opacity. Light signifies various distinct spatial or temporal locations. Artificial light is often placed in contrast to natural illumination (defining indoors and outdoors). The pattern of illumination phases with, and marks off, natural and cultural diurnal rhythms of human activities taking place on either side of the glass partition. Illumination is a controller of social behavior. Both glass and light (separately or conjointly) enforce social divisions.

GLASS USED IN SHOP WINDOWS/ COMMODITIES IN SHOP WINDOWS

The glass used for the showcase displaying products, isolates the consumer from the product at the same time as it superimposes the mirror-reflection of his own image onto the goods displayed. This alienation, paradoxically, helps arouse the desire to possess the commodity. The goods are often displayed as part of a human mannequin – an idealized image of the consumer. Glass isolates (draws attention to) the product's surface appeal, "glamour," or superficial appearance alone (attributes of "workmanship" that link craftsmen to a specific product being lost), while denying access to what is tangible or immediately useful. It idealizes the product. Historically, this change in the appearance of the product corresponds to the worker's alienation from the products he produces; to be utilized, the product must be bought on the market in exchange for wages at a market value, with the conditions of its production obscured. Glass is helpful in socially alienating buyer from producer, thereby concealing the product's connection to another's real labor and allowing it to acquire exchange value over and above its use value.

> In a sort of way, It is the same with Man as with commodities ... man sees himself reflected in other men. Peter only establishes his own identity as a man by first comparing himself with Paul as being of the same kind, and thereby Paul, "in hide and hair," Paul in his Pauline corporality, becomes entirely to Peter the phenomenal form of the genus of Man.[6]

> Capitalistic society makes all personal relations between men take the form of objective relations between things.... Social relations are transformed into "qualities of ... things themselves" (commodities).[7]

Under capitalism, just as the ego is confused with the body image in the mirror, so that ego is confused with the commodity. The individual is made to identify himself (in his feeling for "himself") with the image of the commodity. The commodity object is a substitute (fetish) for his lack—the lack his desire expresses. The glass and mirrors of the shop window beckon the potential customer by arousing doubts and desires about his self-image/self-identity. It is as if in looking at the product behind the glass showcase, the consumer is looking at an ideal image of himself (in the mirror). Or he sees in the reflections that he deviates from the ideal (represented by the mannequin), but is given the possibility of acquiring attributes of this ideal if he buys the merchandise. The commodity reflects his desire for a more complete "better self," identified with the *alter ego*.

Inseparable from the goods the consumer desires is the illusion that buying them will "complete" that which is "incomplete" in himself. This desire is never satisfied (as the market system must continue to function), but because the consumer identifies himself with (his projection onto) the commodity, he infuses the commodity with a psychological value which now becomes part of its market value.

In the showcase display the prospective customer's point of view, his sense of "self," is equated not only with the object centered in his view, but with the System (which created the device). The showcase window as a framing or optical device replicates the form of the Renaissance painting's illusionary, three-dimensional "space." Like a painting's perspective, it frames a determined view (determines a view), creating a point of focus—meaning—organized around a central vanishing point. The customer's gaze is focused upon the centered object's external form; focus creates value. The spectator's "self," unseen, projected into the space, is identified with the thing(s) represented. The spectator's gaze, his "self-projection," organizes meaning around the centered object, meeting his centered look.

The material components of the showcase affect the viewer slightly differently from the painting. First, glass becomes a screen upon which a partial mirror-image of the observer himself (accentuated by the use of mirrors in the back of the case facing the front plane) is imposed. By means of strong over-head lighting, the faint reflection of the spectator, as well as that of the outside, real world, is superimposed on the glass in front of the visually highlighted objects seen within. The glass of the showcase is optically halfway between the invisibility (which hides the spectator's and the original painter's self-image) of the Renaissance painting and the reflectivity of the mirror (which shows the spectator himself looking, plus that part of the real space which is normally invisible behind him).[8] Often a rear mirror or smaller fragments of a mirror are positioned behind objects displayed in showcases, to fracture the ideal image of the spectator, partially glimpsed on the glass surface and rear mirror. By these means a viewer's initially desired ideal "self"-image is focused and imposed upon—identified with—the inaccessible, but visually desired, commodity for sale; the object seems imaginarily complete, while the "self" is de-totalized, incomplete, lost, not graspable, except through its visual projection upon the object. The shop window thus captures, focuses, and efficiently employs the latent desires of the casual passerby, to confer a subjective, overdetermined meaning upon the goods it "objectively" places on view.

GLASS BUILDINGS: CORPORATE "SHOWCASES"

At the same time that glass reveals, it conceals. If one looks into a glass showcase, one can have the illusion that the container is neutral, without apparent interest in the content of what it displays; or, conversely, the appearance of what is contained can be seen as a function of the qualities of the container itself.[9] In the ideology of modern functionalist architecture, an architectural form appropriates and merges both of these readings. First, because symbolic form, ornamentation, is eliminated from the building (form and content being merged), there is no distinction between the form and its material structure; that is, the form represents nothing more or less than the material. Second, a form or structure is seen to represent only its contained function, the building's structural and functional efficiency being equated with its real utility for those who use it. Aesthetically, this idea is expressed in the formula: efficient form is beautiful and beautiful form is efficient. This has a "moral" dimension: "efficient" connotes a melioristic, "scientific" approach seemingly uncontaminated by "ideology," which, pragmatically, has (capitalistic) use value. ("Efficiency" is how well a building contributes to the operations of the company housed within it. The look of a building, its cleanness and structural transparency, thus joins the myth of scientific progress to that of the social utility of efficient business practice.)[10] These glass and steel buildings usually house corporations or government agencies. The building's transparent functionalism conceals its less apparent ideological function: justifying the use of technology or bureaucracy by large corporations or government agencies to impart their particular version of order on society. The spectator's view is diverted away from social context by focusing only on the surface material or structural qualities. Glass and steel are used as "pure" materials, for the sake of their materiality. The use of glass gives another illusion: that what is seen is seen exactly as it is. Through the glass one sees the technical workings of the company and the technical engineering of the building's structure. The glass's literal transparency not only falsely objectifies reality, but is a paradoxical camouflage; for while the actual function of a corporation may be to concentrate its self-contained power and control by secreting information, its architectural facade gives the illusion of absolute openness. The transparency is visual only; glass separates the visual from the verbal, insulating outsiders from the content of the decision-making processes, and from the invisible, but real, interrelationships linking company operations to society.

The glass building, in attempting to eliminate the disparity between its outside facade (which conventionally mediates its relation to the outside environment where it is sited) and its private, institutional function, pretends to eliminate the distinction between its outer form and its inner content. The self-contained, transparent glass building denies that it has an outside and that it participates as an element in the language of the surrounding buildings with other social functions which make up the surrounding environmental context. Where other buildings are usually decorated with conventional signs of their function for the public to see, the facade of the glass building is virtually eliminated. The aesthetic purity of the glass building, standing apart from the common environment, becomes transformed by its owner into a social alibi for the institution it houses. The building's transparent "openness" to the environment (it incorporates the natural environment) on the one hand, and its claim to aesthetic hegemony over the surrounding environment (its formal self-containment) on the other, efficiently legitimate the corporate institution's claim to autonomy ("The World of General Motors"). A building with glass on four sides gives the illusion of self-containment. While it appears open to visual inspection, in fact, in looking through glass on all sides, one realizes the particular, focused-upon detail, the "interior," is lost (one looks *through* and not *at*) to the architectural generality, to the apparent materialness of the outward form, or to "Nature" (light, sun, sky or the landscape glimpsed through the building on the other side).

1 One explanation for the form that broadcast television has taken—a centrally originated transmission sent to the passive home viewer on a privately owned TV set—is that television came into being first as a commodity item, mass-produced for the consumer market. When it appeared, the TV set belonged to a new type of inexpensively produced small machines (other examples are automobiles, cameras, electrical appliances, radios) designed to be transportable or provide means to private transportation. The consumer's demand for these goods was a response to the charged work and life conditions of the industrial worker; he was uprooted from his traditional house for a mobile and urbanized pattern. With the aid of these products the newly resettled worker could plug in quickly to whatever urban social environment he found himself in. At the same time, because of the pressures of a more technically organized work life, the private areas of family and house became retreats for the worker in his "time off." Television programming allowed the person in his private space to feel connected to a larger, public world, but remain free of its demands, sheltered in his private home life.

2 The mirror inverts the position of the spectator seeing a Renaissance painting. There the spectator faces the painting and looks forward into its projected space; in doing this, he reconstructs the exterior (and also the "interior") view of the painter at the point in time and space when he made the painting.

3 Five to eight seconds is the limit of "short-term" memory, or memory which is part of and influences a person's (present) perception.

4 Seen by a second observer on the other side of the glass, the first observer appears as an outsider.

5 There is a physical and a dialectical relation between mirrors and glass, each reflecting, accentuating qualities of the other.

6 Karl Marx, quoted in Anthony Witten, *System end Structure* (London: Tavistock Publications, 1972).

7 Herbert Marcuse, *Reason and Revolution* (New York: Oxford University Press, 1941). Marcuse is quoting Marx at the end of this passage.

8 Both the Renaissance painting and the mirror are two-dimensional rectilinear surfaces, conventionally hung to meet the standing spectator's eye-level view and flush with an interior wall, so that the wall functions both as an architectural (structural) support and as support for the painting or mirror. The mirror or painting's back surface and the area of the wall upon which it is hung are hidden from view; in their place is either the reflection of the opposite side of the space or a depiction of an illusionary "space." Both mirror and painting use the frame to orient the spectator's view, necessitating that he turns frontally and faces the picture or mirror surface, focusing his attention toward the center point (defined by the framed edges of the form).

A mirror literally inverts the Renaissance painting's perspective: it flattens the real, present world, reversing it 180 degrees to the spectator facing the mirror, so he can see himself physically in the picture (looking).

9 But an optical focus—which aspect of the world is perceived when one looks – is culturally determined.

10 The technological-utilitarian glass office structure derives from the Bauhaus's vision of an architecture built from elemental, ideal formal and social images. The total, utopian vision in theory could serve as an alternative to the dominant, conservative, bourgeois order, wedding science and aesthetics to a socially just and more rational notion of progress (scientific progress aiding social progress). The vision begins with, and is grafted onto, the mid-19th century notion of "art for art's sake," which proposed an art that would negate the existing world order through the creation of an interior order of art. In this vision, "Art"/ "Architecture" attempts to create another (which is always "its" own) language—in order to transcend that of the existent, real world. The total new order could be seen as a negation of all existing values, the avant-gardist notion being one that radically denies the "old" in favor of the "new" (social-aesthetic principle); this is seen in itself as healthy. The structuralist version of "radical" art devaluation (e.g. Roland Barthes's *Writing Degree Zero*) is to purge the language of its (hidden) ideological contamination by reducing the text to purely elemental structure. The artist was seen as an "underground" but heroic figure, standing apart from the social order—the existence of his art as a radical negation, denial, of this order. It is a paradox, then, that the more willful and heroic the imposition of the art form on an environment perceived as sterile or antagonistically unaesthetic, the more transcendent and utopian the artist's or architect's initial vision (which the building/artwork symbolically expresses), the much more distanced (and arrogant) the message that the building/artwork conveys to the general social body and more impotent is its intended ideological corrective effect.

Katarzyna Kobro

119

KATARZYNA KOBRO
(1898, MOSCOW – 1951, ŁÓDŹ)

A leading figure in the European interwar avant-garde, a creator of Unism and theorist of modern sculpture. Kobro rejected the figurative approach, psychological expression, and symbolism, striving for objectivity and universality of form. In her vision, sculpture ceased to be an autonomous shape, becoming part of a rhythmically organized space. In "Sculpture and Solid" (1929), Kobro formulated her manifesto, opposing the traditional concept of sculpture as a contained and complete form. Sculpture ought not to "lie with its solid," rather it should reveal spatial relations through precise rhythms and proportions. Kobro developed a vision of art as an objective construct subject to numbers, harmony, and function, thus predating the contemporary view of sculpture as a medium of spatial intervention.

Katarzyna Kobro, "Rzeźba i bryła," *Europa*, no. 2 (1929): 60, (modified) trans. Jerzy Jarniewicz in *Katarzyna Kobro (1898–1951): Henry Moore Institute, Leeds, 25 March–27 June 1999*, eds. Elżbieta Fuchs, Alina Kwiatkowska, Penelope Curtis, Stephen Feeke (Łódź: Muzeum Sztuki; Leeds: Henry Moore Institute, 1999), 149.

SCULPTURE AND SOLID[1]

There are few modern sculptors. Are there any material reasons for this? Or does this result from the fact that today sculpture is too directly involved with architecture, so that every truly modern architect should be a good modern sculptor?

In his futurist sculptures, Boccioni showed us how to free sculpture from the weight of the solid. Archipenko opened up the interior of the solid, preserving, however, the closure of its volume. Vantongerloo feels the need for the harmony of dimensions and for modern classicism; he builds up the sculpture out of several interrelated cubes, enclosed within the overall cubic volume.

In his few experiments with painting and architecture, Van Doesburg promised some spatial solutions in the construction of sculpture out of planes and solids, but what he promised was neither painting, nor sculpture, nor architecture. It only gave an idea of what could be achieved. In his dynamic-spatial constructions and his theoretical writings, Malevich raises the issues of balance in the distribution of weight and mass in space. He was the prophet of abstract painting; now he introduces through his architectonic sculptures a new era of architecture, growing out of contemporary sculpture.

Sculpture is the shaping of space. If one wishes to see the true tendencies in the development of sculpture, one should compare the highest achievements of the present. One should not care about the work of the majority of minor sculptors, but only the achievements of those who are paving the way. Secondly, one should realize, once and for all, that sculpture is neither literature, nor symbolism, nor individual psychological emotion. Sculpture is nothing but the shaping of form in space. Sculpture addresses all people and speaks to them in the same language. Its language is form and space. Hence the objectivism of the most economical expression of form. There are not multiple solutions—there is only one—the simplest and the most appropriate.

A sculpture is part of its ambient space. That is why it should not be separated from space. A sculpture enters space, and space enters it in turn. The spatiality of the construction, the bond between the sculpture and space, brings out of the sculpture the sheer truth of its existence. That is why there should be no accidental shapes, only those shapes that relate and bind it to space. A solid is a lie about the essence of the sculpture. It closes up the sculpture and separates it from space; it exists for itself and it treats its interior space as something completely different from the exterior space. In reality, however, space is always the same. Nowadays the solid already belongs to history and is just a pretty tale from the past.

As it becomes united with space, the new sculpture should be space's most condensed and essential part. It achieves this because its shapes, through their mutual interdependence, create a rhythm of dimensions and divisions. The unity of rhythm is achieved by means of the uniform scale of its calculations.

The harmony of units is the external manifestation of number.

Translated by Jerzy Jarniewicz

1 Katarzyna Kobro's text is an answer to a survey by *Europa*. The publication of the text was preluded by the following introduction: "To explicate the issue in modern plastic art, the editors of the journal Europa asked contemporary European artists these two questions:
1. What do you think of the current state of modern art?
2. What tendency in the efforts and explorations of modern art do you regard as the most promising and productive?
From the replies that we received so far we have printed two, the first by the famous Dutch architect Theo van Doesburg, the second by the Polish pioneer of modernism in sculpture, Katarzyna Kobro."

KATARZYNA KOBRO, *Spatial Composition 9*, oil on metal, 50 × 78 × 56 cm, 1933

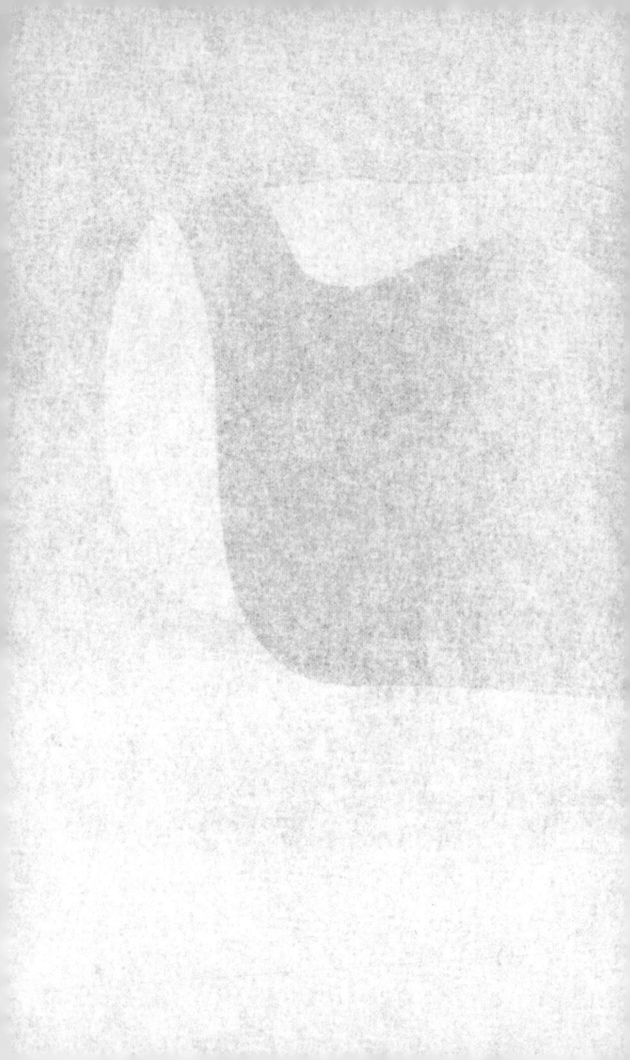

Paul Neagu

127

PAUL NEAGU
(1938, BUCHAREST – 2004, LONDON)

A Romanian-British artist, performer, and art theorist. After emigrating to Great Britain in 1970, he forged ties with London's avant-garde circles, where he developed the concept of "palpable art"—work that was sensory and socially engaged. His "Palpable Art Manifesto!" (1969) declares a radical break with the dominance of vision, considering it to be "tired," "degenerate," and "seduced by the media." In its stead, he offers a total aesthetic, one that is organic and multisensory, based on touch, taste, smell, and physical presence. A sculpture should be experienced not just with the eye, but also through embodied perception, as a form of intense contact with the material.

Text of the *Palpable Art Manifesto* by Paul Neagu (Edinburgh, July 1969), printed in the exhibition brochure of the first show / performance of *Palpable Art* by Paul Neagu at the Richard Demarco Gallery, Edinburgh, Aug-Sep 1969; from: Tom Holert, *Matter For: Paul Neagu*, in *Paul Neagu – The Monograph*, ed. Magda Radu and Georg Schoellhammer, JRPIEditions, Geneva 2023, 26.

PALPABLE ART MANIFESTO!

①THE EYE IS FATIGUED, PERVERTED, SHALLOW, ITS CULTURE IS DEGENERATE, DEGRADED AND OBSOLETE, SEDUCED BY PHOTOGRAPHY, FILM, TELEVISION...

②THE EYE IS LOSING ITS PRIMARY ROLE IN AESTHETIC RESPONSES, WHILE REMAINING SECONDARY IN THIS RESPECT.

③ART MUST GIVE UP ITS PURELY VISUAL AESTHETIC IF IT WANTS TO SURVIVE SPECIFICALLY AS PLASTIC ART, AND MUST MOVE TOWARDS AN ORGANIC AND UNIFIED AESTHETIC THAT WILL MAKE USE OF SENSES THAT ARE STILL FRESH, PURE.

④LET THERE BE ONE, PUBLIC, PALPABLE ART THROUGH WHICH ALL THE SENSES, SIGHT, TOUCH, SMELL, TASTE WILL SUPPLEMENT AND DEVOUR EACH OTHER SO THAT A MAN CAN POSSESS AN OBJECT IN EVERY SENSE.

⑤YOU CAN TAKE THINGS IN BETTER, MORE COMPLETELY, WITH YOUR TEN FINGERS, PORES AND MUCOUS MEMBRANES THAN WITH ONLY TWO EYES!

⑥THESE IDEAS ARE LINKED INSEPARABLY WITH THE CONCEPT THAT ART MUST FUNCTION SOCIALLY, YET NEVER IN A VULGARLY NATURALISTIC WAY.

⑦PALPABLE ART IS A NEW JOY FOR THE "BLIND", WHILE FOR THE "CLEAR-SIGHTED" IT IS THE MOST THOROUGHLY THREE-DIMENSIONAL STUDY...

Paul Neagu
Edinburgh, July, 1969

The first show / performance of *Palpable Art*:
By Paul Neagu – Richard Demarco Gallery
Edinburgh – August – September – 1969

–

palpable art

MANIFESTO!

→ 1. THE EYE IS FATIGUED, PERVERTED, SHALLOW, ITS CULTURE IS DEGENERATE, DEGRADED AND OBSOLETE, SEDUCED BY PHOTOGRAPHY, FILM, TELEVISION...

→ 2. THE EYE IS LOSING ITS PRIMARY ROLE IN AESTHETIC RESPONSES, WHILE REMAINING SECONDARY IN THIS RESPECT.

→ 3. ART MUST GIVE UP ITS PURELY VISUAL AESTHETIC IF IT WANTS TO SURVIVE SPECIFICALLY AS PLASTIC ART, AND MUST MOVE TOWARDS AN ORGANIC AND UNIFIED AESTHETIC THAT WILL MAKE USE OF SENSES THAT ARE STILL FRESH, PURE.

→ 4. LET THERE BE ONE, PUBLIC, PALPABLE ART THROUGH WHICH ALL THE SENSES, SIGHT, TOUCH, SMELL, TASTE WILL SUPPLEMENT AND DEVOUR EACH OTHER SO THAT A MAN CAN POSSESS AN OBJECT IN EVERY SENSE.

→ 5. YOU CAN TAKE THINGS IN BETTER, MORE COMPLETELY, WITH YOUR TEN FINGERS, PORES AND MUCOUS MEMBRANES THAN WITH ONLY TWO EYES!

→ 6. THESE IDEAS ARE LINKED INSEPARABLY WITH THE CONCEPT THAT ART MUST FUNCTION SOCIALLY, YET NEVER IN A VULGARLY NATURALISTIC WAY.

→ 7. PALPABLE ART IS A NEW JOY FOR THE „BLIND", WHILE FOR THE „CLEAR-SIGHTED" IT IS THE MOST THOROUGHLY THREE-DIMENSIONAL STUDY....

PAUL NEAGU
EDINBURGH. JULY. 1969

paul neagu

THE FIRST SHOW/PERFORMANCE OF PALPABLE ART:
BY PAUL NEAGU – RICHARD DEMARCO GALLERY
EDINBURGH – AUGUST – SEPTEMBER – 1969

Morgan Fisher

MORGAN FISHER
(B. 1942, WASHINGTON D.C.)

An American conceptual artist known for his videos, structural films and minimalist painting. In "The Italian Paintings", he describes a series of pictures from gouaches depicting tourist guidebooks. Over time, the artist gave up on replicating books, leaving only the irregular contour of the background, with a trace of their form, as in a photo negative. The result is abstract spaces marked by absence. Books organize the space of the picture as a collection of "breaks," empty contours, and relations. These works recall cartographies of perception: they show how the invisible can shape the field of vision and force us to take a new look at the picture.

Morgan Fisher, "The Italian Paintings," in *Morgan Fisher: Two Exhibitions*, eds. Sabine Folie, Suzanne Titz (Köln: Verlag der Buchhandlung Walther König, 2012), 153–154.

THE ITALIAN PAINTINGS

The Italian Paintings were the result of the series of gouaches I made of pairs of guidebooks. Like the atlases for London, the books in these gouaches were shown on a gray background, the dimensions of which were a standard size of photographic paper. The gray was a middle gray, which I intended to refer to an eighteen percent gray card, a standard reference in photography because it is the middle of the range of grays from black to white.

A typical pair was a Blue Guide and a Touring Club Italiano guide for the same city but with different dates, and there were also other pairings. The books weren't pairs strictly speaking, in the way that a pair of shoes is a pair, but they were in a relation that was sufficiently pair-like that I feel the word is appropriate.

The view of each book was frontal, that is, orthographic. Each book was its actual size, and each had a conventionalized shadow to show how thick it was. A shadow is bound by physical laws to what it's a shadow of, but sometimes the edges or corners of the background intervened in that relation.

Some of the books and shadows extended beyond the gray background on which they were placed, so the overall shape was not a rectangle. But as I say in the note about the London street atlases, there was something about these works I found unsatisfying.

One day, after laying out a drawing in pencil, I began by painting the gray background. When I finished, I realized that the gray was all I needed. The information about the sizes of the books and the shadows was contained in the dimensions of the interruptions in the edges of the background, which was no longer the rectangle it had once implied it was.

I had made a monochrome that was not a rectangle. The Italian Paintings came from this gouache. Like it, the Italian Paintings are not pictures, at least not in the usual way. In each painting the books and shadows are outside the panel, but the panel's contours are the books and shadows as voids, complete enough to make them unmistakable. The books and shadows are present as negative spaces, contiguous with the panel and inseparable from it. Ordinarily the edges of a painting are the boundary between what is inside it and what is outside it. In these paintings this distinction is clear at those parts of the edges that define the rectangles from which the books and shadows have been removed. But at the edges that define the books and their shadows, areas outside the painting but immediately adjacent to it are implicated in the painting and so are part of it.

The ten paintings that make up the Italian Paintings are divided into four groups: two groups of three and two groups of two. In each of the four groups the two books are the same, but in each painting in a group the books and shadows are in different positions.

The paint was wall paint. I put it on with a roller.

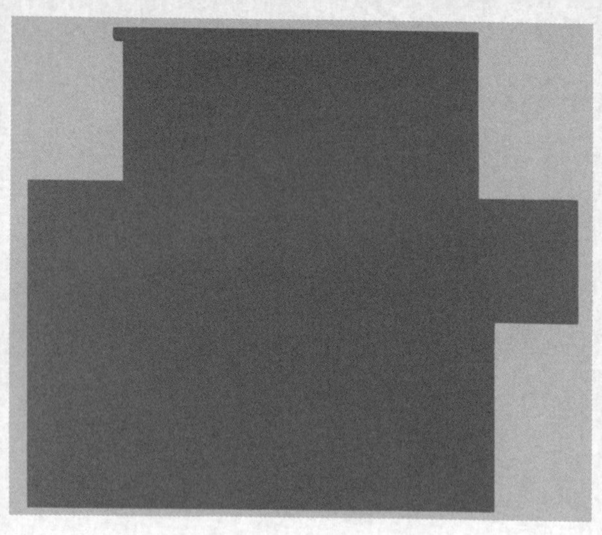

MORGAN FISHER, *Blue Guide Venice, 1957, Blue Guide Venice, 1980*, alkyd enamel on plywood and wood, 50.5 × 61 × 3 cm, 1999

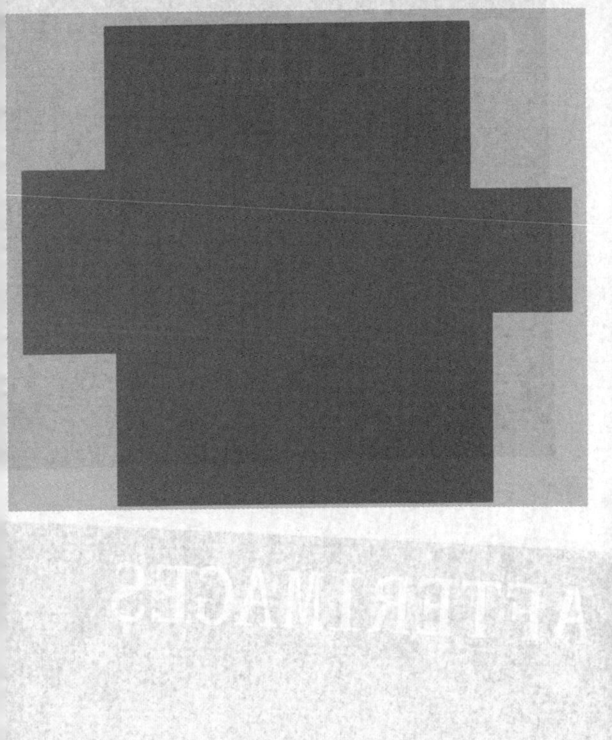

CHAPTER

AFTERIMAGES

IV

Andrzej Wróblewski

ANDRZEJ WRÓBLEWSKI
(1927, VILNIUS–1957, TATRA MOUNTAINS)

A Polish artist, one of the most important figures in postwar painting. His work balanced the abstract and the figurative, Expressionism and realism. Wróblewski made his painting debut at the First Exhibition of Modern Art. In the "Commentary," he shows how the development of science and technology let us see the world anew—more deeply and in detail than ever before. In describing the room of the photomontage for which he used enlarged everyday objects, he passionately analyzes similarities between the works of nature and technology, positing that artists ought not to fear reaching deeper than what is seen at first glance.

Andrzej Wróblewski, "Komentarz do WSN", typescript, private collection, Krakow, from: *I Wystawa sztuki nowoczesnej: pięćdziesiąt lat później*, December 1998 – January 1999, exh. cat. eds. Marek Świca, Józef Chrobak (Krakow: Starmach Gallery, Fundacja Nowosielskich, 1998), 114.

A COMMENTARY ON THE EXHIBITION OF MODERN ART

Please gather in the photomontage room to listen to the explanations.
/repeat/

The photomontages were created using enlarged photographs of the most ordinary objects from our day-to-day environment. These are: the interior of a watch, a starry sky, a blade of moss, a maple seed, an iron structure, a cross-section of a cabbage, and the interior of a pair of human lungs.

Modern technology and science have given us the means to see these objects differently than in centuries past.

Here you see an enlarged view of the interior of a watch. This is not the watch whose golden chain and fob an artist of the last century might have painted on the belly of a respectable burgher squeezed into a fustian waistcoat, simply to add splendor to the portrait and boast of his skill in rendering the gleam of gold. Today, the mechanism—once the sole concern of watchmakers—interests us more than the engraved case. We admire its logic, its purposefulness, its perfect precision, and the infallibility of its movements. We strive to equal it with our imagination as we create our own compositions.

This panel, which at first glance may remind you of a shooting target, is a montage created from photographs of the sky, taken over an eight-hour period. When we look at the celestial vault, we see only shimmering points; yet we know that these are enormous worlds suspended in space, whose apparent movement across the sky is a reflection of the Earth's rotation. Our knowledge of the universe captivates our imagination, leading it beyond the direct impression of navy blue or azure towards the unfathomable, eternally moving depths of time and space.

As we move deeper into the room, we encounter an enlarged photograph of moss on the left, and on the right—a cross-section of a maple seed. How different the internal world of a plant is from its external appearance. Moss, when seen on its own scale, ceases to be a soft, velvety cushion and manifests an unexpected richness of structure and form. An inconspicuous plant seed reveals itself as a complex mechanism.

When we look at nature in this way, a technical structure, such as the one you see next, no longer seems alien or artificial. The logic of construction is the same, both in nature and in human creations.

Let's move on. We all know what a head of cabbage looks like. Yet that knowledge is not enough to recognise it in this photograph, which shows an enlarged view of its cross-section.

The image of a person in an X-ray is different from a photograph in a family album. Is it any less true?

Reality is not limited to what we perceive on the surface. Must the artist's imagination then be worse and any less rich than reality itself?

Translated by Łukasz Mojsak

ANDRZEJ WRÓBLEWSKI, *The Sun and Other Stars*, oil on canvas, 90 × 120 cm, 1948. Courtesy of the Andrzej Wróblewski Foundation

Erna Rosenstein

151

ERNA ROSENSTEIN
(1913, LVIV–2004, WARSAW)

A Polish painter and poet of Jewish origin, she made paintings, assemblages, drawings, and objects. She was linked with the first Krakow Group, from which she took her artistic and political radicalism. Her work drew from Surrealism, often using metaphorical images alluding to themes of memory, history, and war trauma. *Photographs Speak* is the script for a short play in which Rosenstein weaves images of old photographs with poetry and symbolic figures. The past appears as a presence full of shadows and memories whose effects are still felt today.

Erna Rosenstein, "Mówią zdjęcia," typescript with artist's signature from the collection of Urszula Usakowska-Wolff and Manfred Wolff in Berlin, from: POLE. *Dwumiesięcznik literacki*, no. 3 (2023), https://poledwumiesiecznik.com/nr-3/erna-rosenstein-mowia-zdjecia/ [accessed: 16.08.2025].

PHOTOGRAPHS SPEAK

An exhibition of old photographs. The mood of the past. Darkness falls. A poem is heard.

A toast
To you I speak, oh dead ones –
– though you are more and more alive...
A line thinner than the air.
A smile paler than a butterfly.
Words thinner than thoughts.
There is no boundary.
To your health, dead ones!
To our death!
...I carry the fire from the shadows themselves!

After these last words, a red light is increasingly visible. Soft music is heard. (For instance: "Enchanted tales, wondrous tales, told to me by my gray-haired nanny,"[1] or something of the sort...). A lady in an old-world outfit steps out to the strains of this melody. After her, life-sized photographs are carried in.

Various smaller photographs fall like flower petals.

The viewers pick them up. They study them. These are childhood photographs.

The same ones are seen, in different layouts, on a screen in the depths of the stage. They begin to blink. The music grows quieter and quieter... They vanish... Then a great photograph of ruins appears on the screen, brighter and brighter. Silence.

A voice is heard:

The crows are confused.
The silent mud hides.
Nighttime... and again, nothing.
A void tears down all the streets,
it cries for help!

A terrifying clatter. (It might also be the loud, mechanical ticking of a clock.)

Machines come. They have tape-deck heads. They put on cut-out grinning lips. They follow the rhythm of a mechanical and incomprehensible song that plays from a speaker.

The song slowly fades. Everything stops.

A skeleton enters. Turning toward the audience, it cries out:

– Speak up!

A long silence.

A white shroud falls on the procession of machines.

The silence continues.

Again, the skeleton cries:

– Speak!

More silence... We hear a faraway voice:

– Speak straight as a gaze.
Cut the boundary with a flash.
All the voices are from the grammar book.
They don't want to die.
They want to mean something.
Shifted into obsolescence –
they ring out differently.
Their sound again moves and multiplies the shadows.

It knocks on the door.
Opens it with an old-fashioned key.
Rings and decorations fall.
Come in.
Take the shortest word.

The light falls on the tensed figure of the skeleton, who waits a second, then slowly makes a resigned gesture. It picks up a large key and starts to speak.

At the same time, a very old book appears on the screen and we hear a poem by Broniewski.

– If the heart hangs too heavy in the chest,
rip open your chest and tear out your heart.
Line the road with a spring conquest
with a bridge of arms that won't come apart.
Should no blood spray from the song
the scream of hot gun barrels will do.
Strain your eyes. Chomp down strong.
Stand in line. Words are through.[2]

A moment's silence. A second later there is the sound of a procession, distant at first, then louder and louder. Workers with severed heads enter. They raise their clenched fists.

The poem continues:

It won't crack.
Slice the mouth, though it bleeds
bright and beautiful, it bites back.
Then joy and song proceeds.

A black canvas falls and covers everything.

A large and even brighter photograph of ruins appears once more on the screen. In the hall, the wind carries a shower of small old photographs. A moment later, this blizzard appears and flies across the screen as well. Shadows of mourning processions appear. A funeral march is heard:

– You fell in battle...
Great was your toil...

Everything vanishes. Emptiness. A clock ticks. Louder and louder. More and more menacing. Then cocks crow. A bugle call. Distant shots. Smoke. Silence. Suddenly... Bright light.

Various "rubbings," signposts, crosses, hammers, sickles, badges, road signs, illuminated advertisements, telegraph poles appear...

Finally, Don Quixote and Sancho Panza join the whole mess.

The dance draws them in. Pulls them along.

Don Quixote and Sancho Panza doing the most fashionable and unexpected dance moves.

Various lights change in time with the music. Models step in, presenting their conventional faces and magazine outfits.

The light is brighter and brighter. Total silence. Everything grows dark. Things empty out.

The screen shows a banner that reads: "Exiles of all countries, unite!"

This message gets closer and closer. It occupies the whole screen. Shots are heard. After each shot, the inscription tears.

After the last shot, the banner falls apart into scraps.

Everything goes pale. It vanishes. Again, as at the beginning, an exhibition of old photographs.

Translated by Soren Gauger

1 Julian Tuwim, "Bajki. Piosenka" (Warsaw: Publ. Bronisław Rudzki, 1918), 3.

2 Władysław Broniewski, "Pionierom," in *Pionier* 1,2 (March-April 1925): 1.

ERNA ROSENSTEIN, *Paper Starts Softly Speaking with Invisibility*, ink on paper, 22.8 × 32.6 cm, 1984

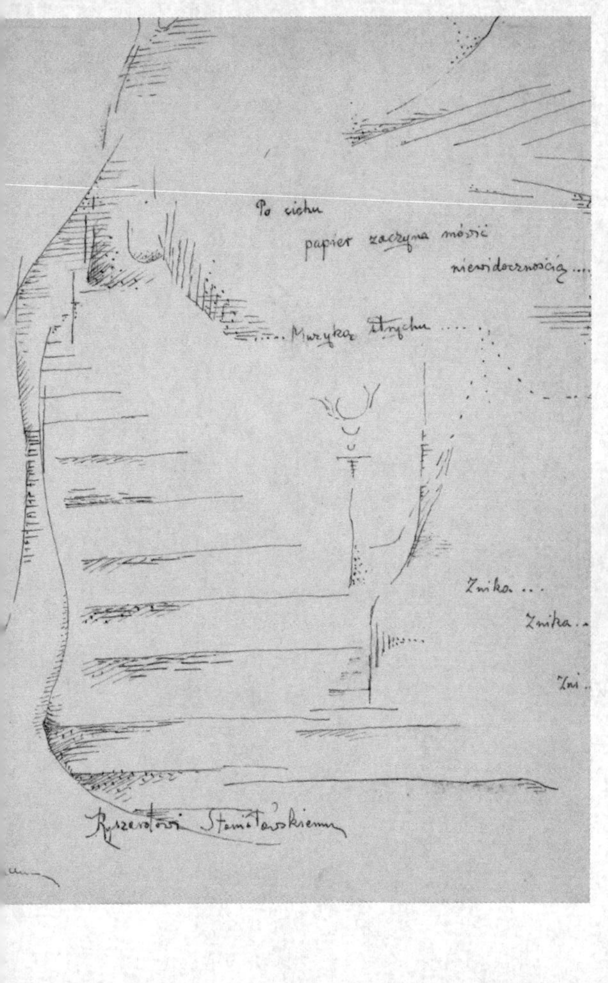

Po cichu
papier zaczyna mówić
niewidocznością....
....Muzyka Strychu ....
Znika...
Znika..
Zni..
Ryszardowi Stanisławskiemu

Aubrey Williams

AUBREY WILLIAMS
(1926, GEORGETOWN – 1990, LONDON)

A Guyanese painter who developed his unique artistic practice from his first solo exhibition in 1954. He combined Abstract Expressionism and inspirations from the pre-Columbian art of the native inhabitants of the Caribbean, and North and South America. In "The Predicament of the Artist in the Caribbean," Williams opposes the primacy of narrative art, suggesting that the art of the Caribbean has developed its own language, capable of expressing the region's unique reality. Along the way, he stresses the key role of visual art in decolonizing the Caribbean identity. He also points to the need to work with artists of other fields, which allowed him to develop an original visual language that was rooted in the region.

Aubrey Williams, "The Predicament of the Artist in the Caribbean," a paper read out at the first conference of the Caribbean Artists Movement in September 1967 at Kent University, Canterbury; it appeared as "The Artist in the Caribbean," Savacou, no. 2 (September, 1970), 16–18 and in *Guyana Dreaming. The Art of Audrey Williams*, ed. Anna Walmsley (Sydney: Dangaroo Press, 1990).

THE PREDICAMENT OF THE ARTIST IN THE CARIBBEAN

I was very disturbed, intellectually, by Professor Elsa Goveia's talk this morning. She made it clear that we have just done a very difficult thing in breaking out of one phase of our development and entering the new freedoms of the different islands and countries in the Caribbean. We will also at the same time have to move from colonialism into the 20th century in one jump, and we will have to do this in our creative arts first.

It always seems in the history of man that the arts give the direction for the technology, the philosophy, the politics and the very life of the people. Art is always in the foreground; it is the true avant garde. The visual arts, being the simplest and the most direct, should be a little ahead of literature, because with emerging peoples you have the problem of illiteracy, and direct contact is the natural level of communication in this society. We have considered the strength of folk-lore in emerging societies. We know that this is direct contact. It is one man or one person sitting in front of a group of other persons. Painting is this kind of direct contact in that the artist must see the object before he can contemplate it, and before it can enter his state of being. Writing will be less effective until we achieve a higher level of literacy.

Now, I am worried about a prevalent conception that good art, working art, must speak, it must be narrative. I do not see the necessity for art to be narrative, in that in thinking about the past and man, art has never been 'narrative' to any great extent. I would not call primitive art in any sense directly representational or figurative. The arts of past civilisations were to a great extent non-figurative. One does not question the validity, or the strength of impact, of so-called primitive abstract designs on shields, on houses, in pottery, in the weave of fabrics; one just accepts them. But strangely, in the West today, one makes demands upon the visual artist, demands that I think are not warranted in many cases. (It was a bit sad for me to see that it was our elder statesman in letters, C.L.R. James, who has turned, over the past two years, into being a champion for the more advanced and adventurous avant-garde in the visual arts. I would have thought that our young writers would have footed the bill far easier as they should be involved in the tensions that would produce an avant-garde in the Caribbean.)

If our intellectuals have not got an automatically functioning visual chain reaction going yet, what must we hope for from our people at home? When I was last in Guyana at the celebration of Independence, I was stopped in the street by a man driving a dray cart that was loaded with people who had come all the way from a village named Buxton on the east coast of Demerara. They had come to Georgetown. And this man came up to me. I was taking photographs, and he made himself known. I did not know him and he told me how glad he was to meet me and he told me of a new function in his life, one that gave him great pleasure. He said to me, 'You see that dray cart there. One day every month I load it up with people from my village and I bring them down to look at your paintings.' I felt very crushed and humble, and I just didn't know what to say. I said to him, 'They are abstract, people say they are abstract.' He used a very strong Guyanese cuss-word. He said 'Abstract, what is that? I don't understand abstract. When I look at your paintings I can think about my days in the bush.' And I thanked him and I went up to the dray cart and I shook everybody's hand and I spoke to the children for a while. And it was one of the most touching episodes of my visit back home. I am not trying to ask Caribbean intellectuals to consider abstraction as 'high art', or the 'art of the future' or anything like that. As a matter of fact I don't even think of my paintings as being abstract. I can't really see abstraction. Abstraction to me would be two colours on a surface, no form and no imprint of the hand of man. I do not think that painters paint abstraction, nor do I think that sculptors sculpt abstraction. I am not very sure that I understand the meaning of the word.

Another much-abused term is 'modern art.' We should see to it that this awful virus does not get a foot-hold in the Caribbean – the attitude to the visual arts that automatically attaches labels to what we see when we look. Much of my work has come out of a long contemplation and a search into the pre-Columbian civilisation in the new World – primarily, the Aztec, the Maya, the Toltec and the Inca. Also, a long immersion in the work of our South American Indians in Guyana. I firmly feel that such art should be automatically appreciated by people from the Caribbean and from Guyana because they share the same environment. The South American and the Caribbean environment as compared to the ordered environments of much of the rest of the world, appears naturally 'abstract'. It is yet, thank Heavens, not rearranged too much by the hand of man. We are losing it fast, but we are lucky to have our roots still in the earth of the Caribbean. We are still in a position to contemplate terrestrial reality. Ours is a beautiful landscape, unbelievably beautiful in some cases; but, as compared with the ordered landscapes in the countries that have been over-lived in, bizarre, unreal, incongruous. It is a very strong landscape and the primitive art that came out of this landscape remains unique. We should be proud of our non-figuration. We should be proud of the essences of human existence that the people from that neck of the woods have produced in the world. We should be very proud of people like Tamayo from Mexico. We should be proud of people like Matta from Chile.[1] We must become more involved with the visual output of our artists in the Caribbean, because they are going to change the real seeing of the world. They are going to do it just as the politicians and the writers will do it.

And I would be far happier if I could see a greater interchange between all the arts in the Caribbean. Caribbean art seems to me up to now terribly isolated. Everybody is in his niche, using up endless energy working alone without the help of his colleagues. We should have more interchange, we should have dialogue between the novelist and the painter, the musician and the dancer, the potter, the weaver; even the artisans should be included in this. And the dialogue with the people would then be automatic.

We come from this environment, we came out of this environment, and we produce the things that belong back to the environment. If our painters must grope and search and forge ahead, we do not as yet know the language they should speak. We will have to grow into this language and it is a movement from a great state of frustration into one of a growing norm. I hope that we will eventually reach what can be called a norm visually, but we must not be too impatient, and I would hope that the interchange between all the arts would promote an atmosphere in which the Caribbean people will find a greater intimacy with the visual arts.

1 Rufino Tamayo (1899–1991) – Mexican painter; Roberto Matta (1911-2002) – Chilean painter. – Ed.

Tadeusz Kantor

169

TADEUSZ KANTOR
(1915, WIELOPOLE SKRZYŃSKIE –
1990, KRAKOW)

A Polish painter, sculptor, performer, director, playwright, and actor who introduced art informel, happenings, and assemblage to Poland. In 1955, he founded the Cricot 2 theater group in Krakow, whose name was derived from the prewar Cricot avant-garde theater created by members of the Krakow Group. In "Picture-Drawing", Kantor recalls his postwar art as intuitive and instinctive. He sees drawings less as a record of something he has seen than an exercise in inward perception, going beyond the senses. Creativity does not come from faithful duplication of reality, but from an intense experience remolded in the imagination.

Tadeusz Kantor, "Obraz-rysunek," in *Metamorfozy. Teksty o latach 1938-1974* (Krakow: Cricoteka, 2000), 126–27.

PICTURE-DRAWING

Our whole dialog about those days is taking place after much time has elapsed. Don't suppose I'd like to take advantage of this fact to fiddle with the facts, now that I'm wiser from the experience of those ten-odd years. At any rate, I'm sure one is "wise" in the present, after something has been discovered and ventured. But many of the intentions of those days, working in the subconscious and mostly suppressed by prevailing conventions, now show me their reasoning with greater clarity.

Despite my faith in the power of the subconscious, I am forever persuaded how far instinct, the subconscious, and intuition faultlessly guide our actions in art. And that consciousness only annexes, and, of course, develops that sphere.

So as not to give the advantage to lyrical idiots, we should also say that without consciousness, which is a rational action that is intensely sharp, critical and radical, those "primary" values swiftly lose their power and are meaningless for Development. Without this, all those inspired intuitionists and "anointed ones" become false idols, working hard to build their own altars.

We see this everywhere. We have so many of them.

In the years right after the war I painted a fair amount, but this was not all I applied myself to. To be honest, a "Cézanne-esque honesty," building a reality in painting, was not especially important to me.

My detractors claimed my paintings were just rough drafts for paintings. They should have been more accurate: they are models. If they were more intelligent, they might have called them "dummies," or traps. Then they could have claimed to have given me an idea, which much later became a basic concept for my work.

Now I would like to clearly lay out my state of mind, whose symptoms were being sketched out even back then, that "defect," from the viewpoint of accepted conventions, which perhaps paved the way for my later work.

This was a difficulty of the imagination. Not the picture, not the work of art, but those zones where a certain sensitivity takes shape, develops, transforms, where ideas, objects, figures, and situations are born...

At the same time, I believed, and this is perhaps most vital, that the realm of the imagination can exist on its own, without coming out in the art object.

I've done masses of drawings. I still do them, to this day. A drawing is a faster, and thus more accurate record. These were in no way like academic studies, meant to be turned into paintings. I find those practices so amusing. Nor is it some intimate expression of my inner life, as most people assume. It is an "exercise" for the imagination. It less materializes the imagination than gives it shape. Owing to the lesser importance accorded to it, it assures the invisible zone of the imagination complete utopian autonomy.

Of course, during this period (1948–55), I painted pictures, but I have to say it was more out of habit. I drew, however, with incredible passion. My countless sketchbooks record my intense, most inward, one might say "subterranean" work, carried out in a kind of mad rush, during the night, totally "disinterested."

We've come to the crucial word: disinterested.

Translated by Soren Gauger

Harun Farocki

175

HARUN FAROCKI
(1944, NOWY JICIN – 2014, BERLIN)

A German director, film essayist, and media theorist, known for his intellectual documentaries that analyze the impact of images and technology on society. He spent decades creating films and video installations that critically explored the mechanisms of power, war, labor, and capitalism. In "Controlling Observation," Farocki analyzes how modern-day prisons become spaces of total control, where supervision technology replaces human contact, and punishment overrides the idea of resocialization. The camera images and training and propaganda materials show prison as a spectacle of violence and obedience, questioning the boundaries between reality and its mediated representation.

Harun Farocki, "Controlling Observation," *From Work To Text. Dialogues on Practise and Criticism in Contemporary Art*, ed. Jürgen Bock (Lisbon: Fundação Centro Cultural de Belém, 2002), 102–07.

CONTROLLING OBSERVATION

In January 1999, Cathy Crane and I started research in the US for a film with the working title *GEFÄNGNISBILDER (PRISON IMAGES)*. We were looking for footage from security cameras installed in penitentiaries, instruction material for prison officers, documentaries, and feature films, which included depictions of prisons. We got to know a private investigator who, as a civil rights activist, campaigns for the families of prisoners killed in Californian prisons: a private detective who reads Hans Blumenberg[1] when he has time to kill. An architect showed us the plans for a new penitentiary for "sex offenders" in Oregon; one-third of the planned buildings—those intended for therapeutic services—had been crossed out from the plans because the legislature refused to fund them. In Camden, New Jersey, near Philadelphia, a guard showed me around the prison; the men gave me disdainful, sidelong glances from behind glass similar to that in the lion house of a zoo. I saw women brushing each other's hair like women in a Pasolini film. The guard told me that there were vents in the ceilings of the day rooms through which tear gas could be introduced, but that this had never been done as the chemicals deteriorated over time.

Pictures from the maximum security prison in Corcoran, California: A surveillance camera shows a pie-shaped segment of the concrete yard where the prisoners, dressed in shorts and mostly shiftless, are allowed to spend half an hour a day. One prisoner attacks another, whereupon those not involved lay flat on the ground, arms over their heads. They know that when a fight breaks out, the guard will call out a warning and then fire once using a rubber bullet. If the prisoners continue fighting, the guard will use live ammunition. The pictures are silent, and the shot is only revealed in the trail of gun smoke drifting across the screen. The camera and the gun are right next to each other; field of vision and field of fire merge. The reason that the yard was built in pie segments is clear—so that there is nowhere to hide from observation or bullets. One of the prisoners—usually the attacker—collapses. In many cases he is either seriously wounded or dead. The prisoners belong to prison gangs with names like "Aryan Brotherhood" or "Mexican Mafia". They have received long sentences and are locked up far away from the world in a maximum security prison. They have hardly anything but their bodies, the muscles of which they work out constantly, and their affiliation to an organisation. Their honour is more important to them than their lives; they fight knowing full well they will be shot at. At Corcoran, brawling prisoners have been shot at on more than two thousand occasions. Some guards claim that their colleagues have often deliberately put members of warring groups into the yard together and placed bets on the outcome of the fights as if the prisoners were gladiators. The surveillance cameras run at a slower speed in order to save on costs. In the footage available to us, the intervals were extended so that the movements are jerky and not flowing. The fights in the yard look like something from a cheap computer game. It is hard to imagine a less dramatic representation of death.

SURVEILLANCE TECHNOLOGY

We obtained the footage of the fights and shootings from a female attorney representing the relatives of the prisoners killed. The guards continually claimed that they feared the attacking prisoner was carrying a weapon, such as the sharpened handle of a plastic spoon. The prisoners in Corcoran are subject to such strict controls, however, that this hardly seems likely. From a central control room it is possible to monitor which cells are occupied and which are empty, which doors are open and in which walkway each person can be found. The guards can send out an electronic identification signal to warn of a prohibited movement by a prisoner.

In the present judicial crisis in the US—despite falling crime rates, the number of prisoners has quadrupled over the past twenty years—many new prisons are being built, including some by private operators. New technologies are being developed and implemented in order to reduce costs. Guards are meant to have as little direct contact with the prisoners as possible, and just as humans in the production sector have turned over war production to machines, prisoners should also be isolated from any direct human contact. There is now a machine available that can check for drugs and weapons in all of a prisoner's orifices. There are metal detectors at every door. An iris scanner is a device that photographs the iris, isolates the significant characteristics, and compares them with a set of data. This equipment can be fixed to doors and identify each individual, prisoner or guard, within two seconds. Meanwhile, a chair embraces a raging prisoner in its steel arms and gags him with gentle force, like something from a fantasy film. This apparatus also expresses a general desire for objectivity, for dispassionate repression.

PUBLIC RELATIONS

The State of California has removed the word "rehabilitation" from its statutes; prisons have given up on correction, they are explicitly and solely there to punish. The justice department commissioned a video for the media, primarily intended to prove that those sentenced to prison do not lead a life of luxury and actually have a tough time there ("The Toughest Beat in California"). The style for this video meant slamming and locking doors extra loudly, guards approaching with loud and ominous footsteps and rattling their keys as if there were an execution about to happen.

They are shown in slow motion, using a long focal length and the accompanying background music is intended to link them with the heroes from Westerns. This video can be compared to a propaganda film the Nazis produced at the Brandenburg Prison in 1943. They have the same message: "The time for leniency is over. Let us no longer speak of correction, but rather of the severity of punishment". Both films show how a prisoner is bound hand and foot like an escape artist in the circus. Both films transform the criminal into a spectacle. In doing so, the California film is even more sensationalist than the Nazi film. The extent of abuse in the Germany of 1943 was of course far greater than in the California of today, but the Nazis were still at pains to maintain at least an appearance of legality. The demand for entertainment has grown immeasurably since then. Even films critical of prisons aim at being entertaining. There are hardly any critical films that manage to do so without the accompanying fearful excitement of an execution.

PRISON AS A SPECTACLE

With the advent of the modern era, punishment underwent a fundamental change when public torture and execution were abolished. Those who break the law today are shut away behind walls, withdrawn from the gaze, made invisible. Every picture from prison is a reminder of the cruel history of the criminal justice system. We see a film produced by the Bureau of Prisons in Washington, D.C., for the further education of the prison staff. A prisoner is raging, and a guard tries in vain to calm him down; he calls his superior who again attempts appeasement. Then the guard fetches a camera to document the procedure completely. A combat unit arrives on the scene together with a physician; having stormed the cell and overwhelmed the prisoner, they tie him up on the bed. (The five members of the combat unit are wearing protective helmets and breastplates, and each of them has the task of seizing a particular part of the raging man's body.) All this is captured on camera so as to document the detachment that the justice apparatus is supposed to maintain towards the prisoner. Precisely because the portrayal is so meticulous, it is also implausible and thus functions as a denial. It insists so emphatically that the personnel were acting indifferently and without emotion, that they took no pleasure in subduing the prisoner. This message is proclaimed so often and so loudly that one ends up believing exactly the opposite.

OBSERVATIONAL CONTROL

In modern prisons, where the aim is to rehabilitate the prisoner, he is not put on display, but the guard's controlling gaze remains. The guard is society's representative, and with this in mind, Jeremy Bentham, the philosopher of punishment, drew up plans for a prison with a central watchtower, providing a line of sight into each cell. The prisoners would be unable to tell whether the tower was actually occupied; they would simply be aware that they were potentially being observed. Bentham thought that anyone could enter the tower and perform the task of supervision. In order for panoptic control to work, cells must be open and have bars instead of walls. This is usually the case in the US. Over the past ten years, prisons in the United States are again being built according to panoptic principles. In point of fact, video cameras could be used anywhere but what is important to prison operators is that the prisoner feels exposed to human observation.

At the same time, there are more and more prisons where the prisoners no longer have direct visual contact with their visitors whether it be through bars or glass. They are only allowed to communicate via videophone. This is justified on humanitarian grounds: relatives no longer need to trek long distances, they only have to go to an office which provides and supervises the videophone connection. This bit of modernisation has meant that one of the central narrative figures of prison films has lost its basis in reality. How often have we viewed movie scenes where the visitor and prisoner are talking together and the vigilant guard steps in? Or of a parting couple symbolically touching longingly through the glass pane that separates them?

STUDIO PLAY

Silent films prior to D.W. Griffith, set in prisons: these films are related to theatre and the cell usually resembles a sitting room. Like the fireplace in a sitting room, the bars in the cell are like stage props that the actor playing a prisoner is better off not rattling for fear that they will fall apart. Without a fourth wall, a cell becomes no more than a scene in a peepshow; especially if the actors involved are "acting as if", instead of acting.

Because there are few visitors in prison, it is difficult to develop dramatic intrigue. This is why silent films often make the prison cell the setting for visions. The condemned man imagines his execution or pardon, the desperate recall their lost happiness, the vengeful picture their hour of revenge. The imagination is portrayed using superimpositions, double exposures, and other film tricks. Seen in this manner, the prison cell is a spiritually rich location. We come to understand that the origins of the cell are related to monastic solitude. "Alone in his cell the prisoner is delivered up unto himself; in the silence of his passions he descends into his conscience, questions it, and senses within the awakening of that moral feeling which never completely dies in man's heart." The cell then is designed not just as a grave, but also as a scene of resurrection.

REMOVING WALLS

More than anything else, electronic control technology has a *deterritorialising* effect. (Companies no longer have to be concentrated in one location; and production at these locations can be quickly switched to making different products.) Locations become less specific. An airport contains a shopping centre, a shopping centre has a school, a school offers recreational facilities, and so on. What are the consequences of this development for prisons, themselves mirrors of society as well as its counter-image and projection surface?

On the one hand, electronic technology makes it possible to constrain a person even when he is outside prison, it can supervise and punish him, and with electronic foot tagging it can keep someone under house arrest while it allows him to go to work or attend school. On the other hand, some two hundred years after Europe tore down its city walls, ever increasing numbers of people are closing themselves off in so-called "gated communities". The residents of these communities are by no means exclusively from the upper classes. Security technology is no longer restricted to selectively regulating access to "sensitive" nuclear or military facilities; today it is also used to control access to normal offices and factories. Throughout a thousand years of urban history, streets have always been public space; twenty-five years ago in Minneapolis the first system of inner-city skywalks was established with private security firms to exclude undesirables. Deregulation does not by any means imply a reduction of control. In one of his last writings, Gilles Deleuze outlined the vision of a society of controls which he said would replace disciplinary society.

THE END OF THEMES AND GENRES

We have already mentioned that the prison visitation scene will soon correspond to nothing in reality. The introduction of electronic cash will make bank robbery practically impossible as well, and if it turns out that in the future all weapons will be electronically secured and only capable of being fired by the licensed owner, the end of movie shoot-outs will be just around the corner. With the introduction of iris scanners that identify an individual *en passant*, the comedy of errors becomes an endangered genre. It will be almost impossible to tell the story of a man going to prison for a crime he did not commit or of a visitor exchanging clothes with a prisoner, allowing him to walk free. With the increase in electronic control structures, everyday life will become just as hard to portray and to dramatise as everyday work already is.

PRISON – WORKHOUSE

In the prison film, work scenes are more commonly shown than in other genres. In the Netherlands of the seventeenth century, there were cells in which water kept rising and whose inmates had to bale themselves out to keep from drowning; this demonstrated that man must work to live. In eighteenth-century England, many prisoners had to work the treadmill—today many prisoners can again be found on treadmills, keeping themselves physically fit. Prison labour has seldom been economically significant and at best had some educational value. Prison trains prisoners to do industrial work, because factories are organised on similar principles: to concentrate, to distribute in space, to order in time, to compose a productive force within the dimension of space-time whose effect will be greater than the sum of its component forces.

It is worthwhile to compare images of prison with those of work-research laboratories: opening the cell doors, prisoners leaving their cells, role call, marching to the yard, circling around the prison yard, etc. Experiments were carried out for the organisation of Fordist factories on how a wall should be built. Should one worker lift the stone and do the mortaring, or is it better for one worker to do the lifting and a second worker to do the mortaring? These tests present a picture of abstract work while the pictures from the surveillance cameras yield a picture of abstract existence.

1 1 Hans Blumenberg (1920-1996) – German philosopher. – Ed.

CHAPTER

THE EYE

V

& THE EAR

Stefan Themerson

189

STEFAN THEMERSON
(1910, PŁOCK – 1988, LONDON)

A writer, poet, philosopher, filmmaker, composer, and publisher. He and his wife, Franciszka Themerson, created pioneering experimental films and were co-founders of the Gaberbocchus Press. His work evolved at the crossroads of art and languages—from the interwar avant-garde to British Modernism. In his book, *The Urge to Create Visions,* Themerson formulates a concept of art as an act of apprehending and creatively distorting perception. These "visions" are neither hallucinations nor simple images—this is an active process of transforming the world through the senses, language, and the imagination. The author analyzes the relationship between the word, the image, and sound, stressing the role of montage, rhythm, and understatement as ways of knowing reality from various angles at the same time.

Stefan Themerson, *The Urge to Create Visions* (Amsterdam: Gaberbocchus + De Harmonie, 1983), 37, 59–62.

THE LUMINIFEROUS EYE

Aboriginal mythography, mediaeval imagery, Joanna-Dorota's reverie, gave way to the new world of vision. The world of the phantasies of Meliès[1] and the realisms of *La Zone*;[2] the expressionisms of *Caligari*[3] and the new realisms of *Changes of Streets*; the sur (?) realisms of René Clair, Jean Vigo, Buñuel, and the lyricism of Cocteau, Germaine Dulac, Blakeston,[4] and Eisenstein's *Sentimental Romance*;[5] the world composed of moving lines of Richter and Eggeling and Szczuka, and of light shapes of Chomette, and of mechanized blacks, greys & whites of Moholy Nagy;[6] the world of 'pure' rhythms constructed from non pure realistic rushes, like Léger's mechanical ballet or Jalu Kurek's[7] rhythmical calculations *(O.R.)*; the visions of the spirit of our age in Ruttmann's *Symphony of the Great City*, and of the ideas of our age in Bartosch's *L'idée*, and of the beauty of the world of Nature in Painlevé's *Hippocampus*, and of the beauty of the world of artefacts in Ivens's *Glassworks*...[8]

In their search for visions, some went the way of the *camera obscura*, some went the way of the *laterna magica*, – and the synthesis of both + the main element of this Changing World: motion. Nature gave us vocal cords but neglected to give us a light-producing organ. We had to build it ourselves: the projective luminiferous eye.

YES, BUT...

'Yes, but what is it, actually, this new "eye", this apparatus for producing visions, this "projector"? Where is it, where does it begin and where does it end in the complicated process of making a film?'

'Well, my dear sir or madam, what I'm talking about is much more than the piece of machinery in the projection room of a cinema. If Berkeley were alive today, and said that the reality seen on the screen is the idea in the mind of the film-maker, these words would define where our organ of lumination ends and where it has its beginning'.

***

To sing images, like a luminous fish does in the dark depths of the ocean, not with a reflected but with one's own light.

(Warsaw, 1936)

THE UNIQUENESS OF PHOTOGRAMS

Photograms are as old as the world. When the apple was still green, a little leaf got stuck to its surface. The sun shone, the apple reddened, but not under the little leaf. And when Eve took the apple, which was pleasant to the eyes, she flicked off the little leaf, but she didn't notice that a beautiful pale shape of the little leaf was created there, on the peel of the apple. Neither did the serpent notice it. Nor did Adam. Nor the author of Genesis (otherwise he would have mentioned it, and he didn't).

Some 3761 + 1727 = 5488 years later, a medical man called Schultze of Halle,[9] took a pair of scissors, cut some letters out of a sheet of black paper, placed them on some flat surface covered with silver chloride, and exposed it to the sunlight. Silver chloride darkened where it was uncovered, and when he removed the letters, their shapes stayed clearly there, white on black. But he (a contemporary of

Chardin) didn't consider it to be a work of art. Anyway, its life was short, the shapes of the letters darkened and vanished, he didn't know how to fix the image.

112 years later, in 1839 (years at the time moved slowly, nobody was in a hurry) an English philologist and archaeologist, William Henry Fox Talbot,[10] laid a few pretty ferns and some other little objects on paper treated with silver chloride, and obtained their 'photogenic', negative, white on black, picture, which he knew how to fix (by immersing it in the boiling solution of kitchen salt in water). But he (a contemporary of Turner and Delacroix) didn't regard it as a work of art either. Later on when dry sensitized paper was invented, hundreds or thousands of photographers must by sheer mistake have exposed a sheet or two to light at a moment when some objects of various shapes (including their own fingers) happened to throw their shadows on paper, and still they wouldn't consider any of those strange new white grey and black shapes as a work of art. Because a work of art is a curious thing. Curious, because the same object may be art and may not be art. Because a work of art isn't, it becomes. It is not enough to know how to manufacture it. There is, in the Platonic Heaven, no formula stating its precise nature. To be art, it has to be (1) recognised as art, and it has to be (2) introduced as art into our life.

It was probably Christian Schad[11] in Geneva who, in 1919-1920, was the first to recognise as works of art some bits of 'spoiled' photographic paper he produced himself; and it was Man Ray who had the courage to proclaim that sort of thing to be art.

PHOTOGRAMS + TIME

The strange thing about a photogram is that the essence of it isn't in it, it is in your eye. Either you see it or you don't. And, even when you can recognize in it the meek, humble objects that have created it – a comb, a flask, a leaf, a tea-strainer, – it is not a representation of any combs, or flasks, or leaves, or tea-strainers, it is what it is, its reality is its own.

But it's not enough to put your humble 'actors' on a sheet of photographic paper and switch the lights on for a second. Your light-source has to be active, – it is it that 'paints' the picture. You can use a naked bulb, or a torch, or a candle, or a lighted match, you can move it and observe the dance of the dark shadows (which will become white), you can caress with it 3-dimensional objects to make their shadows turn round, and elongate, and shrink, you can move it near the paper and brighten it (which will produce deep blackness). And that play, that projective geometry drama of growing, becoming and vanishing, is lost in the final product – the static photogram. We (Franciszka and I) decided to record the whole process as it takes place in time, to make 'photograms in motion'.

What we did was as follows: Instead of putting various objects on photographic paper, they were placed on a sheet of translucent paper on a horizontal sheet of glass, and photographed (frame by frame) from below. Movement was achieved by changing the position of some sharp naked lights, from above. For very big and heavy objects, and sometimes for human beings (as in the film *Zwarcie*) the translucent sheet was spread vertically. The film was printed and the print was used as the negative. The camera was an old (1910) yellow wooden box. I loved it. You could force it to do what you wanted to achieve. A modern camera would force you to do what it is capable of doing.

The first film we made by using that method was *Apteka* (1931), the last, *The Eye & The Ear* (1946). But photograms-in-motion played their role in all our other films.

A man, not very old, (and it was not so very long ago, in the 30s), told me that he felt lost when watching even an ordinary Hollywood film. 'Well,' he complained, 'here I see her eating her breakfast in the kitchen, and a moment later she's already galloping across the desert. How come? She wouldn't have time even to open the door to get out!' That sort of 'editing' didn't bother him in a novel, but it did in a film.

There is another sort of editing which people accept in poetry but don't accept in a film. The sort of editing where pictures are put together not one beside the other, like in a photomontage, but one after another – in a 'temporal collage'. Such sequences of images do not form statements of the sort: 'she's sitting and eating her breakfast', 'she's galloping across the desert'. Their very syntax is different. But I don't attempt to define it. It serves a different purpose. But I wouldn't know how to describe it.

Old words are not meant to deal with this kind of vision, and philosophers haven't yet invented new categories of thought that would. The syntactical relation of images to images is not the same at that of words to words. An image is not exactly the same as a noun, a movement is not exactly the same as a verb, and a collage is not exactly the same as a statement. The latter may be true, or false, necessary, or contingent, or self-contradictory. The former can not. Semantically also they are different. While syntactically words refer to words and semantically words refer to things, images in a collage refer neither to words nor to things, their meaning is to be born in a non-verbal, non-referencial, ostensive way.

What I have just said does not apply to 'ordinary' motion picture images. A motion picture: *Hitler kissing a child* refers to the same factual occurrence to which the verbal statement 'Hitler is kissing a child' does. A collage made of an image of Hitler + child + bouquet of flowers, – does not. It does not refer to authenticity. It is an 'abstract' picture composed of 'real' images. And don't tell me, please: 'That's a bit sophisticated, isn't it?' When Moholy Nagy saw our film *Europa* (in 1936, in London), he also said the film was sophisticated. I was too young then to tell him that he was wrong. That the film was primitive. And that he couldn't see this because he was sophisticated. For what can be more primitive than the juxtaposition in time of the picture of a loaf of bread, and a close-up of a woman's hips, and a view of her face? Or, a solitary blade of grass squeezed up between two paving stones, its roots struggling with their hardness, breaking them, and the blade of grass growing visibly into a tree that falls down on to the roofs of the houses? Primitive people would have taken it in as it was meant to be taken. Would have seen it as it was shown. Without further interpolation. It was only sophisticated people who searched for symbolism, or what not! There was no symbolism there. It was an ordinary visual statement expressed in a simple visual syntax of cinematographic poetry. Its non-verbal language was more concentrated, just like the language of poetry is more concentrated than that of prose. Maybe that's why most of the films I've mentioned were so short. Some were as short as 3 or 4 minutes, not many were longer than 15. (Even *Le Chien Andalou* was only 2 reels = less than 30 minutes long). And nearly all were silent films. Which is a pity.

Because the poetic lyricism of photograms and the concentrated poetic dynamism of temporal collages both have some common denominators with the rhythmical patterns of music. Well, I know that using an analogy to poetry I am committing the fallacy of explaining one unknown by another (*ignotum per ignotum*) – but that's the best I can offer.

The movement of a racing car eulogized by Marinetti,[12] of a butterfly in *All Quiet on the Western Front*,[13] of Marlene Dietrich's[14] eye, winking, are all movements recorded by the camera. But there exist also movements *created* by the camera.

When a man turns round in front of you, it is his movement that the camera records. But when he stays still, and the camera travels around him, or along him, up and down, exploring for you various facets of the reality of his existence, it is the camera that creates the movement, and the movement becomes the property of the screen, and not of the outside world.

A stone in a snapshot is, by its nature, still. But if you observe it from sunrise to sunset, though the stone itself remains static, its image changes gradually, as the light fades in and out. In the motion-still-life, all movements are the property not of the object but of its image. A stone, a sculpture, a book, a photograph of a gauleiter, the dome of a cathedral, a gallows, are not 'presented', they are 'described' by innumerable cinematographic means, – by altering their shape gradually, modulating from one colour to another, passing from solitude to multiplicity, changing their intensity and sharpness, timing their appearance and vanishing, phrase after phrase, till the camera becomes an autonomous visual instrument which has such affinities with musical instruments that it wouldn't feel estranged in an orchestra.

O yes, colour! *Calling Mr. Smith* (London, 1943) was our first film made in colour. (I did try to make some experiments in colour before, in 1939, in Arceuil, near Paris, using colour lights, till a neighbour came and warned us: 'Méfiez-vous de la populace,' people in the bistrot on the corner are starting to say that some colour signals are being sent from your window, and the war is approaching. The war came indeed, and stopped the silly colour fantasies. I don't even remember what I was trying to do and how, using 3 b/w films probably?) In *Calling Mr. Smith* some wartime texts and music (Bach, Szymanowski, a distorted *Horst Wessel Lied*) were integrated with bits of documentary films, pictures and static objects whose motion was achieved by purely photographic means. Mixed colour lights were used all through. (The Dufay-colour people didn't like it. Their ambition was to prove that Dufay-colour was as good as Glorious Technicolor in rendering faithfully the natural colour of the skin, the complexion, and our screen images lit by many colours seemed to disprove it).

1 Georges Méliès (1861-1938) – French illusionist, director, creator of, among others, *A Trip to the Moon*. – Ed.
2 *La Zone* – French documentary from 1928 directed by Georges Lacombe. – Ed.
3 *The Cabinet of Dr. Caligari* – German film from 1920 directed by Robert Wiene. – Ed.
4 René Clair (1898-1981) – French film director, screenwriter and actor; Jean Vigo (1905-1934) – French avant-garde filmmaker; Luis Buñuel (1900-1983) – Spanish-Mexican film director and screenwriter; Jean Cocteau (1889-1963) – French poet, playwright, filmmaker and painter; Germaine Dulac (1882-1942) – French film director and screenwriter, theorist and pioneer of avant-garde cinema; Oswell Blackeston (Henry Joseph Hasslacher) (1907-1985) – British writer and avant-garde artist. – Ed.
5 *Sentimental Romance* –a 1930 film by Sergei Eisenstein. – Ed.
6 Hans Richter (1888-1976) – German filmmaker, one of the exponents of Dadaism; Viking Eggeling (1880-1925) – Swedish artist, representative of Dadaism; Mieczysław Szczuka (1898-1927) – avant-garde artist, one of the Polish Constructivists; Henri Chomette (1896-1941) – French actor, screenwriter, and director; László Moholy-Nagy (1895-1946) – Hungarian painter, photographer, and Bauhaus professor. – Ed.
7 Fernand Léger (1881-1955) – French painter; Jalu Kurek (1904-1983) – Polish writer and translator. – Ed.
8 *Berlin: Symphony of a Great City* – a 1927 film by Walter Ruttmann; *L'idée* – a 1932 film by Berthold Bartosch; *Hippocampus* – a 1934 film by Jean Painlevé; *Philips-Radio* – a 1931 film by Joris Ivens. – Ed.
9 Johann Heinrich Schulze (1687-1744) – German scientist, discoverer of the photosensitivity of silver chloride. – Ed.
10 William Henry Fox Talbot (1800-1877) – archaeologist, chemist, botanist, linguist, mathematician, pioneer of black-and-white photography. – Ed.
11 Christian Schad (1894-1982) – German painter and photographer. – Ed.
12 Filippo Tommaso Marinetti (1876-1944) – Italian poet, publisher, and one of the theoreticians of Futurism. – Ed.
13 *All Quiet on the Western Front* – film adaptation of Erich Maria Remarque's novel, directed by Lewis Milestone in 1930. – Ed.
14 Marlene Dietrich (1901-1992) – German-American actress and singer. – Ed.

STEFAN THEMERSON, ***Photogram,***
photographic paper, 25.3 × 20.1 cm, 1928

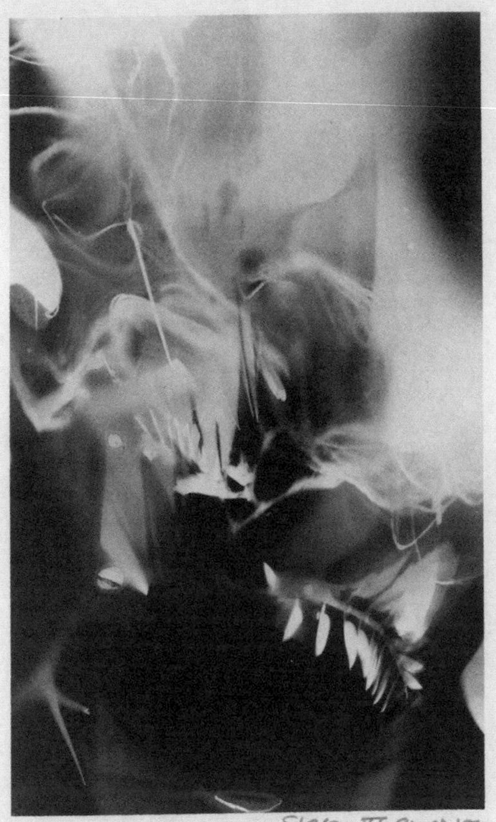
Stefan Themerson

Katalin Ladik

KATALIN LADIK
(B. 1942, NOVI SAD)

A Hungarian poet, performer, and sound and theater artist, a key figure on the experimental arts scene in Eastern Europe. Her work combines visual, sonic, and physical poetry. The poem "Concerto" is a kind of sensual score in which words work like audio images, and language is subordinate to the rhythm, color, and physicality of the voice. The structure of the text recalls a classical form of music: the division into parts (*allegro, largo, vivace, adagio, finale*) structures a series of synesthesic impressions, based on the tension between sound and meaning.

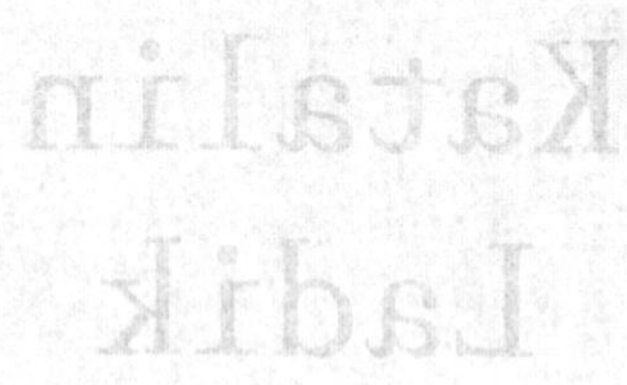

Katalin Ladik, *A négydimenziós ablak. Válogatott versek* (1962-1996) (Hague: Mikes International, 2004), 76–78.

CONCERTO

allegro

shining metal plates
struck
subtle trembling
at the nearest wall
human voice
freezes on impact

largo

nozzles of colored plastic
sealed in crystal

vibrato

bouncing
tiny spirals

the narrowing circle of
pain

a drop of water repeating itself

vivace

shards of warm glass
erupting
in the mouth

vox humana

stretched out
in the center of space
showing both faces
to two gods

con variazione

a narrow human voice
incomprehensible
to the bluest sky

piano

spider
on shards of pale blue
glass

adagio

blinding
screaming ropes

finale

the operating table
at full speed
in the exploding labyrinth of a
bend

Translated by Josef Schreiner

Milan Knížák

MILAN KNÍŽÁK
(B. 1940, PLZEŇ)

A Czech conceptual artist, performer, composer, teacher, and pioneer of experimental performative art in Eastern Europe. Since the 1960s, he has been affiliated with the Fluxus movement, whose ideas—combining life with art, collective action, deconstruction of music and openness of forms—he helped create in a Czechoslovak context. The *Idea* score (1978) is an action based on collective imagination and telepathy—participants are all meant to think about the same things at once. These are sonic concepts ("the sound of C," "melodies"), as well as pictures, physical sensations, or emotional states. Knížák suggests that by a joint act of thinking, it is possible to create an intangible, yet intense aesthetic experience.

Milan Knížák, “Idea (Mental Image, Notion),” in *The Fluxus Performance Workbook*, eds. Ken Friedman, Owen Smith, Lauren Sawchyn (Aberystwyth: Performance Research, 2002), e-book, 67–68.

IDEA (MENTAL IMAGE, NOTION)

A given number of people, at a given, precisely determined time, think of a given, precisely determined thing.

Create a collective idea (mental image, notion).

Examples: think together about:

a headache

a handshake
the warmth of the sun
the note C
the flight of a bird
beauty independent of objects and phenomena
joining
the warmth of skin
melodies
an eye
the spirit
nothing
a black cloud
a blue sky
a collective brain
a collective heart
an earth that is getting smaller
an earth that is stretching etc.

First variation: the people are together when they do this.

Second variation: each person is alone (in their own home).

1978

CHAPTER

ACCELERATION

VI

CIRCLE

Bridget Riley

BRIDGET RILEY
(B.1931, LONDON)

A British painter and a leading figure in the Op art movement, creating illusory pictures with geometrical patterns and color contrasts. Her work focuses on exploring visual perception and optical effects, making the viewer take an active role. Riley sees Mondrian's work as an inspiration to join structure with movement. Her practice, much like his, composes dynamics and harmony to strike a visual balance between tension and contrasts. Riley appreciates how Mondrian transforms the basic elements of painting—lines and colors—into dynamic forms that engage the viewer and create a dialog between universal and individual artistic expression.

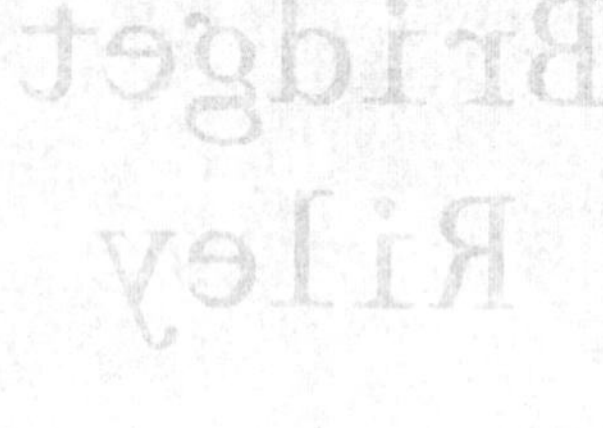

Bridget Riley, "Mondrian Perceived," *Mondrian Evolution*, ed. Sam Keller, Ulf Küster, Susanne Gaensheimer (Berlin: Hatje Cantz, 2022), 186–91. This essay is slightly adapted from the previously published "Mondrian Perceived," in *Mondrian: Nature to Abstraction: from the Gemeentemuseum*, The Hague, ed. Bridget Riley, exh. cat. Tate Gallery (London, 1997), 9–20.

MONDRIAN PERCEIVED

An artist's early work is inevitably made up of a mixture of tendencies and interests, some of which are compatible and some of which are in conflict with each other. As the artist picks his way, rejecting and accepting as he goes, certain patterns of inquiry emerge. His failures are as valuable as his successes in that by misjudging one thing he confirms something else, even if at the time he does not know what that something else is. In that sense, although Piet Mondrian may sometimes fail, he never makes mistakes; everything in his development is of use and contributes to that development.

There are two conflicting traits in his temperament, in the sense given to the word by Charles Baudelaire and Paul Cézanne[1]—"temperament" as an artist's own particular and ineradicable nature. One is a feeling for rhythm, which quickens to the pulse of life and seems somehow to be connected with his positive sense of the new; the other is a love of order and balance, which is at the root of his search for unity and fullness. Both these traits can also have an obverse side: the lively quality may lead to an extreme dynamism and fragmentation, while the insistence on order can sometimes turn into a bland and almost schematic statement. These two temperamental qualities ebb and flow throughout the various preoccupations and styles of his development—one now in ascendancy, and then the other, until they slowly find a resolution in the late abstract works.

The early landscapes painted in Holland are predominantly tonal in treatment and have a low-key, moody character. Trees and buildings reflected in water produce self-contained symmetrical images that cut recession short and pull the field of vision up close. Evening light is frequently chosen, and there is a marked interest in visual phenomena bordering on the apparitional. The tree in *Evening on the Gein*, from around 1906, far from calling on natural similitude, looms over the dark shape of the riverbank and its reflection like some ominous sign; and in *Trees on the Gein: Moonrise*, from 1907-08, the five trees are treated as a spectral frieze spread flat against the light of the moon.

This up-closeness is carried further in a choice of subjects in which the sense of an unencompassable presence and an overpowering scale dominate. In his "Trialogue" (1919-20), Mondrian, under the guise of the abstract-realist painter, says about *Mill*; *The Red Mill*, from 1911: "Indeed, I find this windmill very beautiful. Particularly now that we are too close to it to view it in *normal* perspective and therefore cannot see it or draw it *normally*. From here, it is very difficult merely to reproduce what one sees."[2] The final painting conveys the sensation of something grand towering up above the spectator's viewpoint.

The recurrent subject of sea, sky, and dunes provides a theme of vast, uncentered openness. The lack of differentiation in such motifs gives a singular prominence to the horizon line and its reverberations. By stacking and interlocking horizontal divisions of different weights and distances, Mondrian creates a fluctuating, impalpable envelope of space.

From very early on there seems to have been a special attraction to trees and to the pictorial problem of how branches, sky, and foliage or blossom interact and interpenetrate. Being essentially a subject that cannot be treated "realistically," the tree offers a marvelous pretext for the fabrication of a rhythmic structure of shallow recessions and advances that have little or nothing to do with the void and solid of the original motif. The potential of this subject was to be most fully realized in Mondrian's Cubist work.

But before that, Mondrian discovered color. It first entered his world through Vincent van Gogh and Divisionism. Both the vibrancy of autonomous brushwork and the abstract intensity of color contrast must have appealed to his feeling for rhythm and dynamism. In *Evening: The Red Tree*, of 1908–10, the sensation of evening light has shed its moody aura and Mondrian fairly crackles the painting into life with equivalents of red and blue and short, energetic brush marks. From there it is only a small shift to the liberation of color from any descriptive or representational function. This Fauvist approach can be seen in *Mill*; *Mill in Sunlight*, of 1908. The dazzling heat and light of a midsummer day is recast in stabbing strokes and blotches of red and yellow shot through with pale blue and violet.

But Mondrian's development is not simply one of a young painter finding out what to paint and how to paint it. Like van Gogh, he comes from a Dutch background deeply involved with religious matters, and in a similar way his fulfilment as an artist is inseparably connected with transforming these roots. The parallel is striking because it shows that even a cultural basis as alien and unsympathetic to artistic aspiration as fervent Protestantism is not necessarily an obstacle. It is a question of whether an artist is strong enough to turn this predicament to advantage. Van Gogh was able to transform his religious zeal and empathy with the people working in the coal mines into preaching a virtual gospel of the power of the sun. Whereas Mondrian, who initially engaged in Theosophy and all sorts of attempts to reconcile philosophical speculation with Christianity, had to discover in the basic properties of painting the means that allowed him to fulfill his spiritual quest.

The crucial painting in this context is *Evolution*, from 1911. It is something of an embarrassment to many people who love Mondrian as an abstract purist; and for those who claim that Mondrian is a Symbolist and not really an abstract artist at all, this painting serves as the basic reference point. In fact, it deserves neither of these responses. It is a unique and revealing failure on an imaginative scale only comparable to Cezanne's early expressive works such as *The Eternal Feminine* and *A Modern Olympia*. No fashionable or well-behaved artist would ever dare risk something like this; it takes an unselfconscious and uncompromising imagination to go to such awkward lengths. Over and above its obvious pictorial shortcomings, the failure of the work is objective. In *Evolution* Mondrian attempts to make a universal statement about life—a task of a dimension traditionally only accomplished through the agency of biblical subjects and antique mythology. The fact that this whole sphere of representation was no longer available had been an essential mainspring in the formation of modern art in the nineteenth century. Mondrian had to discover for himself that literary Symbolism and personal invention could not make up for this loss. The creation of a common social language does not lie within the scope of an individual, and the lack of such a basis has to be accepted by modern painting.

It would have been almost impossible for a young artist to deal with this gigantic problem on his own, particularly when living in a provincial context. Soon after *Evolution* was completed, Mondrian left for Paris, where, through the daring and brilliance of its pioneers, the modern movement had already begun to make its response to this crisis. Just as van Gogh had found liberation in the Divisionist approach to color that nineteenth-century Paris offered him, so Mondrian, following a similar pattern of emancipation, found a key to spatial organization through Cubism in twentieth-century Paris. However, as some contemporary critics observed, his interpretation of Cubism was clearly very much his own. His work was recognized for being "extremely original in conception" (Leo Faust) and for the mark that it bore of temperamental distinction, while his complete indifference to the Cubist "laws of volume" (André Salmon)—that is to say, the remarkable flatness of his paintings—drew the criticism of other reviewers.

In Paris, Mondrian worked first from the lattice-like drawings of trees previously done in Holland and then from small diagrammatic notes he made of the planes of interior walls exposed in the demolition of large houses near his studio. These walls bore the remnants of the wallpaper and paint that had once decorated rooms on each floor and presented patches of color placed haphazardly on a flat surface. Both motifs were treated close up, filling the visual field, and provided Mondrian with a loose, informal grid within which he could articulate planes of subdued colors: the warm-cold binaries of classic Cubism, his own lightly colored grays, or muted shades of red, yellow, and blue. Ultimately, the two aspects of his Cubist paintings that were to prove most important to the development of his later abstract work were the dynamic relationships of these areas within the picture plane and the new role assigned to the spectator in assessing these relationships. That is to say, the way in which we "read" the paintings is a constituent part of their formation.

Within a few years, Mondrian had absorbed influences from three seminal movements of Modern art—Divisionism, Fauvism, and Cubism. The impact was clearly very strong. To sort out this experience, he needed time and reduced exposure to the Parisian art scene. He returned to Holland for the summer of 1914, and when World War I broke out in August he was unable to return to Paris until 1919, when it was over. This enforced break enabled him to take stock; to reflect on the various phases and changes that had taken place in his work, and gradually to find his own footing with greater certainty. In 1915 he made a distinction between the human spirit in its role as a builder within the realities of an artistic medium and the "moody" quality of emotion with its expressive dependence on external reality: "Emotion is more outward than spirit. Spirit constructs, composes; emotion expresses mood and the like. Spirit constructs most purely, with the simplest line and the most basic colour."

In Holland, Mondrian at first continued with the facade motifs, now based on the church at Domburg, but the dunes and the sea soon exerted their pull. We have a friend's account of strolling with Mondrian on the beach:

> On a walk beside the ocean, late in the evening, under a radiant, starry sky, he took a tiny sketchbook out of his pocket and made a scribbled drawing of a starry night. For days he worked over that suggestive little scribble. Every day he took a tiny step further away from reality and came a tiny step nearer to the spiritual evocation of it. (autumn 1914)

This gradual shift from an emotional response to a spiritual realization gave rise to the beautiful series of preparatory drawings leading up to *Composition 10 in Black and White*, also known as *Pier and Ocean*, from 1915. In the final painting, an immensity of sensation opens up; one feels oneself surrounded by the sparkling stillness and the rhythmic movement of some boundless continuum. Here, Mondrian's lines take on a wider range of functions, they act as breaks, points, and accents. At one stage in the development of *Pier and Ocean* Mondrian thought of adding color, but in the end decided against it. However, in the very next painting, *Composition*, of 1916, he did precisely that. A pervasive gray with red, yellow, and blue patches—sometimes light, sometimes darker, but always adjusted—support and contradict the beats crosses, and intervals of the lines.

Slowly the work loosens its moorings in what Mondrian refers to as "given in nature" and begins to make its way autonomously. Color planes are simply arranged on a white ground, gray lines are added to provide a context for the spatial movement of these planes without destroying their dynamism. The introduction of regular grids was strongly objected to by friends such as Theo van Doesburg for being repetitious and denying composition; but Mondrian defended them on the grounds that he reworks the regular division considerably, and in the case of the "checkerboard" paintings he maintained that he achieves contrast through the weight and disposition of his color planes. However, he also had reservations about this direction, as he later admitted, for being too "vague": "The verticals and horizontals cancelled each other; the result was confused, the structure was lost."

During this period in Holland, Mondrian wrote and published "The New Plastic in Painting" (1917), in which he sets forth his criteria. Part speculative thinking, part soliloquy, and part reverie, this book has done almost as much to confuse as to enlighten his followers. However, although it does not provide a complete framework with all its reference points in place, the expressions and definitions Mondrian uses offer important clues in themselves. One gets nearer to the nature of his endeavor by starting from these basic terms than by trying to grasp an overall system or find a comprehensive theory.

On his return to Paris in June 1919 the effects of this reflective and withdrawn period in Holland soon became apparent. Of *Composition A*, from 1920, on which he worked for the best part of a year, he said: "I have now made a painting that pleases me more than all my previous work. . . . It has been a long quest." Although, in the light of his classic period in the 1920s, this work can be seen as transitional, it is more revealing in many ways than those highly accomplished paintings. The peculiar flatness of his pictorial space that had already been observed in his Cubist work is now developed and clarified. The color planes take up different positions in space—some advance, some recede; and this is not a simple matter of a particular hue always taking up the same spatial position wherever present. It is a question of context. Take the three yellows for example: the yellow in the top right corner is on a different plane from the yellow in the center, and both of these are again on different planes from the yellow in the lower right. Although one customarily thinks of yellow as a light color, these three yellows have different visual weights—that is to say, the block in the top right appears slightly heavier than the central yellow, which in turn weighs visually more than the yellow rectangle in the lower right. These three yellows, therefore, perform two principal tasks simultaneously: they take up different spatial planes and they exert pressures through their different weights. The same applies to the reds, the blues, and blacks, and of course to the grays and whites (although there it is perhaps less easy to see). This brings about a field of forces in which the various weights and planes are building up dynamic relationships and tensions.

Such dynamism could easily lead to a sort of visual anarchy. But Mondrian practices a form of ordering that he later referred to as "the equivalence of the dissimilar." The disparate visual qualities—each in itself completely "real," or as he would say "determinate" —are balanced in such a way that they both build a whole and yet retain their individuality. "I had just got that large work right," he writes to van Doesburg[13] about *Composition A*: "I made that blue square on the right and changed that yellow one on the left to white; I painted over the gray, the black and the white. I wish you could have seen it like this." And as the final result shows, he altered the painting again. In this way an "equilibrated relationship" is achieved which, in his words, "most purely expresses the universal, the harmony, the unity that are proper to the spirit." So anxious was he to preserve the individual characteristics within this unity that he worried for quite a while about the intensity of the large red in the lower left of the painting: "I am not absolutely sure that it ought to be so totally homogeneous. In theory it should be, but in practice ... ?" Eventually he decided to leave it alone.

Gradually it becomes clear that this abstract way of ordering forms the content of Mondrian's work. His paintings are not symbolic or transcendental, but perceptually accessible and plastic in the sense that he builds a structure of relationships that places us, as spectators, in an analogous "equilibrium." We are invited to participate in a visual interplay between weights, forces, and tensions held together by a balance that is neither symmetrical nor systematic. In a remarkable essay of 1923, "No Axiom but the Plastic Principle," Mondrian describes this balancing between the individual elements and their dynamic unity as the plastic principle and purpose of his art in a period when, as he says: "Everything is seen «relatively» ... Moreover, the relativity, the mutability of things creates in us a desire for the absolute, the immutable." Far from resolving this conflict by offering a new "absolute," he turns the inbuilt contradiction into a dynamic relationship that becomes something of an absolute in itself and which has to be rediscovered and reestablished in each particular instance; that is to say: painting by painting. *Composition with Red, Blue, Black, Yellow, and Gray*, of 1921, shows with what awesomely simple means Mondrian can achieve his objective. There is no explicit center to the painting, and yet the peripheral events do not drift apart. With their differing characteristics they form a correlation of forces that hold the square in tension, being both open and defined at the same time.

As the body of Mondrian's mature work grew throughout the 1920s, this plastic principle gave rise to a tremendous richness and variety. Quite apart from changes in the proportion of the rectangular canvases and the dramatic shift in orientation of the diamond paintings, Mondrian pursues, alongside these changes, a number of themes in the almost serial manner he had sometimes employed in the past. He may explore the weights and tensions that can hold an empty center, as in the painting just described; or the reverse, as in *Tableau I*, from 1921, where the linear divisions cut across the central area and the visual forces are turned inside out, as it were. As a result, the color weights and planes, being well within the pictorial field, provoke relationships that concentrate or diffuse attention. Other areas of investigation include an even greater reduction of his already simplified means, such as just black bands of varying width with just white planes of varying proportion; or compositions with only one or two color planes occupying the spatial compartments provided by the linear divisions.

For a long time, this period was regarded as the zenith of Mondrian's achievement. Certainly, the monumental stability and grandeur reflects one side of his temperament. However, the other, the lively feeling for rhythm, was soon to assert itself and to dramatically increase the dynamic element in his work. In 1932 he made his first "double line" paintings, among them *Composition with Double Line and Yellow*. The rapid repetition of the horizontal line adds a new and different quality of plane, a kind of outlined band, to the relationships in the painting—and one so subversive that it puts the stability and coherence of the painting at risk. But when, as in *Composition C (No. III), with Red, Yellow, and Blue*, from 1935, he widens the interval between the two lines, the ambiguous duality of this new relationship is reduced, and the plane thus created sits more easily with the others in the painting. However, the friction of the "double line" is there to stay, as Mondrian is obviously fascinated by its rhythmic potential and repetitive insistence. In the following year, 1936 he painted *Composition in White, Blue and Yellow: C*. There, a centralized black vertical cuts the pictorial field in half and is repeated to the left to form a "double line," while a pair of horizontal "double lines" (with slightly wider but equal intervals) crosses these verticals, setting up virtual flashing points at the intersections. But now Mondrian directly tackles those aspects of repetition that perhaps seemed most problematic to him: the accumulated intensity of the overall dynamism, which threatens to diminish the "particular" at the expense of the "universal." By adding a large yellow plane and a small blue one he introduces a strong asymmetrical bias that checks the evenness of the rhythm.

In 1937—the year before he left France for England and New York—he made *Composition de lignes et couleur: III*, a most beautiful painting that reconciles the increasing role he was giving to rhythm with a new sense of scale and tectonic strength. Generated by various black verticals and their intervals, the movement sweeps across the painting and is brought to a complex, rhythmic close on the right. A subtle countermovement of horizontal intervals modifies and harmonizes the drive and tempo of the painting. As a finishing stroke, an implied diagonal descending from the top left is pulled up for attention by the deep blue rectangle it carries, the only color plane in the painting.

During the last few years of his life, spent in New York, Mondrian carried on with his explorations, which more and more amounted to a reversal of the priorities that had governed his work in the 1920s. In his writings and in conversation he repeatedly insisted on "dynamic rhythm" and "creative destruction," by which he meant the transformation of the actual elements—the basic colors and lines—into the "purely plastic" agents of an expressive dynamism. His last completed painting, *Broadway Boogie Woogie*, of 1942-43, seems to sum up his entire endeavor in one amazing statement. Earlier tendencies, such as those revealed in *Composition 10 in Black and White*, the diamond, and the "checkerboard" paintings are integrated with interests that previously seemed to contradict and exclude them. The striving for constancy and immutability coexists with the love of rhythm and movement. It can be taken as a proof of Mondrian's rigorous and somewhat antiquated effort to achieve the "equilibrium of the universal and the particular" that his paintings have not been rendered obsolete by history. However frail and modest their physical appearance may be, they shine among the best works of this century with a unique vitality and mysterious timelessness.

1 Charles Baudelaire (1821-1867) – French poet and critic; Paul Cézanne (1839-1906) – French painter. – Ed.

2 References throughout are made either to Piet Mondrian, *The New Art – The New Life: The Collected Writings of Piet Mondrian* ed. and trans. Harry Holtzman and Martin S. James (New York, 1993); or to Yve-Alain Bois et al., *Piet Mondrian*, 1872-1944, exh. cat. Haags Gemeentemuseum, The Hague; National Gallery of Art, Washington, DC; Museum of Modern Art, New York (Boston, 1995).

3 This relationship was the subject of my paper given at a symposium on November 20, 1995, during the run of the Mondrian retrospective at the Museum of Modern Art, New York. It has been published under the title "Mondrian: The 'Universal' and the 'Particular,'" in *Burlington Magazine* 138, no. 1124 (November 1996), pp. 751-53.

Simone Forti

SIMONE FORTI
(B.1935, FLORENCE)

An American dancer, choreographer, and visual artist. She is considered a precursor of postmodernist dance. Her innovative *Dance Constructions* of the 1960s joined movement, improvisation, and everyday actions, redefining the boundaries between dance and performance art. *Handbook in Motion* is a guide to her approach to dance and movement. In the extract provided, Forti details her experiences taking psychoactive substances, which caused changes in her perception and showed her various paths of knowledge. The artist analyzes the perception of music in this context, casting doubt on its rational and mathematical nature.

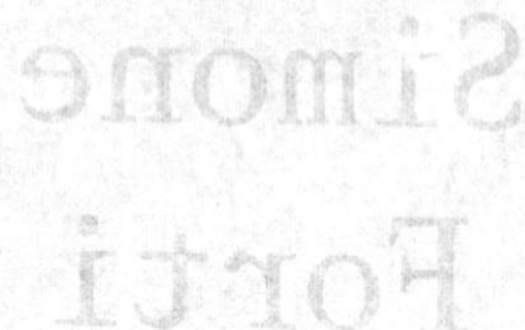

Simone Forti, an extract from *Handbook in Motion: An Account of an Ongoing Personal Discourse and Its Manifestations in Dance* (Middletown: Wesleyan University Press, 2021), 118–20. Simone Forti, *Handbook in Motion*, copyright 1974 Simone Forti. Originally published by Presses of the Nova Scotia College of Art. Now published by Wesleyan University Press, and used by permission.

HANDBOOK IN MOTION: AN ACCOUNT OF AN ONGOING PERSONAL DISCOURSE AND ITS MANIFESTATIONS IN DANCE (EXTRACT)

Several months ago, at a party, I tried to tell Emmett[1] about a problem I was having in making this book. I guess I was feeling that up to the time of doing acid I had seen the world in a certain way. Then, with acid, I had seen other things. And I didn't know how to correlate these two visions. I didn't know how to throw a net of words over this problem. And I felt that if I did manage to exploit my stoned vision in the service of my straight vision, I would be made to pay a fearful price. Emmett listened to me and nodded, said "just a minute", and put on a record of dogs barking *Jingle Bells*.

As I've worked on this book, I've kept expecting a system to form in my mind. I think that the acid had polarized my perceptions. I was recognizing patterns which previously I had left unrecognized. To my amazement, it seemed that the somatic threshold decisions of whether to contract or expand were a common root of both perception and the orgasm. And somewhere in that maze seemed also to be the story on magic and on the oracle as a reading of the pulse of the moment.

The whole question of measurement seems to lie at the center of what I'm trying to understand. When I was in college, I attended a teacher education course called *New Math*. The emphasis was on the fact that to perceive properties of quantity is one thing. To make notes of these perceptions is another. And to manipulate notation is still another. But even the materials which the children handled to obtain their first hand perceptions of aspects of quantitative variation seemed to be modelled after the standard ideal foot-long rod. Absolute position seemed to be the underlying assumption regarding what constituted perception of quantitative variation.

I understand Duchamp's *Three Standard Stoppages* as reference units which are less arbitrary than the meter or the yard. But there seems to be nothing arbitrary about harmonic breakdown. In the Raga, an ancient musical form of India, the tamboura holds a droan. The droan breaks into harmonics and, being constant, provides a grid in relation to which the voice moves. The voice and its harmonics must be in phase with the droan. This is achieved by compensating for all the forces acting to disrupt this state of dynamic equilibrium. I've always felt that droan could never be recorded. It is exactly specific to its live time and to all the elements of that moment. It requires the immediate living faculty of perception and compensation. As a point of equilibrium it does not seem to admit to absolute position or to lend itself to agreed upon notation. When the mind's eye stays focused on that situation of equilibrium, the active compensations become a negative mirror of the world and a way of being in touch with things that one cannot encompass with one's conceptual structure.

Also in college, I was reading about experimental psychology and learned to take for granted the method of studying one element of behavior by setting up two situations which would be considered identical. One situation would be held constant while in the other the factor in question would be somehow altered and the unfolding of both situations would be compared. It seems to me that my early pieces come out of this climate. The *Huddle* and the *Slant Board* are each a unit defined by its own uniformity of process. They are more closed systems than not, arrived at by abstracting and reordering elements of one situation to create another which is of a new order. The elements of the situation are elements of its definition and of cultural agreement.

In the western musical scale the intervals are positioned so as to avoid a predominance of the natural harmonic breakdown of tones. I've wondered if systems based on organically arbitrary units tend to reinforce a territoriality of exclusive space through an arrangement) vibrational disinfectants. And I wonder if certain functions can atrophy causing an imbalance in the powers that reside in the human animal. And if the precarious state of health of the ocean can be a result of a disproportionate development of the powers that come of standardized measurement.

It seems to me that when the polar bear swings his head, he is in a dance state. He is in a state of establishing measure, and of communion with the forces of which he is part.

One day I talked to Les[2] about my two apparently different images of what the world must be. I used the words "conceptual" and "vibrational". I wasn't clear about what I was thinking, I'm not clear about what he said. But one clue came through to me. I think he said something like "You can just follow harmonics, and you can keep doing that until you run into a barrier." And this started me thinking about conceptualization as a tool for choosing the dimensions in which to place those barriers which do and must exist. There are harshnesses involved in lasting from season to season. Each culture seems to deal with this complex of harshnesses with its own particular complex of definitions, measurements, and controls. Control over birth, over territory, over incest, control over killing, control over succumbing to death. Each of these control networks is reflected in and aided by that culture's movement conventions. Placement of center is one key to the survival network. Rhythmic structure is another key. For the body has a different geometry and measures differently in time according to at what point along the spine is located the center of movement. The movement that has come to me from ancient America, from Africa, and from Asia, has come as systems of relating to the duality that life support seems to imply as a competitive struggle against entropy. One principle of Tai Chi that has very much interested me, prescribes the way in which an opposing force is to be met. One must not counterpose with one's own force, but simply pivot on one's own center just slightly deflecting the opposition and letting it fly past of its own momentum.

1 Emmett Williams (1925-2007) – an American poet and visual artist. – Ed.

2 Les Levine (1935) – an American artist, featured in this volume, see pages: 411-429– Ed.

SIMONE FORTI, *Past Future*, pencil on paper, 22.1 × 30.3 cm, 2013

PAST
Future

Roman Opałka

241

ROMAN OPAŁKA
(1931, ABBEVILLE – 2011, ROME)

A Polish painter, likewise adept at drawing, who began conceptualizing time in the 1960s in *Chronomes*—a series of pictures filled with tiny points. In 1965, Opałka began carrying out a program he called *OPAŁKA 1965/1--∞*, which, after 1972, became his sole focus. In his text, he explores an issue that determined his artistic practice: the visual inscription of time. For Opałka, reversible time is the eternal, cyclical movement and transformation of matter, where events can flow in both directions, creating infinite returns without lasting traces. Irreversible time appears as constant evolution and memory of material transformation, where every moment is unique, creating an unbroken, logical chain of events with no chance for reversal or change.

Roman Opałka, [untitled], in *Miejsce sztuki*, ed. Curatorial team of the Muzeum Sztuki in Łódź (Łódź: Towarzystwo Przyjaciół Muzeum Sztuki w Łodzi, 1991), 93.

Ryszard,[1] do you remember the allusion,
you made with regard to my
platinum-blond hair during
one of our many Venetian
meetings at the Biennale?
In this allusion I caught the suspicion that my hair
color was not entirely natural,
so I quickly responded:
Yes it's the chemicals of time that whiten my hair.

REVERSIBLE TIME

Matter is forever transforming singularity into quantity—quantity into singularity—a *panta rhei* of the same; the waters of rivers and oceans, a *perpetuum mobile* of stars and planets in infinite space and time measured by the wisdom of calendars and clocks, the time of eternal returns—as reversible as an hourglass. Time as a product of our being; identical to our knowledge about it—a world without beginning, without end, without time. Time relativized into four-dimensional space, chasing itself in all directions, leaving no trace of its coming. With total impunity, humanity will always be determined to show an inexhaustible capacity for interfering with the record of the world, seemingly already stripped of all its mysteries, with no limits to the realm of cognition, with a horizon eternally shifting along with the progress of god-like humanity.

IRREVERSIBLE TIME

The memory of footprints in a traveled desert—time etching matter, with its genius for self-creation—with its memory of information and its whimsical errors and forgetting, with its evolution of always the same other, like the idea of "counted images" of a detail 1965/1 → ∞, the idea of visualizing the phenomenon of time in an unbroken chain of logical signs, always conditioning one another, with no interference in another value in the structure of the self-defining quality of a shattered illusion of something different and better, a quality liberated from quality, as it is its own truth of perfection, like the idea of the perfection of the philosopher's stone, a thesis that is its own proof, like God; an expression of the inexpressible, the idea of finding sense in the senselessness of existence, the relationship of the infinitely small to the infinitely huge, the finite to the infinite, singularity to multiplicity—the past and the impression of the present to the future, a meditation on our limits in time and space, dazzled by the brightness that comes from the black darkness to the blinding glare of the white light of declining existence.

Translated by Soren Gauger

1 Ryszard Stanisławski (1921-2000) – director of the Muzeum Sztuki in Łódź in the years 1966-1991. – Ed.

CHAPTER VII

DESCRIPTION OF A PHOTOGRAPH

DESCRIPTION OF A PHOTOGRAPH

Marcel Broodthaers

MARCEL BROODTHAERS
(1924, BRUSSELS – 1976, KÖLN)

A Belgian conceptual artist, poet, and filmmaker. He combined a poetic language and analysis of pictures with systems of representation, probing the boundaries between text, film, installation, and museum as a space of meanings. In the poem "My Memory Is a Film in Colour" (1958), Broodthaers uses the image of an inner cinema to trump the experience of a real film. Memory emerges as a dynamic and unpredictable medium, full of hallucinations, distortions, and poetic visions. The artist opposes the "commercial picture" to individual perception. He shows perception as a poetic, fluctuating, and non-linear process, eluding rational control, yet resisting reality.

Marcel Broodthaers, "Ma mémoire est un film en couleur," 1958, in *Marcel Broodthaers: Cinéma*, ed. Manuel Borja-Villel (Barcelona: Fundació Antoni Tàpies, 1997), 26–27.

MA MÉMOIRE EST UN FILM EN COULEUR

Ma mémoire est un film en couleur,
d'une technique supérieure à celle des
films commerciaux. Je n'ai pas encore
vu une couleur sur pellicule
qui ait un éclat, une richesse de
tons qui puissent rivaliser avec les miennes.
Je vais donc au cinéma quand je le désire,
mais cette facilité cinématographique
m'ennuie plutôt. Je préfère les
instants où l'image s'éteint en moi,
et la brume s'épaissit. Il fut un
temps où je ne pouvais empêcher ses
terribles apparitions et
son déroulement soudain.
J'avais alors des rendez-vous bizarres
avec un cheval d'argent.
Je fuyais avec cette monture
les images qui me poursuivaient,
des foules, des soldats armés de lance-flammes.
Je préfère le film en noir et blanc
plus conforme à mon goût de
l'analyse et plus sévère, ensuite
il est différent des images
accumulées en réserve.
Je pouvais finalement conduire ce
délire inférieur à la façon
dont A.R. conduisait ses
Illuminations. J'inventais la tempête qui s'élevait
de l'alphabet,

le miroir de la pluie, et
l'allée des cortèges.
Ce pouvoir des visions,
fabriqué par la méditation et la
mauvaise volonté devant mes devoirs
me permettait de rencontrer qui je voulais.
Des [monstres] célèbres, des cantatrices...
Eh bien Prométhée me
dit un jour le directeur d'une prison
faites de l'évasion objective.
Et Prométhée son vautour sous
le bras faisait la ronde
en chantant intérieurement dans
une cour dont les murs très hauts
semblaient en barrer son destin. Et
tard dans ses nuits le soleil se couchait.

Prométhée que fais-tu là ?
Je me coupe la gorge.
Prométhée sois patient dit le vautour.

D'autres rapportent que Prométhée dormait.
Sa tête trouait la nuit et ses yeux exorbités
voyageaient avec les astres morts.

Un peu de café fort dit le bon dinosaure
et il le ranima avec ce cordial des
familles pauvres. Prométhée
revint à lui et se jeta avidement
sur les nouvelles fraîches que
lui apportait le préhistorique.
L'actualité est importante quels
que soient les projets.

MY MEMORY IS A FILM IN COLOUR

My memory is a film in colour,
one that is technically superior to
commercial films. I have yet to
see a colour on film
with tones vivid and rich enough
to compare with mine.
So I go to the cinema when I feel like it,
but this cinematographic facileness
rather bores me. I prefer those
moments when the image within me
fades and the fog thickens. There was
a time when I was unable to prevent its
terrible apparitions and
its sudden unfolding.
I used to have these bizarre rendezvous
with a silver horse,
on which mount I fled from
the images that pursued me
crowds, soldiers armed with flame-throwers.
I prefer black-and-white film,
which is more suited to my taste for
analysis and more severe, and which
is also different from this
reserve stock of images.
In the end I was able to conduct these
inferior figments the way
A.R. conducted his
Illuminations. I invented the storm that blew up
from the alphabet,
the mirror of rain and
the alley of corteges.
With this visionary capacity
fabricated by meditation and
recalcitrance over my homework

I could meet anyone I wanted.
Famous [monsters], opera singers...
Well then, Prometheus,
the director of the prison
said to me one day,
make an objective escape.
And Prometheus with his vulture
under his arm trudged round and round,
singing inwardly, in
a yard whose very high walls
seemed to bar his destiny. And
late in his nights the sun set.

Prometheus, what are you doing?
I am cutting my throat.
Prometheus, be patient said the vulture.

Others tell that Prometheus was sleeping.
His head pierced the night and his staring eyes
travelled with the dead stars.

A drop of strong coffee said the good dinosaur
and with this cordial he revived
families of poor folk. Prometheus
came to and with relish tucked in
to the fresh news brought
him by the prehistorical. Current affairs are important,
whatever your plans.

1 Arthur Rimbaud (1854-1891) –
French poet. – Ed.

Andrzej Partum

ANDRZEJ PARTUM
(1938–2002, WARSAW)

A poet, performer, conceptual artist, and cultural organizer. He saw poetry as a field of free play between word, image, and sound, exploring the limits of perception. His "Blink of an Eye" and "Depicting" are examples of his early poetry, where language works as a perceptual instrument. In "Blink of an Eye" color is described in terms of sound and fading; seeing and hearing meld into one process. "Depicting" analyzes the relationships between the shape of the object and its spatial "distribution," undermining the evident nature of seeing. Both pieces display Partum's intermedial imagination, joining visual and acoustic concepts in a poetic experiment that not only describes perception, but also engages it in the viewer.

Andrzej Partum, "Obrazowanie, Okamgnienie," in *Powodzenia nieurodzaj. Zwałka papki*, Warsaw: self-published, 1965), 28, 31. Courtesy of Antoni, Berenika, Pia and Piotr Partum

DEPICTING
from where views
of objects
join a deployment
of their own size
from there
authenticity
is subject to the likeness
of the calculated gauge
which assigns them
their shape

BLINK OF AN EYE
the fullness of the perceptible
color
generates a phonics within
the hollow hue of the phono-malleable
circuit
because of this fade
of the playback
the sound engineer ties on
immersive fringes
visualizing them in eye overload
Translated by Soren Gauger

Zdzisław Jurkiewicz

ZDZISŁAW JURKIEWICZ
(1931–2012, WROCLAW)

A painter who likewise had a flair for drawing, he was also an art theorist and lecturer, associated with Wrocław's conceptual art circles. He was one of the first artists in Poland to introduce conceptual practices based on the everyday experience of time and perception. The poem "Painting," dedicated to Ryszard Stanisławski, is a meditation on the condition and future of painting. The author wonders about the possibility of a second revelation of a picture that surprises and moves us, despite the historical saturation with novelty and the language of delight. This text shows perception as an act of hope—of anticipating "sights beyond prediction," which might yet appear before the artist and the viewer.

Zdzisław Jurkiewicz, "Malarstwo," *Miejsce sztuki*, ed. Curatorial team of the Muzeum Sztuki in Łódź (Łódź: Towarzystwo Przyjaciół Muzeum Sztuki w Łodzi, 1991), 67.

to Ryszard Stanisławski[1]
with gratitude, always –

PAINTING

I ask you, Painting,
will you emerge
once more
to show places that are unpredictable,
nameless, terrifying us
with astonishment?
So many times now we've seen
new spaces
of painterly sensitivity,
but all of today's revelations
have already been named—
we want no more new names
no delight at past accomplishments.
And so, oh Painting, are you
still possible?
For I still believe,
though I despair,
that Other Windows will still open up
onto
sights I cannot foresee...

Wrocław, 1982

Translated by Soren Gauger

1 Ryszard Stanisławski (1921–2000) – director of the Muzeum Sztuki in Łódź in the years 1966–1991. – Ed.

Wojciech Bruszewski

265

WOJCIECH BRUSZEWSKI
(1947, WROCLAW–2009, ŁÓDŹ)

An artist, director, theorist, and pioneer of media art in Poland, associated with the Workshop of the Film Form. His work included experimental film, installations, photographs, and elaborate sound and language projects. In "The Satori Problem" (1973), he sets out a model for an alternative film narrative, going beyond the linear logic of montage. Diagrams, instead of illustrating the plot, visualize meetings and the continuity of observations. Bruszewski treats film as a philosophical tool, capable of depicting "unknowable situations" and transcending cognitive inertia. The titular "Satori"—a Zen term—suggests a moment of clarity, a look that goes beyond narrative structures, achieved through a precise analysis of perceptual and temporal relationships.

Wojciech Bruszewski, "Problem satori," in *Wojciech Bruszewski. Fenomeny Percepcji*, eds. E. Fuchs, J. Zagrodzki (Łódź: Miejska Galeria Sztuki w Łodzi, 2010), 65–67.

THE SATORI PROBLEM

There are at least two ways to perceive the world. One, let us conventionally call it "Euro-American" and another, speaking just as conventionally, typical of the "Far- East". Both are said to have appeared in the art of our cultural region. My aim is to demonstrate a certain misunderstanding associated with this issue, with reference to examples from the field of film.

The traditional film narration consists, generally speaking, in a combination of larger or smaller fragments of recorded events into one time course based on a linear consequence.

It is assumed that there is a hypothetical observer, that is the viewer at the moment of synthesizing fragmented storylines during the screening. It is necessary to appeal to the linguistic tradition typical for the viewer's cultural region which allows such synthesizing.

A film made with this method can be represented graphically as the sum of segments of unequal lengths where the gaps between the segments mean any editing figure and the total length–the duration of a screening. Missing time intervals are supplemented by the viewer's imagination thanks to the knowledge of the code, often not even consciously realized, for example, the first shot ends with person A looking to the left from the axis of the lens and the second shot begins with person B looking in the opposite direction; the viewer deciphers: persons A and B are looking at each other, etc.

Owing to this ability the psychological time continuum is realized in the imagination of the viewer, though the actual running time is not equal to the duration of events presented.

Some avant-garde film experiences from the past ten years, particularly the New American Cinema, led to the replacement of this type of narration with another. A hypothetical observer has been assimilated with the recording camera. By giving up the material preparation, and therefore specifically giving up editing, camera movements, illustrative music, etc., the viewer has been released from the obligation to engage the—thus-far necessary—linguistic apparatus in the reception. And finally—the running time of the screening is equal to the duration of events presented...

It can be assumed that this is the result of self-reflection of cinema on the essence of its record. This reflection could have two aspects: the moral and the cognitive one... The second aspect of the case, which seems more important, that is, the cognitive reflection, could be accompanied by the hope of rejecting the conventional barrier of language, which, like a glass pane, reveals and separates from the tangible concrete...

What is *satori*?

In his essays on the psychology of religion, Erich Fromm[1] gives the following description: "If we would try to express [satori] in psychological terms, I would say that this is a state in which a person is completely tuned to the reality outside and inside of him, a state in which he is fully aware of it and fully grasps it...".

The new treatment of film, pure recording, did not cease to be a narration. The system of signs compared to the traditional narration has only become less clear. At this point the entire confusion with Zen Buddhism begins. In my opinion, our feelings during the screening have nothing to do with the experience of *satori*.

Film, still limited by the rectangular frame and the duration of the showing, has not ceased to interpret reality. By showing something while not showing what is beyond the frame or outside the length of time; instead of merging—it separates, instead of bringing closer—it drives further away. The choice itself, even when it is not controlled by man, is inevitably a process of indicating or marking. A meaningful structure is being created. The final consequence of such narratives were the experiments, conducted this year by the Film Form Workshop in Łódź, with direct, mechanical, unscripted television broadcast and the transmission of acoustic space. In the case of a film recording the screening running time is equal but it is not identical to the time of the events presented. In direct broadcasts reality and its image function synchronously. Transmission time can be unlimited. In the case of transmission of acoustic space there even are no clear boundaries of the areas broadcast. Let us assume, however, that we reject all technology and all media.

Experiments with recording and transmission, however, provoke a suspicion that our perception of the world, shaped by European culture, our way of contact with reality is not direct but linguistic. Language, in turn, is a category of thought.

In this situation, the *satori* experience is not available to a European equipped with, as Roland Barthes puts it, sign imagination...

We can run a series of such laboratory operations on recorded images, which have nothing to do with the traditional preparation of information material and, while meeting the conditions for transmission in the direction of their designation, would confirm the real existence of such reality which we never experience, and whose presence we can only guess.

Translated by Katarzyna Gucio

1 Erich Fromm (1900-1980) – German philosopher and psychologist. – Ed.

CHAPTER

DEMONSTRATION PAINTINGS

VIII

OF

Fred Sandback

FRED SANDBACK (1943–2003, NEW YORK)

A pioneer of minimalism, known for his spatial installations using thin acrylic threads that made geometrical shapes and set limits in space without material form. His works explored the viewer's perception and the intimate relationship between line, space, and light, pushing the envelope of sculpture and conceptual aesthetics. Sandback's text shows how his minimalist thread sculptures create spaces to encourage careful and active observation and to discover the relations between form and surroundings. Through simplicity of material and construction, his works teach us to see a space as a dynamic phenomenon, open to multidimensional perception and active interaction.

Fred Sandback, "Children's Guide to Seeing," *Fred Sandback. Sculpture*, ed. Lesley K. Baier (Houston: Contemporary Arts Museum, 1989).

CHILDREN'S GUIDE TO SEEING

We all need a place for play, whether it's jump rope, baseball, or making a sculpture. I'm lucky enough to have the whole Contemporary Arts Museum in which to build my sculptures that are made out of knitting yarn.

I need a big space like this because I mean my sculptures to take space and make it into a place—a place that people will move around in and be in.

Knitting yarn is great for making the proportions, intervals, and shapes that build the places I want to see and to be in. It's like a box of colored pencils, only I can use it to make a three-dimensional sculpture instead of making a drawing on paper.

My knitting-yarn sculpture is a somewhat distant cousin to some other string games. Maybe the one that uses the most space is kite flying. But the one that is the oldest, and the most universal, is cat's cradle. Indians, Eskimos, Bushmen, and many other cultures around the world have had games like cat's cradle since before anyone can remember.

Often cat's cradle is about making a little place—just for yourself, or to share with someone. If you don't know any of the moves, you can probably learn some from a friend, a relative, or from your mom or dad, if they remember them.

If you ask the attendant here in the Museum now, he or she will give you some yarn to use while you are here and to take home. Your fingers might do some thinking while you wander around and look at my sculptures.

[...]

Cat's cradle is nice because you can put it in your pocket when you're busy with something else, and take it out again when you're not. Although, as you can see, it's not so hard to build big things like my sculpture. All it takes is a ball of string. If you were feeling a little adventurous, you could even wrap up your whole house.

FRED SANDBACK, *Untitled*, acrylic yarn, 1981

Marysia Lewandowska

MARYSIA LEWANDOWSKA
(B.1955, SZCZECIN)

A conceptual artist whose practice focuses on the relationship between art, intellectual property, and the institutions producing knowledge. Through designs based on collaboration and archiving, such as *Open Hearing* or *Free Trade*, she redefines concepts of authorship, access, and communal participation in culture. In "Blind Spots, Search Lights," Lewandowska analyzes how the choice and placement of the lighting, including the types of lamps and their parameters, affect the visual and emotional feel of a space. The essay is based on the transcript of a conversation with a light expert. She treats lighting as a key element in creating atmosphere and forms, capable of transforming the same interior into a range of visual experiences.

Marysia Lewandowska, "Blind Spots, Search Lights," in *Strip Light* (London: Photographers' Gallery, 1992), 15.

BLIND SPOTS, SEARCH LIGHTS[1]

...the thing about light, as I see it, is that some people are blind to its powers. I am playing here, but what I mean is they never look at it, or can't. Most people remain ignorant of its potential, the way it can alter things. Right here under these lights, I'll show you. If you know what lighting you need in order to control these things, you can begin to supplement what is there, you can build a scheme. Essentially if you want a low budget, low maintenance scheme, Hypnos are brilliant. You can have the whole perimeter lit, you can touch the entire surface. The only problem is if you have poor ceilings or poor walls it will show up, the light will compromise appearances. In that situation you would need to suppress the surface, wash it away. If you have a nice clean space they are wonderful, everything becomes clear, precise. On raw brickwork they are really great. Then you can have much more localised spots in the centre for bringing out depth and structure, they modulate the light and create a volumetric effect. Texture wise, with a smaller lamp it's the same as with a pinhole camera, the smaller the hole the sharper the image. With L-V's you get very defined shadows, a lot of contrast. It does depend on what you're lighting. It's always nice if you can use light-fall, they are more permanent than spots. But there are systems that also look attractive in themselves, they are either solid and look very dedicated, or are small dinky things. These would be great for very dramatic lighting, localised pooling, they are really quite intense. You can have a very generous beam or a very tight beam picking up focal points, they are also quite low glare. Glare can be a problem, but with these lights if someone is looking at this and then they turn around they don't get a blinding light in their eyes. They are also positioned in such a way that if they are standing here they don't get a shadow of themselves in the picture. Are you after a particular effect visually? Do you want the lighting to be evocative rather than ... here is the lighting, here is the floodlit wall, that type of thing. Let me show you, because lighting can entirely change the same space. Overall what you want to create is a powerful environment, not just a little light here and there, you want atmosphere. These are L-V on a dimmer, so they are warm, where as these are directional within a void, very low glare, very efficient. They are in a tight target arrangement. These are spots on a very absorbent surface, very soft, moody, sensuous. The same space, with white walls for instance, can look totally different under the same lighting conditions. You can have dramatic shadows with these, they can create luxurious effects. They are supplemented with L-V to give you more depth. With spots you don't get coverage, but if you need coverage that's a different concept altogether. You can see here, these two are quite tight while these are much broader, so with exactly the same fitting, just change the lamp. You can have localised light and then open the units if you want to brighten the space. If you wanted a warmer feel here, they could go on dimmers. That's a chandelier, we just pushed a spot through a chandelier creating its shadow on the wall, and there you have blue crystal glass on the bottom. Here, with the more general lighting, visually the space looks brighter, it's simply because you don't get the contrast, light to dark, which warms things up. You see that type of thing, it's very warm, very exotic. So you have the same beam here, although these have a bit more spill. There is exactly the same intensity in that pool, and that pool. This has more light on, so this image is totally changed, more candle-like. It just shows how manipulative it can be. Here totally different things, broad beams, just to liven it up. You can still be effective, and still get that softness. A lot of people feel that lighting is a utility, fixed and that's it. They think that if you want change you have to have track. That is just not the case, now you actually alternate dramatic effect lighting with general floodlighting using down-lighters. You can accentuate the image, or the feeling of what the lighting is about. This is about science, it's very clinical, so the lighting is very clinical. Alternatively you've got this sort of thing, it's antique and much more evocative, it's a warmer thing. Lighting can control whatever you see. These are designed for either giving you an effect, and accent lighting for focal qualities, drama. Fluorescents can be used for brightness. You can see here there is no contrast at all, no drama with fluorescent, zero shadow. The thing with fluorescents is that although you get a good colour rendering, they are visually unacceptable, unless they are shielded. Because it's an unnatural quality of light and most people are used to seeing things, particularly in an interior, lit under warm lighting, while warm fluorescents actually look quite pink. That's daylight, that's blue, and if you saw that outside it's exactly like daylight, but when it's inside it's totally out of place. This is really, really stark. Main voltage compared to L-V is very yellow. There is a kind of psychological resistance. You see main voltage is much warmer on reds, and L-V is much better on the cool colours by comparison. L-V gives better control, and put them on a dimmer, because sometimes the texture of light is too stark, and it assumes a brilliant quality. You see, you are limited by fluorescents size-wise. Although you can get lots of different types, you can get a light box, a little dinky thing you can carry around in your briefcase. You have a cable here, starter here, ballast here, fitting there, and then your glass here. But when it is larger you get more options. In fluorescents you get 70 or 80 different colour temperatures, but most of them you cannot distinguish just by looking at them. There is a lamp for instance specifically made for butchers' windows, that's all it's made for, and that's all it's bought for. So it's very dedicated. These are of pretty limited use, utility lighting, toilets, that sort of thing, very grim, institutional. So the colour temperature is not that great. Those butchers' tubes, they are called Rosetta, they make things look very red, although the best thing would be the neutral white. North light is blue, it looks like ice-cubes, tropical daylight looks natural, while pink incandescent homelight is very warm. Artificial daylight, they are like deluxe natural...

1 Marysia Lewandowska would like to express her gratitude to Max von Barnholt. – Ed.

CHAPTER

GAZE
A

IX

IS BRIDGE

Käthe Kollwitz

KÄTHE KOLLWITZ
(1867, KOENIGSBERG– 1947, MORITZBURG)

A German graphic artist, sculptor, and painter, known for her compelling works on suffering, poverty, and social injustice, particularly concerning war and the place of women. The excerpt from the artist's diary in this publication reflects on the choice of subject matter in art as an expression of sociopolitical involvement and aesthetic sensitivity. Kollwitz's fascination with the lives of the working class came not from ideology, but from finding a special beauty and power in them, as opposed to her perception of the middle-class world. This gaze focuses on the everyday gestures and fates of ordinary people.

The Diary and Letters of Kaethe Kollwitz, [extract], ed. Hans Kollwitz (Chicago: Henry Regnery Company, 1955), 46.

THE DIARY AND LETTERS OF KÄTHE KOLLWITZ [EXTRACT]

[...]

I should like to say something about my reputation for being a "socialist" artist, which clung to me from then on. Unquestionably my work at this time, as a result of the attitudes of my father and brother and of the whole literature of the period, was in the direction of socialism. But my real motive for choosing my subjects almost exclusively from the life of the workers was that only such subjects gave me in a simple and unqualified way what I felt to be beautiful. For me the Koenigsberg longshoremen had beauty; the Polish *jimkes* on their grain ships had beauty; the broad freedom of movement in the gestures of the common people had beauty. Middle-class people held no appeal for me at all. Bourgeois life as a whole seemed to me pedantic. The proletariat, on the other hand, had a grandness of manner, a breadth to their lives. Much later on, when I became acquainted with the difficulties and tragedies underlying proletarian life, when I met the women who came to my husband for help and so, incidentally, came to me, I was gripped by the full force of the proletarian's fate. Unsolved problems such as prostitution and unemployment grieved and tormented me, and contributed to my feeling that I must keep on with my studies of the lower classes. And portraying them again and again opened a safety-valve for me; it made life bearable.

[...]

KÄTHE KOLLWITZ, ***Self-Portrait***,
printing ink on cardboard, 27 × 23.5 cm, 1920

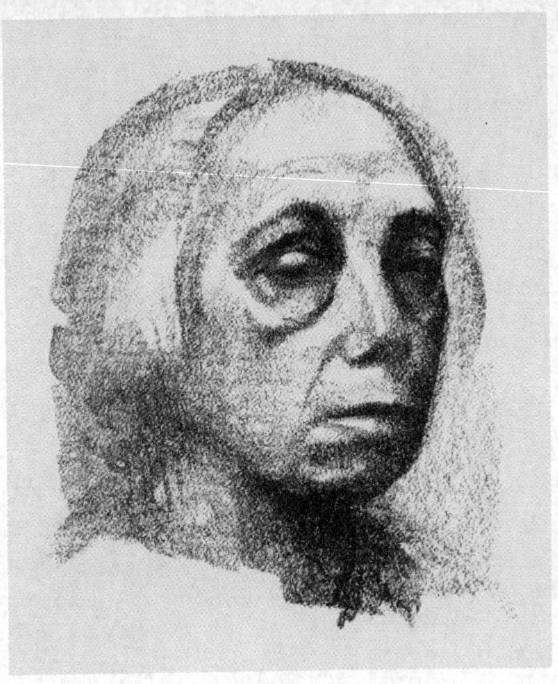

Zofia Kulik

ZOFIA KULIK
(B.1947, WROCLAW)

A Polish visual artist working in photography, installation art, and performance, one half of the KwieKulik duo (along with Przemysław Kwiek). Since the 1980s, she has created monumental photography compositions, broaching the subjects of power, the body, history, and the role of women. In the passage quoted here, Kulik describes the process of creating complex compositions through repeating and multiplying parts of the human body, as a symbol of subjugation and power. By juxtaposing monumental pictures and everyday gestures, Kulik confronts the viewer with history and symbolic meanings that appear gradually, revealed upon careful examination and interpretation.

Zofia Kulik, [untitled], *Camera Austria International* [Graz] no. 47/48 (1994): 36–44.

[UNTITLED]

I would now like to quote some passages from texts I have written about my artistic work.

"I am interested in building structures, composing more complex wholes. I am fascinated by closed forms, centricity, symmetry, multiplication, order, figural ornament, imposing upon myself certain already existing patterns of structures (...) that I try to fill with my own madness [I wrote this in 1989; now I feel it should be a different word] –these are my form-shaping rules of composition."[1]

"Their purpose is to humiliate 'the spectator' and bring him to his knees. But for whom are you to humble yourself today? There is no god, no leader, no mystery. So whom are you to serve? That is a question. I am afraid of myself–that I can feel and visualize subordination so well. I do not show an individual man; the man is a splinter which I can divide and multiply at will and then build a composition of it. But it is neither free nor fanciful (...). First, I search for a pattern, and then while composing according to that pattern I begin to feel the sense of what I am doing (...). Do I appreciate and praise 'subordination' by depicting it, or do I deride and refute it? Having accepted 'subordination' as my problem and motive, but being fearful and hateful of the situation marked by compulsive subordination, I take my artistic revenge by grabbing every symbolic and formal weapon that has been used against me. I love the grass which I love to cut down."[2]

In a letter to Christine Frisinghelli about my work *All the Missiles Are One Missile*, which is shown in the Neue

Galerie in Graz,[3] I wrote, "The whole composition has the form of a carpet, a photographic carpet, as it were. Its 'decorativeness' is built up of photographic images chosen from my collection of b/w negatives. These include images of socialist monuments, cemeteries, landscapes, photo still lifes composed by me, human gestures performed by my models, and 'real' events taken from TV – wars, protest marches, executions, marches past, riots, etc. I copy the images from the negatives onto the surface of the photographic paper by covering and uncovering different parts of the surface, according to plans and stencils I have made before. The complete work is made up of a number of photographic sheets 60 cm by 50 cm in size.

In the second letter to Christine Frisinghelli I wrote, "When you look at all these real and definite things in the photographs, remember that they show not only real and definite things and events but that they can be seen without their background – they show what they show." So, in the work in the Neue Galerie, you have on the left a monument from Leningrad, entitled *Fatherland-Mother*, dating from 1960, and on the right, the monument *Back and Front*, erected in Magnitogorsk in 1979. In the first case, what you see is a woman wearing a garland, in the second case, a man with a sword.

1 Zofia Kulik, "KwieKulik", in: *Exit. Nowa sztuka w Polsce* (New Art in Poland), no. 5, January – March 1991, p. 161.
2 Ibid.
3 Contribution to the "Austrian Triennial on Photography 1993", Neue Galerie am Landes-museum Joanneum and Forum Stadtpark, Graz, 17.9. -31.10. 1993, see: Wemer Fenz, Christine Frisinghelli (ed.), WAR., *Austrian Triennial on Photography 1993*, exhibition catalogue, 2 vol., Edition Camera Austria, Graz 1993, vol. I, p. 97, vol. 2, p. 18.

Sergei Eisenstein

303

SERGEI EISENSTEIN
(1898, RIGA – 1948, MOSCOW)

A film director and theorist considered a pioneer of cinema montage. His films, such as *Battleship Potemkin* and *Alexander Nevsky*, revolutionized the language of cinema and had a vast influence on the development of the art. According to Eisenstein's concept, montage, based on a clash of frames, forces the viewer to take active part in creating the meaning between images. Much as a gaze unites two banks of a river, the juxtaposition of contrasting shots makes a bridge that gives birth to a new idea.

Sergei Eisenstein, "Montage is Conflict" (1929), in *Cinematic*, trans. Jay Leyda, ed. David Campany, Whitechapel (Cambridge, London: The MIT Press, 2007), 30–32.

MONTAGE IS CONFLICT

The shot is by no means an *element* of montage.

The shot is a montage *cell*.

Just as cells in their division form a phenomenon of another order, the organism or embryo, so, on the other side of the dialectical leap from the shot, there is montage.

By what, then, is montage characterized and, consequently, its cell - the shot?

By collision. By the conflict of two pieces in opposition to each other. By conflict. By collision.

Before me lies a crumpled yellowed sheet of paper. On it is a mysterious note:

'Linkage—P' and 'Collision—E'.

This is a substantial trace of a heated bout on the subject of montage between P (Pudovkin[1]) and E (myself).

This has become a habit. At regular intervals he visits me late at night and behind closed doors we wrangle over matters of principle. A graduate of the Kuleshov school, he loudly defends an understanding of montage as a *linkage* of pieces. Into a chain. Again, 'bricks'. Bricks, arranged in series to *expound* an idea.

I confronted him with my viewpoint on montage as a *collision*. A view that from the collision of two given factors *arises* a concept.

From my point of view, linkage is merely a possible *special* case.

Recall what an infinite number of combinations is known in physics to be capable of arising from the impact (collision) of spheres. Depending on whether the spheres be resilient, non-resilient or mingled. Amongst all these combinations there is one in which the impact is so weak that the collision is degraded to an even movement of both in the same direction.

This is the one combination which would correspond with Pudovkin's view.

Not long ago we had another talk. Today he agrees with my point of view. True, during the interval he took the opportunity to acquaint himself with the series of lectures I gave during that period at the State Cinema Institute ...

So, montage is conflict.

As the basis of every art is conflict (an 'imagist' transformation of the dialectical principle). The shot appears as the cell of montage. Therefore it also must be considered from the viewpoint of *conflict*.

Conflict within the shot is potential montage, in the development of its intensity shattering the quadrilateral cage of the shot and exploding its conflict into montage impulses between the montage pieces. As, in a zigzag of mimicry, the *mise-en-scène* splashes out into a spatial zigzag with the *same* shattering. As the slogan, 'All obstacles are vain before Russians', bursts out in the multitude of incident of *War and Peace*.

If montage is to be compared with something, then a phalanx of montage pieces, of shots, should be compared to the series of explosions of an internal combustion engine, driving forward its automobile or tractor: for, similarly, the dynamics of montage serve as impulses driving forward the total film.

Conflict within the frame. This can be very varied in character: it even can be a conflict in - the story. As in that 'prehistoric' period in films (although there are plenty of instances in the present, as well), when entire scenes would be photographed in a single, uncut shot.

This, however, is outside the strict jurisdiction of the film-form.

These are the 'cinematographic' conflicts within the frame:

Conflict of graphic directions.

(Lines—either static or dynamic)

Conflict of scales.

Conflict of volumes.

Conflict of masses.

(Volumes filled with various intensities of light)

Conflict of depths.

And the following conflicts, requiring only one further impulse of intensification before flying into antagonistic pairs of pieces:

Close shots and long shots.

Pieces of graphically varied directions. Pieces resolved in volume, with pieces resolved in area.

Pieces of darkness and pieces of lightness.

And lastly there are such unexpected conflicts as:

Conflicts between an object and its dimension—and conflicts between an event and its duration.

These may sound strange, but both are familiar to us. The first is accomplished by an optically distorted lens, and the second by stop-motion or slow-motion.

The compression of all cinematographic factors and properties within a single dialectical formula of conflict is no empty rhetorical diversion. We are now seeking a unified system for methods of cinematographic expressiveness that shall hold good for all its elements. The assembly of these into series of common indications will solve the task as a whole. Experience in the separate elements of the cinema cannot be absolutely measured.

Whereas we know a good deal about montage, in the theory of the shot we are still floundering about amidst the most academic attitudes, some vague tentatives, and the sort of harsh radicalism that sets one's teeth on edge. To regard the frame as a particular, as it were, molecular case of montage makes possible the direct application of montage practice to the theory of the shot.

And similarly with the theory of lighting. To sense this as a collision between a stream of light and an obstacle, like the impact of a stream from a fire-hose striking a concrete object, or of the wind buffeting a human figure, must result in a usage of light entirely different in comprehension from that employed in playing with various combinations of 'gauzes' and 'spots'.

Thus far we have one such significant principle of conflict: *the principle of optical counterpoint.*

And let us not now forget that soon we shall face another and less simple problem in counterpoint: *the conflict in the sound film of acoustics and optics.*

1 Vsevolod Pudovkin (1893-1953) – Soviet director and art theorist. – Ed.

2 Lev Kuleshov (1899-1970) – Soviet film director and film theorist. – Ed.

Barbara Hammer

BARBARA HAMMER
(1939, LOS ANGELES – 2019, NEW YORK)

An American film director, visual artist, and pioneer of lesbian and queer cinema. Her film experiments of the 1970s broached subjects like the search for freedom and discovery of female and lesbian sexuality. In "The Politics of Abstraction", Hammer analyzes experimental cinema practices that use the abstract as a tool for expanding the field of meanings and reception in response to a lack of lesbian representation in visual culture. She stresses that a lack of linear narrative and figurative references does not equal a lack of meaning. She notes the significance of the abstract and the active reception of film as a way of freeing the imagination, broadening discourse, and making room for diverse forms and identities.

Barbara Hammer's text "The Politics of Abstraction" was first published in 1992 in the journal *Women & Performance: A Journal of Feminist Theory*. It was later included in the anthology *Queer Looks: Perspectives on Lesbian and Gay Film and Video*, edited by Martha Gever, John Greyson, and Pratibha Parmar, and published by Routledge in 1993. Courtesy of the Estate of Barbara Hammer, New York

THE POLITICS OF ABSTRACTION

As an experimental filmmaker and lesbian feminist, I have advocated that radical content deserves radical form. In 1979 I had my first screening outside the supportive lesbian feminist community when Terry Cannon, then programmer at Film Forum in Los Angeles, asked me to show my films in a venue of experimental films. I had already completed several experimental films with lesbian feminist content and had shown them regularly in the Bay Area of San Francisco. They were also distributed by early women's film cooperatives. In both cases I was called upon to explain my unorthodox form and content. To the feminist community, I introduced my films in light of the formal concerns of experimental filmmaking. To the experimental film community, I spoke about the importance of unrepresented content.

It is my belief that a conventional cinema, such as classical narrative, is unable to address the experiences or issues of lesbian and gay perceptions, concerns, and concepts. When an audience awaits the image on the screen it expects a heterosexual narrative to unfold, and the audience is not disappointed. Even if the characters are lesbian, the script projects lesbian characters within a heterosexual world of role-playing, lovemaking, and domestic and professional life. The numerous films that purport to be "lesbian films" have failed to address me as a lesbian spectator. The romance, the onscreen gaze, the plot, and the character development are all situated within a heterosexual life-style or a Hollywood imaginative life-style made for the cinema. Certainly the women I have seen on the screen, their issues, the story, and the mise-en-scène do not relate to the personal experiences I live and have lived as a lesbian woman for twenty-three years in the Western world.

Lesbian cinema is on an invisible screen. By the "invisible screen" do you mean pictures drawn in lemon juice backward that, when heated, can be read through a mirror? asked a friend. It has been that difficult to see lesbian representation in cinema. The lesbian imaginary is carried in a back pocket inscribed in invisible lines until heated by the projector lamp.

How could this be, in an age where we have films like *Desert Hearts*, *Lianna*, and *Personal Best*? These are films where the onscreen space is filled with seeming "lesbian representation." But my reading of these films is that there is no lesbian to deconstruct, as the discourse of the gendered subject is within a heterosexist authority system. The lesbians act out heterosexual gender roles and positions rather than claiming any difference, and even sexual practices are situated within heterosexuality.

As a runaway from the political regime of heterosexuality, I and other lesbian filmmakers began to construct a lesbian cinema in the early seventies. Visibility was the central concern for lesbians making cinema at this time, for the simple and profoundly sad reason that there were few or no pictures, images, or representations available. The screen space, on and off, was blank. Not just marginalized, but not there. There was no cinema to deconstruct. There was no gaze to analyze. Lesbian image-makers in the seventies were forced by critics into the "camp of essentialists" because of the extreme urgency of their need to make lesbian representation. A marginalized and oppressed group must make a mark first, define a form, and make a statement that they exist. As we began to make films of lesbian representation, we were categorized by the emerging feminist semioticians and theorists (newly emerged themselves from French studies with Christian Metz[1]) as "essentialists." Because we made representations of lesbians, the false assumption was made that we invested these representations with biological, essential "meaningness" separate from ideology or social construction.

I, for one, as a lesbian cineaste, take a more eclectic and I hope eccentric view of the lesbian representations I made in the seventies. The lesbian women I imaged in film were constructed by the general and dominant society, as well as the marginal society of the lesbian community. In the process, we also discovered who we were, as we stepped into the void, the invisible, the blank screen, and named ourselves "lesbian." That was the first step. There could be no semiotics if there were no sign. The lack we felt as we began this early naming process was not the lack of a phallus but the singular and significant lack of any representations. The image did not exist, the picture was not made, the word scarcely heard in discourse nor seen in text.

Until recently the dominant discourse of feminist criticism has not addressed this issue but has continued to ignore it, and by doing so perpetuates the invisibility and repression of lesbian cinema. To dismiss the early naming and identity films with the highly charged and emotive term "essentialist" further removes the opportunity for discourse in a climate where deconstruction, Marxist, psychoanalytic, and Lacanian theories prevail.

The reidentification of a lesbian self through lesbian sexual experience is one part of lesbian representation. There are many parts and practices of lesbian experience to be represented. In physics, light can be understood through wave and particle theories at the same time. So too can there be multiple, coexisting, and different theories and understandings of "lesbianisms" through a variety of readings. One of these readings is experimental cinema: the cinema that makes its own construct where form and content are inseparable. I don't think one can make a lesbian film using a patriarchal and heterosexist mode such as the conventional narrative. Plot points are male points. We are radically changing people, and we cannot reproduce that radicality using conventional forms.

I have chosen images rather than words for the act of naming myself an artist and a lesbian because the level of meanings possible for images and image conjunctions seemed richer and held more ramifications. I have broken rules, studied the construction of norms, and questioned restraints since I was a little girl. It was not strange that I chose to practice in the longtime artistic tradition of breaking or modifying the status quo in an attempt to advance the dialogue. Generally speaking, my films made in the seventies, *Dyketactics*, *Multiple Orgasm*, *Double Strength*, *Women I Love*, and *Superdyke*, as well as others, were made with this intention that grew from an unconscious impulse to a conscious insistence on lesbian naming.

Once named, and identities established as artist and lesbian, I wanted to get on with other areas of expression that I had left unexplored. The second ten years of my nonnarrative film production focused on my perceptual interests. In my early films, I chose "realism" by using the camera as an eye, capable of defining form, outline, and depth to depict the lesbian body. The social realism of the scenes was contrasted with the dreamlike, metaphoric, and imaginative images of freedom. In the urgency to make lesbian imagery, I neglected my thrill of simply projected light even without images, and my love for abstraction.

Abstract or nonrepresentational art appeals to me for several reasons. I have deeper emotions when I'm working beyond realism because there are no limits, and I enter and engage with the dialogue between light and form. I am not presenting a statement or an essay, but a more amorphous work that allows the maker and the viewer *the pleasure of discovery*. Meaning is not apparent at first glance and often requires repeated screenings, promising *challenge*. The *satisfaction* that comes from study and understanding of a complex work of *multiple references* and *perceptual insights* is a very rich fullness that can't be compared to linear journalism or narrative. Film allows me to express perceptual, intellectual, and emotional configurations that provoke pain and give pleasure.

The contributions of postmodernism have challenged the singularity and uniqueness of individual expression through the "utilization of forms over and above content due to the production of works in concrete historical circumstances."[2] The forms I choose are marked by the historic period in which I live, but the content of my work has not been remarked upon by modernists or postmodernists. Lesbian difference is ignored by both schools of theory. While I may enjoy the multiplicities of abstraction in form, it is still continually necessary to state my difference in content in my films, videos, performances, and writing. It is true that I bear the mark of the construction of perception by the social forces and institutions in which I live. Architecture, advertising, educational systems, family rearing, and Hollywood movies have all shaped my construction of knowledge and perception.

All these authority systems have "authorized certain representations while blocking, prohibiting, or invalidating others."[3] So even while I find pleasure and ambiguity in the formal characteristics I select for my films, I am still compelled to work from my experience from which my "subjectivity is semiotically and historically constructed."[4]

As a working lesbian artist, I am using abstraction not only for the perceptual pleasure and multiple possibilities of meaning. but also because I believe the viewer must be active. The supposition I have made is that participatory behavior in one area can lead to participation rather than passivity in another. The passive reception of non-challenging visual media—broadcast television, commercial film and the pulp press, static or moving—encourages passivity in other modes of living (on the job, at home, in the streets, in politics). An active audience engaged in "reading the text" will also be active in making their own decisions about campaigns, elections, issues, and demonstrations. I also use abstraction because of the uncertainty principle that is the locus for a certain type of play. There is linear play, where each person accepts rules of behavior, dialogue, and dress, such as children playing nurse and doctor. Then there is an abstract kind of play which requires the active imagination, where the only rule is: anything goes. There can be abrupt changes of scenes and locations, gender, names, and all possibilities of expression are possible. This form of play for children or adults requires a strong sense of self. In abstract play, everything around you can be turned upside down, and the most unimaginable combinations of words might be spoken; the disruptions, flights, costumes, and fantasies will swirl around you. You must know you won't be destroyed by letting go. Similarly, in letting the abstractions of light and texture, image and voice swirl around you and carry you into a filmic experience, you become aware of what you are experiencing. The active audience members don't lose a sense of themselves while engaging in the physical sensations of abstract cinema, but feel more the possibility of being.

Finally, multiple readings, understandings, and namings are promoted by abstractions providing richness, diversity, and complexity. If it is any worldview we need right now to allow for preserving difference, it is a worldview that embraces flexibility, possibilities, and multiple understandings of phenomena. There is not a feminism but feminisms, not a lesbian cinema but lesbian cinemas, and there is not abstraction but multiple manifestations of abstraction.

1 Christian Metz (1931-1993) – French film theorist from the semiotic school. – Ed.

2 Craig Owens, "The Discourse of Others: Feminists and Postmodernism," in *The Anti-Aesthetic: Essays on Postmodern Culture*, ed. Hal Foster (Seattle: Bay Press, 1983), 58.

3 Owens, p. 59.

4 Teresa de Lauretis, *Alice Doesn't: Feminism, Semiotics, Cinema* (Bloomington: Indiana University Press, 1984), 182.

BARBARA HAMMER, *Big Eye*,
photographic paper, 34.2 × 27.3 cm, 1980

Mary Kelly

MARY KELLY
(B. 1941, FORT DODGE)

An American artist, a pioneer of conceptual art with ties to the second wave of feminism, psychoanalysis, and the theory and practice of experimental film. In “Desiring Images/Imaging Desire”, she analyzes pictures from a psychoanalytic perspective, showing how the visual is enmeshed in mechanisms of desire and identity. Here the gaze is a space of negotiation, between what the picture reveals and what desire adds to it. Meaning is born from the tension between the visible and the imaginary.

Mary Kelly, "Desiring Images/Imaging Desire," *Mary Kelly*, eds. Homi Bhabha, Douglas Crimp, Margaret Iversen (London: Phaidon, 1997), 120–125

DESIRING IMAGES/IMAGING DESIRE (EXTRACT)[1]

"In this matter of the visible", said Lacan, "everything is a trap".[2] The field of vision is ordered by the function of images, at one level, quite simply by linking a surface to a geometric point by means of a path of light; but at another level, this function seems more like a labyrinth. Since the fascination in looking is founded on separation from what is seen, the field of vision is also, and most appropriately, the field of desire. Here the viewer enters the realm of lost objects, of vanishing points determined, not by geometry, but by what is real for the subject; linked not to a surface but to a place—the unconscious; not by means of light but by the laws of primary process.

In this matter of images of women then, it would seem that everything is doubly labyrinthine. Desire is embodied in the image which is equated with the woman who is reduced to the body which in turn is seen as the site of sexuality and the locus of desire ... a familiar elision; almost irresistible it would seem judging from the outcome of so many conference panels and special issues devoted to this theme. Nevertheless, it is a dangerous and circuitous logic that obscures a certain "progress"; a progression of strategies, of definitions made possible within feminist theory by the pressure of a political imperative to formulate the "problem" of images of women as a question: how to change them. The legacy is not a through-route, but a disentangling of paths that shows more clearly their points of intersection and draws attention to the fact that it is not obligatory to start over again at the beginning.

Discourses of the body and of sexuality, for instance, do not necessarily coincide. Within the modernist paradigm, it is not the sexual body, but the phenomenological (Husserlian) body that takes precedence; what belongs to me, my body, the body of the self-possessing subject whose guarantee of artistic truth is grounded in "actual experience", often deploying the "painful state" as a signature for that ephemeral object. Thus, the contribution of feminists in the field of performance has been, exactly, to pose the question of sexuality across the body in a way which focuses on the construction of the sexed subject, and at the same time problematizes the notion of the artist/auteur. The body is decentred, radically split, positioned; not simply my body, but his body, her body. Here, no third term emerges to salvage a transcendental sameness for aesthetic reflection. Yet, these artists continue to counterpose a visible form and a hidden content; excavating a different order of truth–the "truth" of the woman, her original feminine identity. Although the body is not perceived as the repository of this truth; it is seen as a hermeneutic image; the enigma of femininity is formulated as a problem of imagistic mis-representation which is subsequently resolved by discovering a true identity behind the patriarchal facade.

The enigma, however, only seems to encapsulate the difficulty of sexuality itself and what emerges is more in the order of an underlying contradiction than an essential content. The woman artist sees her experience as a woman particularly in terms of the "feminine position", that is, as the object of the look, but she must also account for the "feeling" she experiences as the artist, occupying what could be called the "masculine position" as subject of the look. The former she defines as the socially prescribed position of the woman, one to be questioned, exorcized or overthrown, while the implication of the latter (that there can be only one position with regard to active looking and that is masculine) cannot be acknowledged and is construed instead as a kind of psychic truth—a natural, instinctual, pre-existent and possibly unrepresentable femininity.[3] Often, the ambivalence of the feminist text seems to repudiate its own claim to essentialism; it testifies instead to what extent masculine and feminine identities are never finally fixed, but are continually negotiated through representations. This crisis of positionality, this instability of meaning revolves around the phallus as the term which marks the sexual division of the subject in language. Significantly, Lacan describes the woman's relation to the phallic term as a disguise, a masquerade.[4] In being the phallus for the other, she actively takes up a passive aim, becomes a picture of herself, erects a facade. Michèle Montrelay suggests "that the woman will disguise herself with the lack, throwing into relief the dimension of castration as *trompe-l'oeil*".[5] Behind the facade, finally, there is not "true" woman to be discovered. Yet, there is a dilemma: the impossibility of being, at once, both subject and object of desire.

Clearly, one (so-called post-feminist) response to this impasse has been to adopt a strategy of disavowal. It appears in the guise of a familiar visual metaphor: the androgyne. She *is* a picture; an expressionistic composite of looks and gestures which flaunts the uncertainty of sexual positioning. She refuses the lack, but remains the object of the look. In a sense, the fetishistic implications of not-knowing merely enhance the lure of the picture, effectively taming the gaze (a *dompte-regard*, as Lacan proposes), rather than provoking a de-construction. Another (and perhaps more politically motivated) tactic has been to assume self-consciously the "patriarchal facade"; to make it an almost abrasive and cynical act of affirmation. By producing a representation of femininity in excess of conventional codes, it shatters the narcissistic structure which would return the woman's image to her as a moment of completion. This can induce the alienating effect of a mis-recognition, but the question persists: how can she represent herself as subject of desire?

The (neo-)feminist alternative has been to refuse the literal figuration of the woman's body, creating significance out of its absence. But this does not signal a new form of iconoclasm. The artist does not protest against the "lure" of the picture. In another way, however, her practice could be said to be blasphemous in so far as she seeks to appropriate the gaze behind it (the place of gods, of auteurs and evil eyes). In her field of vision femininity is not seen as a pre-given entity, but as the mapping out of sexual difference within a definite terrain, a moment of discourse, a fragment of history. With regard to the spectator, it is a tactic of reversal, attempting to produce the woman, through a different form of identification with the image, as the subject of the look [...]

Desire is caused not by objects, but in the unconscious, according to the peculiar structure of fantasy. Desire is repetitious, it resists normalization, ignores biology, disperses the body. Certainly, desire is not synonymous with images of desirable women; yet, what does it mean, exactly, to say that feminists have refused the "image" of the woman? First, this implies a refusal to reduce the concept of the image to one of resemblance, to figuration or even to the general category of the iconic sign. It suggests that the image, as it is organized in that space called the picture, can refer to a heterogeneous system of signs—indexical, symbolic and iconic. And thus, that it is possible to invoke the non-specular, the sensory, the somatic, in the visual field; to invoke, especially, the register of the invocatory drives (which, according to Lacan, are on the same level as the scopic drives, but closer to the experience of the unconscious), through "writing". Secondly, it should be said that this is not a hybrid version of the "hieroglyph" masquerading as a "heterogeneity of signs". The object is not to return "the feminine" to a domain of pre-linguistic utterance; but rather, to mobilize a system of *imaged discourse* capable of refuting a certain form of "culturally overdetermined" scopophilia. But why? Would this release the "female spectator" from her hysterical identification with the male voyeur?

Again, the implications of suggesting that women have a privileged relation to narcissism or that fetishism is an exclusively male perversion should be re-considered. Surely, the link between narcissism and fetishism is castration. For both the man and the woman this is the condition for access to the symbolic, to language, to culture; there can be no privileged relation to madness. Yet there is difference. There is still that irritating asymmetry of the Oedipal moment. There is Freud's continual emphasis on the importance of the girl's attachment to her mother. And there is Dora.[6] What *did* she find so fascinating in the picture of the Sistine Madonna? Perhaps, above all, it was the possibility of seeing the woman as subject of desire without transgressing the socially acceptable definition of her as the mother. To have the child as phallus; to be the phallic mother; to have the pleasure of the child's body; to have the pleasure of the maternal body experienced through it; perhaps, in the figure of the Madonna, there was a duplication of identification and desire that only the body of another woman could sustain.

For both the man and the woman, the maternal body lines the seductive surface of the image, but the body *he* sees is not the same one *she* is looking at. The woman's relation to the mother's body is a constant source of anxiety. Montrelay claims that this relation is often only censored rather than repressed. As a consequence the woman clings to a "precocious femininity", an archaic oral-anal-vaginal or *concentric* organization of the drives which bars her access to sublimated pleasure (phallic *jouissance*). [7] Similarly, with regard to the artistic text, and if pleasure is understood in Barthes' sense of the term as a loss of preconceived identity, rather than an instance of repletion; then it is possible to produce a different form of pleasure for the woman by representing a specific loss—the loss of her imagined closeness to the mother's body. A critical, perhaps disturbing sense of separation is effected through the visualization of exactly that which was assumed to be outside of seeing; precocious, unspeakable, unrepresentable. In the scopic register, she is no longer at the level of concentricity, of repetitious demand, but of desire. As Lacan points out, even the eye itself belongs to this archaic structure since it functions in the field of vision as a lost object.[8] Thus, the same movement which determines the subject's appearance in language, that is, symbolic castration, also introduces the gaze. And the domain of imaged discourse.

Until now the woman as spectator has been pinned to the surface of the picture, trapped in a path of light that leads her back to the features of a veiled face. It seems important to acknowledge that the masquerade has always been internalized, linked to a particular organization of the drives, represented through a diversity of aims and objects; but without being lured into looking for a psychic truth beneath the veil. To see this picture critically, the viewer should be neither too close nor too far away.

1 First presented as a paper at the conference "Desire" at the Institute of Contemporary Arts, London, 1983. Published in *Wedge*, no. 6, New York, 1984 and re-published in *Instabili: la question du sujet*, La Galerie Powerhouse, Centre d'information Artexte, Montreal, 1990, pp. 24-28, and in *Imagining Desire, Mary Kelly Selected Writings*, MIT Press, Cambridge, Massachusetts, 1996.

2 Jacques Lacan, "The Line and Light", *The Four Fundamental Concepts*, ed. M. Masud, trans. R. Khan, Hogarth Press, London, 1977, p. 93.

3 Mary Kelly, "Re-Viewing Modernist Criticism", *Screen*, Vol. 22, No. 3, London, 1981, pp. 53-56. Republished in this volume pp. 112-19.

4 See Jacques Lacan, "The Signification of the Phallus", 1958, *Feminine Sexuality*, eds. Juliet Mitchell, Jacqueline Rose, Macmillan, London, 1982.

5 Michèle Montrelay, "Inquiry into Feminity", *m/f*, no. 1, London, p. 92.

6 See Sigmund Freud, "Fragment of an Analysis of a Case of Hysteria", 1901, Standard Edition, Vol. VII, trans. James Strachey, Hogarth Press, London, 1968.

7 Michèle Montrelay, op. cit., pp. 86-99.

8 Jacques Lacan, "What is a Picture", *The Four Fundamental Concepts*, op. cit., p. 118.

Leon Chwistek

LEON CHWISTEK
(1884, KRAKOW – 1944, MOSCOW)

A philosopher, logician, and painter. As a member of the Artes group and co-creator of Formism, he integrated artistic practice and theoretical reflection on the status of representation. His concept of the multiplicity of realities attempted to build an epistemological groundwork for stylistic pluralism in Modernist art. In this text, Chwistek explores characteristic attributes of children's art, calling attention to its spontaneity, independence from conventional rules, and links with "primitive" forms of expression. He stresses that children's art, which is free from traditional aesthetic standards, has authenticity and freedom of expression; its potential could inspire artists in search of innovative means of expression.

Leon Chwistek, "Elementy twórcze sztuki dziecka," *Wiadomości Literackie*, no. 42 (1936): 8.

CREATIVE ELEMENTS OF CHILDREN'S ART

Gauguin[1] gave professional artists in the latter half of the nineteenth century an original model for art. In the same period, theoretical studies on the art of dilettantes and children began to emerge (Lombroso, Ricci, Sully[2]). Initially, these influences were fairly minimal and opinions rather slight. Over time, some striking phenomena emerged.

It began with the fantastic success of a typical dilettante, Henri Rousseau.[3] This success was, perhaps, the most interesting event in the history of modern art.

We must confess right off the bat that at the core was an oversaturation, caused by the naturalist canon and the cold, aesthetic relationship to art that came with it. The Impressionists had, of course, managed to break through the canon of colors, but the naturalistic model of drawing still held sway. This duality both delighted and disquieted, but in a relatively short time it grew dull. Overkill and boredom are harbingers of a new epoch.

A new epoch had indeed begun, but this time the birth proved extremely strenuous. First there was the matter of abstract forms, as these were about to shift into the foreground (in Cubism). This issue made artists move their efforts into a field of experiments that were notable, but fundamentally opposed to the postulate of enthusiasm. Cubism was just as cold and aesthetic as naturalism, though it was incomparably more interesting. The same goes for Constructivism and Unism (Strzemiński). A yearning for the primary enchantment of the child's art, brought into the light of day by Henri Rousseau, exploded along with the individual efforts of various artists, and ultimately led to Expressionism. This school succumbed too quickly to the influence of metaphysics and magic. It all ended with the Expressionists' canvases drowning in a mood of horror and perverse sensuality.

Formism was born of the combination between abstract tendencies and a primitive instinct. I think this composite direction is bound to be decisive in the future.

Nonetheless, its history makes for a thoroughly tragic picture. An over-emphasis on a naturalistic reaction, combined with unfortunate professional ambitions, caused the breakdown of the first explosion. Then came a second standstill. Right now, we may observe an attempt at a new offensive.

The rebirth of Formism can only be achieved through a conscious and bold assertion that the professional artist is not, and cannot be fundamentally superior to a child. On the contrary, we should openly declare that the child or the dilettante, who are spiritually alike, have more direct contact with the summits of art than the professional artist, as they need not contend with deleterious influences like the desire for recognition and the struggle to put food on the table. If, however, the artist can overcome the dangers of professional ambition, if they gain an approach to art as sincere and passionate as a child's, then they will not only be able to find the enchantment of a child's art, they will also be able to expand the field of ready opportunities without giving up their essential value.

One of these attempts to introduce the viewer's perspective is in *The March of the Artillery Through the City*. It is my pleasure to report that Mieczysław Wallis,[4] the seven-year-old nephew of Karol T., came up with the same idea.

I quote the note loaned to me by Mr. Wallis (the steamship with the big funnels in the foreground is smaller than the bridge and the human figures in the background).

"Why did you draw it that way? Aren't the things that are further away from us supposed to be smaller than the ones that are near?"

"That's how I drew them. One of those people standing on the bridge is me, the other one's you. So, since we're standing on the bridge, which is close to us, it seems bigger than the steamship, which is far from us."

I later concluded that the Expressionist artist Spies[5] took the very same approach to perspective in some of his pictures, even if his constructs can be fairly accidental (*Carousel*, *Slide*). Spies's pictures are full of a demonic horror that is foreign to children and encroach on what we call literature. An approach to this subject that excludes these features strikes me as compelling.

I am only raising one of a great many possibilities here. I want to show that a child's art is not a rigid structure that breaks down when one turns fourteen, On the contrary—it can provide us with infinite perspectives. The task of the artist is to combat the tragedy a child undergoes in their fourteenth year.

It would be impossible to address all the urgent matters that go together with the mystery of children's art, but I will call attention to several points.

First, the matter of emulation. Many have stated that the folk primitive is incompetent when it emulates professional art. We do indeed find incompetent emulation, yet the strange fact is that incompetent emulation is more fascinating than the original. Indeed, in professionals the effort to be original too often leads to unconscious imitation, worse than the model. I have kept a notebook with pictures copied from my history book when I was six. I believe these scribbles are more compelling than the staid German etchings on which they were based. We should note that the influence of the model modified my primitive approach, bringing results that were well beyond the ordinary child's drawing capabilities. I think the struggle against naturalist tendencies, fought through the charm of children's art, could lead to an evolution in the Primitivist approach and bring about striking results.

We should add that evolution takes place automatically, with no effort from the experimenter. I have found it in my daughter, whom I managed to preserve in an atmosphere of children's art, and in many dilettantes whose works hang in my collection. For instance, I attach a pastel drawing by Fanny Grossmannówna.

FANNY GROSSMANNÓWNA:
Lekcja gimnastyki

An analysis of this drawing leads us to the basic premise of repeating related forms, which is one of the most important aspects of the theory of Zonism. This tendency to create zones, based on joining related forms into a whole, is found most prominently in children and dilettantes, as well as in purebred artists. One of the most radical examples is reproduced by Dr. Prinzhorn[6] in his study. Here I attach an etching by Leopold Lewicki, a leading exponent of the Krakow Group.

To conclude, I would like to return to a thought that has plagued me in recent years. Our nation is constantly producing great talents, cut from an original cloth, simply because civilization is less smothering here than in the West. The original model played a major role in the Formist period (the Pronaszkos, Czyżewski. Mierzejewski, Winkler, Makowski, Gwozdecki, Halicka[7]). At the moment it can be seen with great force in the art of Streng and Hahn, Lewicki, Blonder, Osostowicz,[8] and many members of the Krakow Group. It plays a great role in the work of artists who have achieved recognition recently (Stryjeńska, Malczewski[9]). Nonetheless, as usual, here too we have been unable to rouse ourselves to make a conscious and concerted effort. For this to happen, we must revise some fundamental concepts. Above all, we must finally understand that we ought not to look at children's art with a forbearing smile, nor should we say that when they grow older they will understand how they ought to paint. We must understand that the secret of great art is held by none other than children and that they should be our maestros. Then we will surely have the great renaissance of art we dream of, and have long awaited.

We should remember that this is not about imitating children, but about uncovering the same creative instinct, the one that is found so plentifully in them and is so dampened in ourselves.

Translated by Soren Gauger

1 Paul Gauguin (1848-1903) – French painter. – Ed.

2 Cesare Lombroso (1835-1909) – Italian psychiatrist; Corrado Ricci (1958-1934) – Italian archaeologist and art historian; James Sully (1842-1923) – British psychologist. – Ed.

3 Henri Rousseau (1844-1910) – French painter. – Ed.

4 Mieczysław Wallis (1895-1975) – Polish philosopher, art historian and art critic. – Ed.

5 Walter Spies (1895-1941) – German painter, composer and musicologist. – Ed.

6 Hans Prinzhorn (1886-1933) – German psychiatrist and art historian. – Ed.

7 Andrzej Pronaszko (1888-1961) – painter, set designer, Formist; Zbigniew Pronaszko (1885-1958) – sculptor, painter, co-founder of Polish Expressionism and Formism; Tytus Czyżewski (1880-1945) – painter, poet, Formist, and Futurist; Konrad Winkler (1882-1962) – painter and graphic artist, Formist; Tadeusz Makowski (1882-1932) – painter, representative of synthetic and naive painting; Gustaw Gwozdecki (1880-1935) – painter and graphic artist, associated with the École de Paris; Alicja Halicka (1889-1974) – Polish painter, associated with the École de Paris. – Ed.

8 Henryk Streng (Marek Włodarski) (1903-1960) – painter, illustrator, teacher, co-founder of the Artes group; Otto Hahn (1904-1942) – painter, member of the Artes group; Leopold Lewicki (1906-1973) – painter, graphic artist, sculptor, co-founder of the Krakow Group; Aleksander (Sasza) Blonder (1909-1949) – Polish painter of Jewish origin; Stanisław Osostowicz (1906-1939) – painter, creator of collages, drawings and scenography. – Ed.

9 Zofia Stryjeńska (1891-1979) – Polish painter and illustrator who worked in the Art Deco style; Jacek Malczewski (1854-1929) – Polish painter, representative of Symbolism. – Ed.

CHAPTER

MULTIPLE

X

PORTRAIT

X

PORTRAIT

Stanisław Ignacy Witkiewicz

STANISŁAW IGNACY WITKIEWICZ
(1885, WARSAW – 1939, JEZIORY)

A painter, portraitist, novelist, and playwright, a total artist, for whom art was not just creativity, but also an expression of a painful sense of the disintegration of values and the world. In his final, unfinished novel, *The Only Way Out*, Witkacy forged a pessimistic vision of the future and an attempt to deal with a sense of inevitable destruction—both personal and civilizational. In the quoted extract, Marcel, an artist possessed by a vision of pure form, is the embodiment of both artistic intuition and total social alienation. His painting comes from a "weave of initially undefined forms" and "metaphysical terror."

Stanisław Ignacy Witkiewicz, *Jedyne wyjście* (critical edition), ed. Anna Micińska (Warsaw: Państwowy Instytut Wydawniczy, 1993), 138–42.

JEDYNE WYJŚCIE (THE ONLY WAY OUT) AN EXTRACT

Marceli threw himself into his work. Suffretka was due to arrive at midday, and by then the composition that he had begun a few days prior had to be completed – its time was already running out. Every work of art must be executed within its own specific timeframe. The process is as precise as the progression of childbirth. The artistic intuition of the creator (and here, the concept truly has meaning) consists, among other things (and quite apart from the resolution of purely formal problems), in the execution of the work within that one, singular interval of time. Every artist knows with absolute certainty that a given work must be initiated at a specific moment, and knows, more or less, how long the process may last, and during which precise hours it must be created. He who fails to heed this voice is a charlatan and a scoundrel, a mere fraud pretending to be an artist. Inspiration is truth – contrary to the fables spun by over-intellectualized creative impotents, who artificially manufacture their creations (for whatever secondary purpose: fame, money, etc.) only after they have achieved recognition in certain spheres, or even universally, and have found that such production pays dividends for them in other, non-artistic dimensions. But, as one of America's presidents once said: "You can fool all the people some time, you can fool some people all the time, but you n e v e r can fool all the people all the time." It is, in all probability, analogous to childbirth: something mature both wishes and is compelled to tear itself from the substrate upon which it arose, in order to make way for something new. To miss such a moment is to risk the putrefaction of the foetus within the creator, or to risk stillbirths; the premature violation of this process's natural course in the name of some secondary, mundane affairs leads also to severe artistic maladies, and even to complete creative impotence. But one must truly possess this "intuition" and not squander it for the sake of, for instance, a game of bridge, an assignation with some lady, or a pleasant little constitutional; while at the same time, one must do everything in one's power to facilitate the conditions for its very emergence. I have the impression that Polish writers and artists – with the exception of the aforementioned intellectual drudges (and I mean "intellectual" in the most pejorative sense: namely substituting inspiration for a paltry intellect) – proceed in a manner precisely contrary to the principle axiomatically posited above. But no matter: nothing will save Polish culture from its flaccidity and sluggishness if the intellectual development of both exceptional individuals and the infra- and semi-intelligent masses is not accelerated. The point is not to annihilate the potential for the next creative onslaught during the lulls in between. The sole means to this end is intellectual labour – not sitting around in cafés, cracking jokes, reading newspapers, and swilling vodka.

And so, Marceli was possessed of this fundamental intuition,[1] for which reason he hurled himself directly upon the composition entitled *The Omphaloskepsis of the Vexers*, a work that only with respect to its inessential, biographical content had anything in common with the title as such – this, of course, assuming the comprehensibility of the term "vexer" itself (is it a "she" or a "he"? no, a "he"—a male vexer—like a fixer, not a vixen) and of the more recognisably human act of "omphaloskepsis". One might, of course, be accused of "incomprehensibilism" here, and with good reason – and yet, on the other hand, in a certain sense everything is indeed comprehensible, provided one does not construe that term as an understanding in the purely logical sense, one predicated upon the exact, strict definitions of the relevant concepts. For one can, after all, have a direct sensation of a thing; and perhaps this sensation will not be synonymous with the state experienced by the "creator" of a given, unspecified symbol, but something will indubitably have been felt. Words are centres, each possessing a smaller or larger aureole of indefiniteness around it, the radius of which is inversely proportional to the strictness of its definition. These constant digressions are insufferable, yet on the other hand, so many interesting things exist (or perhaps not, you cretin? How about a fist in your gob?) that no one knows about, and then the intellectual rabble comes along and spouts the most preposterous bilge on the subject, further befogging the already none-too-illuminated craniums of their milieu. But what is to be done – one must return to life and, within life itself (or then again, perhaps not at all), demonstrate what this is all about.

This composition, like every vital painterly creation (damn it!), had materialized before Marceli as a still-imprecisely-defined nexus of initially indeterminate forms, possessing directional tensions that were faintly delineated by a not-yet-unambiguous similitude to certain at-first-nebulous objects. A ganglion of potential force, as in an undetonated bomb, yet one already bearing a faint adumbration of directional-dynamic – that is to say, vectorial – possibilities. It had manifested itself to him, in point of fact, at the precise moment a naked and heretofore unprecedented metaphysical terror had descended upon him; while returning at night from Suffretka Nunberg's, he had suddenly felt himself absolutely alone on an u n k n o w n planet – and this w i t h o u t r e c o u r s e t o m e t a p h o r, without any of the hideous, repulsive literary contrivances and stratagems calculated to impress a reader, and a second-rate one at that;[2] he was utterly alone on a s u l t r y s u m m e r n i g h t, walking from the city's periphery towards its centre, and his slow encroachment into streets that were illuminated yet, in these districts at this hour, utterly dead, did nothing to diminish his sense of a b s o l u t e solitude. And in addition to this, the full consciousness of not belonging to any multiplicity, to any species of similar beings – that had been terrible. But what had been more terrible still was the fact that the appearance of a belated passer-by in some side-street – an inevitable eventuality, given the circumstances – did not alter by a hair's breadth the uncanny impression of solitude and of non-belonging to the human species whatsoever. This was not a state of affairs that could be encapsulated by the judgment "I am not human" – that problem, as such, did not exist in the slightest. Marceli had fallen out of nowhere (and who knows how he had materialized in Interstellar Space in the first place) onto some unknown globe. Everything was uniformly incomprehensible, yet this was an incomprehensibility of a higher order: as if a grown man had abruptly been born, or had found himself – having come into existence for the very first time – in some place or other, it mattered not where, that was in any event entirely u n k n o w n . These were experiences that one cannot have without narcotics. And on top of it all, to his usual portion of coke – which in the dead of night sometimes reached 12.0—he had added 0.08 of that other drug Eukodal, *per iniectionem cutanea* (during a visit to his addict friend who was perpetually at work on the stuff). This produced the characteristic shift from cocaine's agitation to a state of slightly moronic delight, a blissfully placid contemplation of the world – the exact condition which is the domain of those who use the aforementioned substance. There was only him, Kizior, and his cane (a Malacca, a counterfeit one it seemed, yet cherished nonetheless). The terrestrial globe itself shrivelled to the size of some plainly stupid little asteroid – one could circumnavigate it in fifteen minutes – and the city seemed an object "from another dimension" of the spirit: an incomprehensible mishmash of forms without a shadow of an idea of any utility, "a pure form of the nonsense of objecthood", specified, but not defined. "Just me and my cane", Marceli told himself with a cold glee and an axiomatic inner conviction. Some little man he passed did not belong to this world and was, by the force of pure judgment (in the logical, not the judicial, sense), summarily excluded from it. And in that, there was a true miracle. Unfortunately, at the very instant the drug is working, you cannot fully grasp the miracle of such a state, for you are sealed inside that compartment, and the prize for this confinement is precisely that improbable and, in any normal state, utterly unutterable perspective.

Translated by Łukasz Mojsak

1 That is to say, the faculty of divining and predicting things, not in any absolute sense, but merely with a certain degree of probability, on the basis of data not yet consciously and precisely apprehended as such – a fact which does not preclude their subsequent discovery by means of an analysis of a relevant complex of experiences.

2 There is literature that is pure unto itself (where the author writes for his own delight, and that is all), and then there is the sullied kind, which implicates the reader. And in that kind, the whole spectacle is laid bare: the hideous little author fawning over his (usually mediocre) reader, bombarding him, zeroing in, correcting his aim, and then letting fly – Ab-hor-rent!! It is with this very literature that you, jokers and jesters, have corrupted the last vestiges of any potential readership we had. And now, the game is up.

Natalia Lach--Lachowicz

355

NATALIA LACH-LACHOWICZ
(1937, ŻYWIEC – 2022, WARSAW)

A creator of photographs, experimental films, installations, actions, videos, drawings, paintings, and objects. Natalia LL's work, often seen as feminist and conceptual art, abandoned themes of physicality and identity, exploring relations between the erotic, consumption, and mass culture. In "Dreaming", which is also the title of a series of photographs, the artist explores the intuitive nature of art, opposing the primacy of thought over the act of perception and postulating their indivisible coexistence. In "Visual Language" she extols separating the experience of everyday life and the reality defined by art. Art should shape a "language" which is untranslatable into other paths of knowledge.

Natalia Lach-Lachowicz, "Język wizualny," *Fotografia*, no. 1 (1976): 14–15.

VISUAL LANGUAGE

If art were identical to life, it would likely dissolve into everyday activities and behaviors. However, the reality that art presents or defines does not align with the image of the world formed by cognition based on our everyday experiences.

I destroy and combat these commonplace and schematic experiences: for to see is not to think.

Art appears to be an operation within highly complex structures: semantic and morphological.

I therefore propose ongoing research aimed at creating structures that are "out of the ordinary" and "impossible" to realise within daily reality.

The goal of this research is to develop (to create) notations that are impossible to concretize, or whose concretization is significantly hindered.

Experiences of reality are needed only to formulate the morphology of signs, thus serving to create signs that are, as far as possible, perfectly transparent to that reality. Ultimately, the visual language will be legible only within the language itself, and any anecdotal motivation will lose all sense. In this way, art will become art.

December 1974

Translated by Łukasz Mojsak

Natalia Lach-Lachowicz, "Śnienie," *Fotografia*, (1978): 20.

DREAMING

The supremacy of the thought process over visual perception is a fiction that must be resolutely opposed in art. The apparatus of visual perception (the eye and the brain) is an indivisible whole, for we cannot look without thinking. The process of perception is holistic and can be regarded as such.

This premise leads me to assert that what art needs is an imaginative and intuitive correction, as the canonised metalinguistic process fails to encompass reality in its full complexity and richness. Conceptualism has diligently cleaned the spectacles; let us now put them on to see the world. I therefore propose an art realised through objectified means – as they are better suited to our sensory structure – yet these means must remain strictly subordinate to artistic intuition. Intellectual cognition, after all, belongs to the domain of science, where each new element is built upon a preceding one that has been carefully proven and described.

Art is a construct in which paralogical operations are possible, for it possesses the ingenious quality of being founded on intuitive cognition. Intuitive photography, examples of which I present here, is therefore an objectified record of intuition, an insight into the irrational world of art's self-awareness. The intuitive nature of art seems to be its fundamental characteristic, distinguishing it from all other forms of human activity. If we are to demonstrate that art has not succumbed to the prevailing trend of dehumanisation, it must be grounded in a conscious intuition, one that precedes any grammatical and canonized analysis.

The inherent limitations of art do not render the cognition it provides less valuable than that of science. Art, being closer to the whole of the human psychological constitution, is, as it were, internally contradictory, much as human beings are themselves. These contradictions, however, attest to human complexity that is the very engine of our transformation and development. Intuitive photography also exposes the inherent contradiction between science and art, whose teleological purposes are entirely distinct.

Translated by Łukasz Mojsak

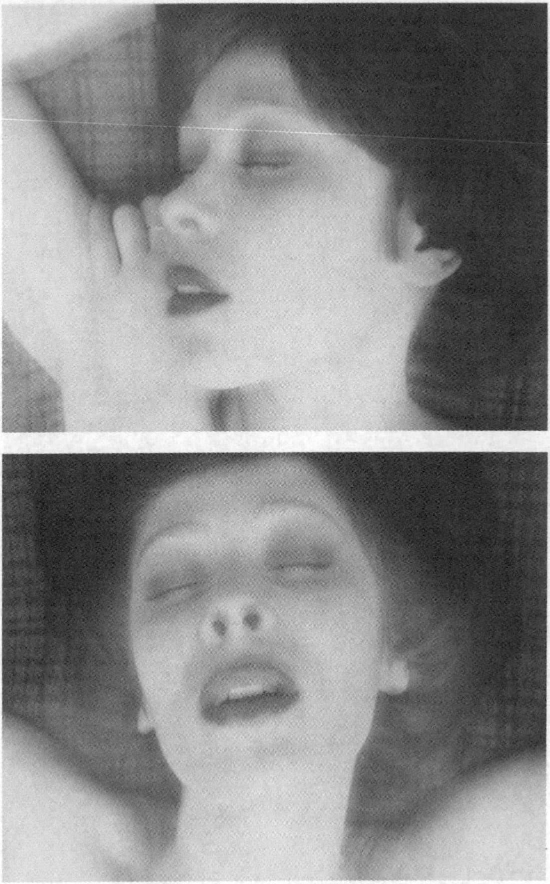

NATALIA LL, *Dreaming*, photographic paper, 49.5 × 59 cm, 1978

Alina Szapocznikow

363

ALINA SZAPOCZNIKOW
(1926, KALISZ – 1973, PRAZ-COUTANT)

A Polish sculptor whose work focused on physicality, transience, and trauma, especially in terms of her own experiences with illness and the Holocaust. In a letter to Ryszard Stanisławski, Szapocznikow stressed the difficulty in depicting a nurse, a symbol of care, in a monumental fashion, as the movement involved in the work would deprive the sculpture of its gravity and solidity. She did not want to romanticize this profession either. She thought that in Socialist Realist art, depicting people at work required strict principles and simplification to preserve the legibility and sublimity of the message.

Alina Szapocznikow, "Szapocznikow do Stanisławskiego 25 X 49 l'hôpital," in *Kroją mi się piękne sprawy. Listy Aliny Szapocznikow i Ryszarda Stanisławskiego 1948-1951*, ed. Agata Jakubowska (Krakow–Warsaw: Wydawnictwo Karakter, Muzeum Sztuki Nowoczesnej w Warszawie, 2012).

SZAPOCZNIKOW TO STANISŁAWSKI 25.X.49 L'HÔPITAL[1]

Rysiu, Rysieńku

I wanted to do a sculpture of a nurse. Without any of what typically surrounds it, like "devotion," "sensitivity," "gentleness" etc. That is all a bunch of very romantic dead weight. These women that care for the sick are professionals as in any other sector of life. They spend 8 hours at their workplace and return to their family and their personal activities and entertainments. Nonetheless, and as in other walks of life, their occupation has impressed its specific character on their entire person. Sometimes this character is strong and truly lovely. Healthily there echoes from the wards of the sick and exhausted their springy step, their eternally energetic legs and strong, often supportive arms. Such a figure, which would join all the qualities of the nurse-woman caring for the sick, a figure symbolizing and typifying the nurse, is a really lovely theme. But... in order for the figure to be representative, it has to depict the nurse in some movement characteristic of her as she does her work. And there is where sculpture robs the nurse of her gravity. Movement destroys monumental dignity. A sculpture of a person in motion ceases to be a sculpture. And this is also why, I think, that same difficulty may arise in all socialist art. Sculpted people shown at work have to have an exceptionally unschematic form, the artist has to limit himself exceptionally in his means of expression and simplify the composition in order to emphasize the dignity of the work, in order for the activity itself to reach the viewer's consciousness, and, basically, in order not to mess up the specifics, that is, of the activity. That is why in Romanesque and Egyptian art we can see the activities of the craftsmen so clearly, and the little sculpted figure is like an embodiment of the entire craft.

But all speculations in one's head are crap, it's only when you start to compose that you see what makes sense and what doesn't, and you destroy and redo as needed until the image corresponds to the felt truth.

Rysieńku, this was supposed to be a letter to you, but what am I supposed to write to you? I could at most caress you in embraces.

A.

Translated by Jennifer Croft

1 l'hôpital – hospital (Fr.).

ALINA SZAPOCZNIKOW, Alina Szapocznikow, *A Difficult Age*, patinated plaster, 189 × 59 × 38 cm, 1954-1956 © ADAGP, Paris. *A Difficult Age*, Courtesy The Estate of Alina Szapocznikow / Galerie Loevenbruck, Paris.

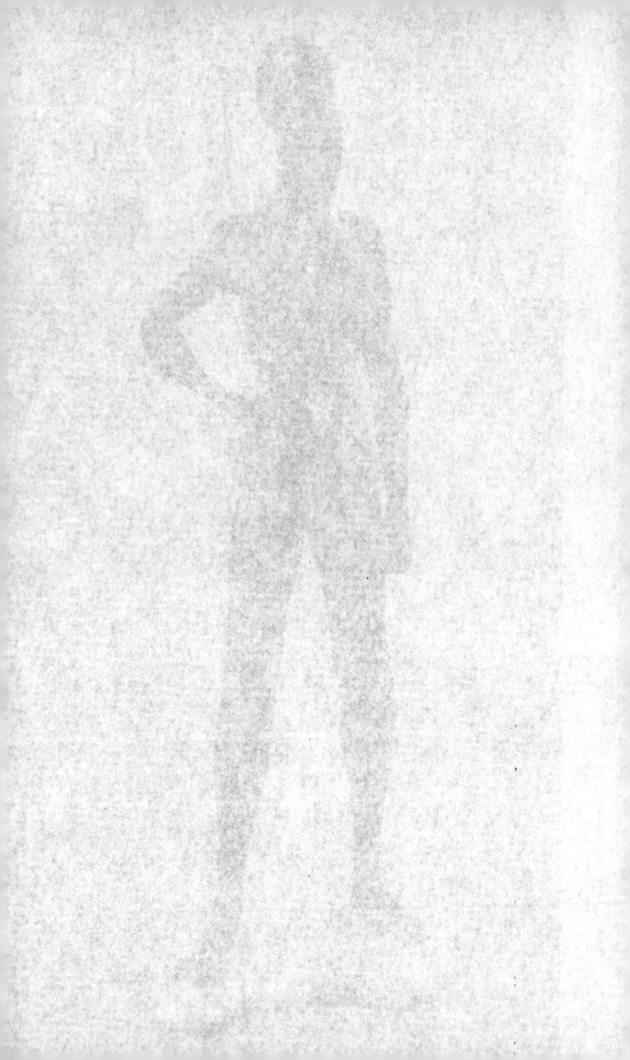

Zofia Rydet

ZOFIA RYDET
(1911, IVANO-FRANKIVSK – 1997, GLIWICE)

A Polish photographer and documentary filmmaker, a central figure in Polish postwar photography. Her work combined a documentary form with aspects of Surrealism and symbolism. In *Sociological Record* (1978–97), she photographed thousands of home interiors and their residents, creating a unique portrait of Polish society. The present text is a testimony of Rydet's artistic philosophy, which she pursued throughout her professional life. Rydet shows that her motivation for taking pictures and desire to capture "the truth of human existence" always preceded her formal and technical concerns. Speaking of her monumental *Sociological Record*, she described it as embalming time and preserving what is irreversibly vanishing for posterity.

Zofia Rydet, "O swojej sztuce," in *Zofia Rydet (1911-1997): fotografie*, ed. Elżbieta Fuchs (Łódź: Muzeum Sztuki w Łodzi, 1999), 34–36. First published in: *Zofia Rydet o swojej twórczości* (Gliwice: Muzeum w Gliwicach, 1993), unpaginated.

ZOFIA RYDET ON HER WORK

Photography has vast capabilities and various faces. The camera is almost **the same sort of tool** for rendering thoughts and visions as the paintbrush or the pencil, as film or even the written word. Most important is **not how, but what** you want to say, and where you find the meaning in the work. I have always wanted to create something that aroused a profound faith in its truthfulness, and thus would have the power to move people and prompt them to think. I would less like people to look at the various photographs than to be able to read the content I want to give them.

Callahan once said **it is not the composition, but the motivation that counts**. My motivation, despite my various statements, is always the same. **People—this is the key word**.

My first exhibition, and then the *Little Man* (1961) photobook, arose from psychological observation, not a fascination for how photogenic children can be. I wanted to show the child in all their multifaceted experiences and reactions, without the stereotypes of idyllic, angelic childhood, speaking of people through thoughtful juxtapositions; as Janusz Korczak once said, all the same things happen in the child's world as in the dirty world of "grown-ups." There's no such thing as children, only people with concepts on a different scale, a different store of experience. A child is a hundred roles, a hundred masks of a talented actor. The exhibition's motif was: seek **a bit of yourself** slumbering in that unfamiliar child, maybe you'll glimpse it, or even develop it.

My second exhibition, *Czas przemijania* [Time of passing], also spoke of people, those at the end of their lives, showing the coarse and ugly old age of average people, pensioners, the vulnerable and helpless, with all the withering and dying, the deep wrinkles covering their faces and bent backs.

Paired with photographs of crumbling houses and dry, wilting flowers, they spoke of the transience of life, its essence and true meaning. The exhibition was meant to prompt understanding and sympathy for people who we fail to see, or often shove aside as we dash around, caught up in our everyday affairs.

In this exhibition I also used juxtapositions to enhance the power and impact of the statements.

Looking for new means of expression, I also turned to photomontage.

Photomontage has a great capacity to transpose your deepest thoughts, feelings, and experiences into a completely different picture, which seems unreal but is made up of real parts.

Photomontages have a Surrealist bent, and though Surrealism is already a classical style in the history of painting, in photography it has entirely different prospects. Through the equipment, reality is brought into the picture; it is composed of real parts, yet extends the range of photography, delving into the realm of our dreams and nightmares.

Świat wyobraźni Zofii Rydet [Zofia Rydet's world of the imagination] (pub. 1979) depicts a person in peril from the moment of their birth, their feelings and desires, solitude and anxiety, from which only love can save them, fear of destruction, and the tragedy of the passing of time.

In 1980, I created *Nieskończoność dalekich dróg* [The endlessness of distant roads], a metaphorical tale of life and the ever-changing roads we must travel, and although they are there, surrounding us with traffic signs, they mean nothing, they are wrapped and illegible. Only the crossroads we encounter are real, and only the path leading to death is certain. It all ends with a gate to the vastness of the ocean, opening wider and wider. The final photos show the deception of life after death—a fuzzy, solarized road, captured on the go, with a bright point on the horizon, in which Christ appears. The second part of the exhibition features ruminating old women on a podium, cut out and processed into spatial sculptures—the women are thinking. Lower on the podium is the book of life, open like an accordion, a record of essential steps in every person's life: birth, first steps, first games, home, school, First Communion, study, adulthood, love, marriage, and new births. Between the photographs are excerpts from real letters, detailing their life. The whole thing is done in sepia. Only the small black-and-white portraits of the changing protagonist show the course of time and the standard path of life. The whole series begins with a large black-and-white photograph of a newborn child in his mother's arms, and ends with an identical shot of the child, now a grown man, holding his own son.

In 1978, I began my *Zapis socjologiczny* [Sociological record].

André Bazin[1] wrote: "Artificially preserving the appearance of a human being means tearing it from the stream of time and loading it onto the ship of life."

My series was meant to be a way of embalming time. It was (or is) supposed to preserve what is changing, for a time when what is now reality ceases to exist and could be very hard to imagine. It is meant to provide a faithful reflection of people in their surroundings, in their environment they create for themselves, which, on the one hand, is the décor of their immediate surroundings (their home interior), and on the other, reveals their psyche, and sometimes says more about them than they do themselves.

Home is a place to which you return, where you find yourself. Whether it's a palace, a cabin, a villa, a mud hut, or a skyscraper, home is always a shelter from the anxieties that plague a person. A home is a reflection of its owner, it also reflects the society, civilization, and culture in which it was built. A home lives according to the wishes of its creator, the person who inhabits it. A home is so saturated with its owner's character that as a result, the home and its owner are one; no two people are alike, and nor are any two homes. Every one has its individual characteristics. A person instinctively and subconsciously adapts their home to their tastes.

People, apartments, belongings.... A person's immediate surroundings that are the most natural, even if they are shaped by civilization and the culture of their life's environment. A space of intimacy, family community, solitude. A place where the world begins, and where it ends. Where times past live on in a small memento, an heirloom, a wedding photograph... and where, through a holy picture or a cross on the wall, a portal opens into a different time dimension, another way of living, into a reality where all the paths of an earthly pilgrimage lead. A place of everyday returns, an asylum of respite from the torments and joys of every stage of this journey—**THE CENTER OF THE WORLD.**

My initial premise was: the objects and interiors are most important, while the people only define the interior, they are to be static, as if objects themselves, and so they have to sit facing the camera and stare into the lens; the photographs always have to be taken with the same camera, the same lighting, and more or less from the same angle. After all, this was to be a simple, objective, authentic record of the existing reality, taken from a detached perspective.

At the same time, I noticed even while I was doing the work that it was taking on an entirely different color, that these ordinary documentary photographs were revealing, before my eyes, **a great truth about human fate**, that I was unable to maintain my detachment; on the contrary, the series was drawing me in more than anything I had ever done before; it was becoming my new love, my passion, bringing me new perspectives and strengths.

The person, who was meant to be just another part of the whole, turned out to be the most important, and their staring directly into the lens created a very strong link between us: model–camera–photographer. The model realized the "gravity of the moment" in staring straight into the camera, that they were being immortalized, the capturing of their personality or even themselves, that they were being ennobled to become a symbol of sorts, though they themselves were not an eminent person. The photographer was a powerful magician with the ability to stop time, defeating the hydra of death for a brief second. The camera was the main instrument, an enchanted box that could freeze an image in time.

And thus it became like a narcotic. Walking all day through villages and towns, entering homes and meeting such varied people, I forgot I was lugging around a heavy camera, that my back hurt, that it was hard for me to walk all day. Those meetings with people, which always felt new and interesting, gave me strength. At the same time, they taught me new philosophies, new values and relationships to the most important matters, that is, to life and death.

I took over thirty thousand photographs in twenty voivodeships, mostly in villages, whose landscapes are changing every year with astonishing speed; the old thatched cottages are vanishing, along with the small wooden houses that typify various regions. The old cottage furnishings, with rows of holy pictures, are also disappearing.

Boxes with flat roofs, the same all across Poland, are being built at enormous speed, often decorated with mirror or glass. There are no wooden walls anymore, and inside there are knick-knacks from trinket shops, glasses painted with gold or cherry patterns, gnomes and dolls, stiff fake flowers, though there are beautiful fresh ones in the garden. This documentation of the truth of modern-day people and their existence shows the transformations in society and in ways of thinking and aesthetic sensibilities and in ways of consumption. This is most evident when we compare the village and the city. Here, too, we see a rich diversity, between bureaucrats, craftsmen, scholars, and artists. To my mind, almost every **HOME** is the image of a person. I have documented this quite precisely. I recently photographed vanishing handicrafts, especially rural ones: blacksmithing, pottery. My *Sociologial Record* is more than interiors. It includes heaps of other series, including photographs of cottages, little houses, villas, etc. The village windows are very decorative from the inside. I did one series about the presence of the Holy Father (a photobook was published on this theme).

In 1988, I spent twelve days in the small French town of Douchy, and I managed to gather fairly in-depth documentary materials, from which I created the *Zapis socjologiczny 1988, Douchy* [Sociological record 1988, Douchy] exhibition. In 1989, I was in Lithuania and in New York, where I also took pictures of people in their homes. That gave me a lot. People are the same everywhere, but their homes show crucial differences.

Last year I started a new series. My *Record* is documented. Having kept careful notes, I decided to return to those homes and people. That was a cruel experience; time is merciless, everything changes. People die, and their homes die with them. People vanish, but so does everything that once surrounded them. Only photography can stop time. Only photography has the ability to defeat the specter of death. This is my ongoing struggle, with death and the passing of time.

These trips of mine (without a car) and meetings with various people have lost none of their fascination. I use my camera to capture what is precious to me, what is astonishing and unconventionally beautiful, and I have the profound hope that I manage to communicate this to others as well, sharing what I myself experience.

Translated by Soren Gauger

1 André Bazin (1918-1958) – French film theorist and critic. – Ed.

Ray Johnson

RAY (RAYMOND EDWARD) JOHNSON
(1927, DETROIT – 1995, NEW YORK)

An exponent of early American Pop art and Neo-Dada. He mainly worked in collage and mail art. Johnson's first collages, in which he used objects taken from pop culture (snapshots, advertisements, magazine and newspaper photographs), as well as abstract features, were created as early as 1955. A "moticos" is an invented, intangible sign or being that could appear on railway cars, but also elsewhere; its meaning remains intentionally vague. It is not meant to be followed, only maybe photographed, kept in a box, or symbolically recreated. "What is a Moticos?" is a poetic, Dadaist game in which the moticos becomes a metaphor for transience, freedom, and imaginative playfulness.

Ray Johnson, "What is a Moticos?" in Ellen Levy, *A Book About Ray* (Cambridge, London: The MIT Press, 2024), 62.

WHAT IS A MOTICOS?

The next time a railroad train is seen going its way along the track, look quickly at the sides of the box cars because a moticos may be there. Whether the train is standing still or speeding past you, a moticos. Don't try to catch up with it. It wants to go its way. But have your camera ready to snap its picture. It likes those moments of being inside the box. When your film is printed and the moticos is finally seen, it will not be seen, unless you paste the photograph of the moticos on the side of a box car so someone can see the moticos or take its picture. It may appear in your daily newspaper. Someone may put it there. Cut it out. Save it. Treasure it. Make sure it is in a box or between the pages of a book for your grand-children to find and enjoy.

The moticos is not only seen on railroad trains, but on It really isn't necessary to see the moticos or know where it is because I have seen them. Perhaps I might point them out to you. The best way is to go about your business not thinking about silly moticos because when you begin seeing them, describing what they are or where they are going is So just make sure you wake up from sleeping and go your way and go to sleep when you will. The moticos does that too and does not worry about you. Perhaps you are the moticos. Destroy this. Paste the ashes on the side of your automobile and if anyone asks you why you have ashes pasted on the side of your car, tell them.

Or write the word moticos on the top of your automobile. It loves moving and rain water. Not so many people will wonder what it means. There will be no questions, hence no need for answers. And if you have an automobile, drive it to pleasant places because Have you seen a moticos lately? Perhaps you have. They are everywhere. As I write this I wish someone were here to point one out to me because I know they exist.

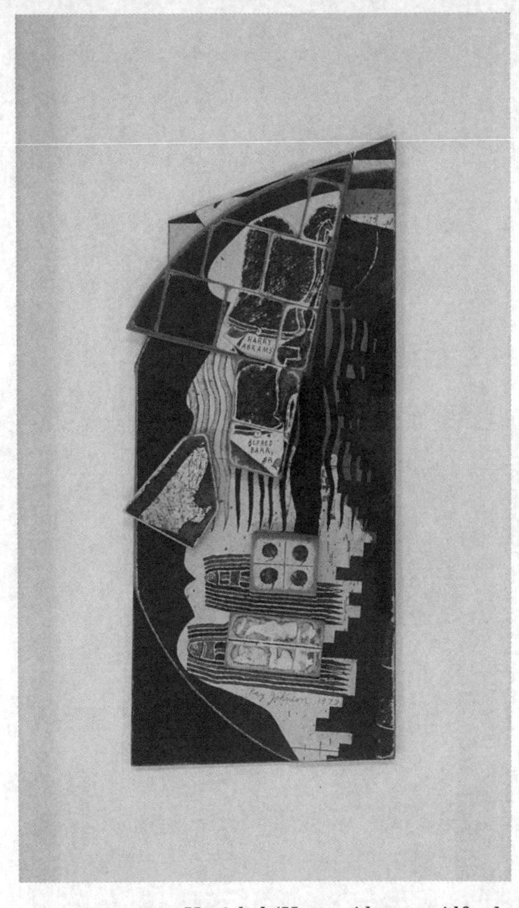

RAY JOHNSON, *Untitled (Harry Abrams, Alfred Barr Jr.)*, watercolor, pencil crayon, ink, paper (assemblage), 32.4 × 14 × 2.5 cm, framed 47 × 29 × 5 cm, 1979

Luis Camnitzer

LUIS CAMNITZER
(B. 1937, LÜBECK)

The Uruguayan-German artist, curator, and art theorist is known for his political and conceptual art, concerning power, education, and social justice. His works, often textual and minimalist, critique institutions and systems of oppression, and promote art as a tool for education and social reflection. Camnitzer's text explores the link between the study of reading and writing and an arts education, stressing that the traditional alphabet model puts more emphasis on reception (reading) than creativity (writing). He criticizes educational approaches that concentrate on a rote acquisition of skills instead of developing individual creativity and critical thinking.

Luis Camnitzer, "Art and Literacy," *e-flux Journal*, no. 3 (2009) https://www.e-flux.com/journal/03/68519/art-and-literacy [accessed: 20.08.2025].

ART AND LITERACY[1]

"You teach a child to read, and he or her will be able to pass a literacy test".

George W. Bush,
in a speech given in Townsend,
Tennessee, February 21, 2001

Interestingly, at least in the languages I know, when one talks about alphabetization there is always the mention of reading and writing, in that order. Ideologically speaking, this prioritized order not only reflects the division between production and consumption, but subliminally emphasizes the latter: ignorance is shown more by the inability to read than by the inability to write. Further, this order suggests that alphabetization is more important for the reception of orders than for their emission.

Of course, this theory—that if one wants to be able to write something, one should know how it is written—has some logic to it. It forces one first to read, then to copy what one reads—to understand somebody else's presentation in order to then re-present it. In art terms, however, this is similar to saying that one has to first look at the model in order to then copy it. Now the logical construction becomes much less persuasive. This is not necessarily wrong, insofar as one really wants to copy the model, or the need to copy the model is well grounded. In essence, if there is no proven need, the logical construction ceases to be one—it becomes a dogma disguised as logic.

This theory establishes first that the model deserves to be copied, second that there is a merit in making a reasonably faithful copy, and third that this process is useful to prepare the artist to produce art. This idea is a leftover from the nineteenth century, and its relevance today is highly questionable. An artist then has to ask whether the problems posed today by alphabetization might not be in need of new and more contemporary approaches. Is there an analysis of these problems informed by the attitudes that removed art from the nineteenth century and brought it into the twentieth? In other words, is alphabetization a tool to help presentation or re-presentation? Where is power located? Is it granted to the literate-to-be or to be found in the system that wants him or her to be literate?

One tends to speak of art as a language. In some cases it is even described as a universal language, a kind of Esperanto capable of transcending all national borderlines. As a universal language, stressing *universal*, art serves the interests of colonization and the expansion of an art market. The notion of art as a plain language, however, underlines a notion of it as a form of communication. In this case, power is not granted to the market, but to those who are communicating.

Educational institutions expect everybody to be able to learn how to read and write. It would follow that, if everybody has the potential to use reading and writing for expression, everybody should also have the potential to be an artist. Yet in art the assumption is different. Everybody may be able to appreciate art, but only a few are expected to produce it—not all readers are writers. Such inconsistent expectations overlook the fact that, just as alphabetization should not aim for Nobel Prizes in literature, art education should not aim for museum retrospectives. Nobel Prizes and retrospectives are more indicative of a kind of triumphal competitiveness than of good education. Put simply, good education exists to develop the ability to express and communicate. This is the importance of the concept of "language" here, the implication being that both art and alphabetization can be linked to nurture each other.

READING, WRITING, AND THE REST

At this moment, we are in the precise middle of the decade that the United Nations has designated as the Decade for Alphabetization (alphabetization here used in the sense of education for literacy). UNESCO estimates that there are 39 million illiterates in Latin America and the Caribbean, roughly 11% of whom are adults.[1] 16 million of them are in Brazil. These statistics only include people who do not know how to read or write. If we add those who are functionally illiterate—people who have the techniques, but are not able to use them to understand or to develop ideas—these figures grow astronomically. In developing countries, one out of every five people older than 15 is considered illiterate. Among developed countries, nearly 5% of the population of Germany, for example, is functionally illiterate. And among literate students in the US, it is estimated that 75% of those finishing high school do not have the reading skills required for college.

The teaching of reading and writing has been a major part of the schooling mission for over two centuries. It has also been on the minds of countless specialists who ponder gaps in formal education in both expected and unexpected sectors of the public. That everybody should know how to read and write is taken for granted. However, beyond vague truisms regarding its function, there is little discussion about how those abilities are used. And yet the problem of illiteracy persists even in countries claiming to have eradicated it.

Art has dealt with illiteracy on amazingly rare occasions, and when it did, it did so mostly of its own accord, keeping within its disciplinary identity and confusions, among them an idea that appreciating art is for everyone while making art is for the few. This means that art's main strengths—speculation, imagination, and its questions of "what if?"—have not really been explored on those occasions. Supposedly art is art and the rest is the rest. Art, however, happens to be the rest, too.

MY IMPERIALISM

Forty years ago, I was invited to organize the art department in a US university. I refused on the grounds that art is not really "art," but a method to acquire and expand knowledge. Consequently, art should shape all academic activities within a university and not be confined to a discipline. I recognize that my position reflected a form of art-imperialism, and this is something I still adhere to. As in all imperialisms, my position was not necessarily based on solid information and I used aggression as a tool for persuasion. Predictably, I was defeated, and shortly after was condemned to solitary confinement in the art department I had so proudly rejected. Yet I am unrepentant: I continue to operate with poorly informed opinions, I continue to be aggressive, and, to be sure, I will continue to be defeated.

My imperialism is based on a generalist view of art in which everything (including the "rest") can be seen as art. I also believe that the social structures that divide us into producers and consumers—those that ensure that our lives conform to the laws of the market instead of seeking a collective well-being—should be demolished. These were the views we developed as students during the late 1950s while I was in art school in Uruguay. These views took for granted that such a broad definition of art, in which everybody could be a creator, would become a tool for improving society. We were defeated then, and today these beliefs are considered anachronistic and out of place.

Regardless of their feasibility, these perspectives had some importance because they introduced an awareness of the role and distribution of power in matters of art and education that should not be ignored. They clarified claims surrounding the ownership of knowledge, how that ownership is distributed, and who benefits from it. Even if these issues are normally considered to be outside the scope of art, it is on their account that the use of language and the means of engaging illiteracy become interesting to art.

INDOCTRINATING SUBVERSION

Both art education and alphabetization have in common the dual and often contradictory mission of facilitating individual and collective cultural affirmation and expression on the one hand, and of being necessary tools to cement and expand forms of consumption on the other. Consequently, education is not only an ideologically fractured field, but one in which each of its ideologies assumes its own particular pedagogical approach to apply to all fields of knowledge, overcoming all irresolvable contradictions. When reasonably progressive, such pedagogies assume that one can ensure the stability and smoothness of the existing society while at the same time forming critically questioning, non-submissive, creative individuals. This approach takes for granted that education will create good, accepting citizens who play by the rules, but who will also be subversive individuals attempting to change that society. In a conservative pedagogical approach, the latter part of the mission will simply be ignored.

As it is, the educational system emphasizes good citizenship during the early stages of formation and postpones any potential subversion until the postgraduate level. Speculation and imagination are allowed only after becoming a good citizen. In order for actual subversion to take place, it would first have to address the earlier parts of the educational process. This explains why alphabetization takes place at the beginning of the educational voyage while true art-making is placed at its end, or is indeed postponed until after formal education is over. The tension that emerges from this built-in stability/instability contradiction creates two main divisions in how education is approached: between "integralism" and "fragmentalism," on the one hand; and between tutorial education and massive education, on the other. Although the two divisions are not necessarily aligned with each other, in traditional education, fragmentation tends to be coupled with massive education. Here information is reified, classified into disciplines, and simultaneously transmitted to large groups of people with the aim of achieving an efficient conformist stability. Knowledge travels from the outside to the inside. The elements are distinct, and their classification and order are presumed to be good and unchangeable. Power lies in the hands of somebody other than the student.

The second alignment is different. In more progressive education practices, integralism tends to be associated with a tutorial style of instruction in which there is more room for interdisciplinary research, encouragement of discovery, and an emphasis on individual processing. While not necessarily seeking either a flexible society or a critical analysis of one's connections to it, there is at the very least this emphasis on individuation.

And inasmuch as it includes the possibility of a permanent critique, there is an empowerment of the individual in the form of an encouraged, self-aware perception of the world.

It is this notion of empowerment that creates ideological differences between the two alignments. As soon as empowerment is introduced, the politics around the distribution of power becomes an indissoluble part of the educational process. This can explain why the most paradigmatic pedagogical figures in Latin America sought to develop not only the basic process of alphabetization within the field of education, but also self- and social awareness. Both the Venezuelan Simón Rodríguez (1769–1854) and the Brazilian Paulo Freire (1921–1997) saw education as a form of building a progressive and just social community. In the 1820s, Rodríguez declared that education had to deal "first with things, and second with those who own them." In the 1960s, Freire wrote that "before learning how to read words, one should learn how to read the world." Both educators underlined the importance of decoding the social situation prior to decoding the disciplines of reading and writing.

It is not surprising that this form of social decoding is easier to achieve through individual exchanges rather than collective ones. Individual tutoring seems to be ideal. When the teacher can focus all his or her energy and attention on one person, it allows for immediate calibration and response to the most minimal signs of incomprehension. Done well, it takes the Socratic method to the level of extreme psychological therapy, making for a tailor-made education for each individual. If the teacher is a good one, this makes for perfection. Seen in terms of efficiency, however, individual tutoring is the least economical strategy. It is no coincidence that having a personal tutor is a symbol of wealth reserved for the upper classes, so it becomes paradoxical to expect this highly elitist mechanism to also be the most appropriate means of achieving a just and classless society.

On the other hand, massive education remains seductive for its apparent economic efficiency as well as its populist appeal. A teacher can form tens or hundreds of individuals with the same investment of time and energy that a tutor makes for one. As far as the empowerment of the individual is concerned, however, massive education has the tendency to disseminate information and indoctrinate rather than to promote investigation and self-consciousness. In other words, striving for efficiency favors cheap output at the expense of qualitative evaluation. Quality becomes assessed within an economic frame of reference. Alarmingly, this distortion is accepted as the norm. Of course, there are tutors who inform and indoctrinate their students, just as there are teachers educating the masses who are able to raise awareness and empower them. In the first case, however, the tutor is betraying the teaching mission; in the second, the ideals are only reached by overcoming built-in obstacles.

CODING AND DECODING HOW AND WHAT

Sixty-five years ago, when I was learning how to write, I was forced to fill pages with the same letter, repeating it over and over again. I had to copy single letters before I was allowed to write words. I was given words before I could express other people's ideas, before I could express my own ideas, before I could even explore what my own ideas might be. It only occurred to me as an adult that, if I know how to write with a pencil, I also know how to draw with that pencil.

For my mother, educated in the Germany of World War I, matters were even worse. She had to use a pen designed specially—not for writing—but for learning how to write. The pen looked as if it had been designed for torture. Oval pieces of sharp tin forced the placement of the fingers into one particular position. If the fingers were not in the required position, they would be hurt. One could speculate that these pens were instrumental in preparing for Nazi Germany's ethos of obedience.

Art education has always been faced with a confusion between art and craft: in teaching how to do things, one often neglects the more important question of what to do with them. The conventional way of teaching how to write concentrates on readability and spelling, which only addresses the how of writing without regard to the what. Exemplified by the practice of teaching someone how to write by concentrating on a frozen aesthetic feature such as calligraphy, this approach fails to first identify the need for a message, which would then open an approach to writing that concerns the structure and clarity of what is being written.

In an exaggerated form, the pen synthesizes everything I hated about my education: the fragmentation of knowledge into airtight compartments, the confusion between how-to-do and what-to-do, the development of communication without first establishing the need for it. It was like learning how to cook without first being hungry—without even identifying what hunger is. After all, education is less about being hungry than about awakening appetite to create the need for consumption. In fact, I believe that this is how cooking is taught.

Why can't one first identify and explore the need to communicate in order to then find a proper way of communicating? Languages themselves are generated in this manner, and this is how they evolve. Words are created to designate things that had hitherto been either unknown or unnamable. Today's spelling errors determine tomorrow's writing. Many of those errors are the simple product of an oral decoding that overlays written coding. Of course, errors should be acknowledged—but they should also be subject to critical evaluation. As a derogatory term, "error" reflects a particular code-centrism typical of our culture. Illiteracy is, after all, only a problem within a literacy-based culture. In general, codes are created by a need to translate a message into signs, and then decoded by a need to decipher the message. Through this coding and decoding, there is a process of feedback in which "improper" or misplaced codings produce evocations that change or enrich the message.

FINDING DISCOVERY

When the reason to read and write is primarily to receive and give orders, it is understandable that the need for learning should not be identified by the person to be alphabetized, but by the same power structure that produces those needs. Knowledge becomes predetermined and closed when both definition and identification are performed within this restricted functional field, while a more open field would stimulate questioning and creation. In essence, one cannot educate properly without revealing the power structure within which education takes place. Without an awareness of this structure and the way it distributes power, indoctrination necessarily usurps the place of education.

While this is true for education in general, it becomes more insidious when applied to the teaching of reading and writing. In this case, indoctrination is not necessarily visible in the content, but instead seeps heavily into the process of transmission: if one is taught to repeat like a parrot, it doesn't really matter what is actually being repeated; only the desired automatic, internalized act of repetition will remain. If we only teach to recognize things by their forms without addressing concepts, it won't matter what generates these forms. Only the recognition of the packaging will remain, and worse, the acquisition of knowledge will stop there.

A real education for an artist consists of preparation for a pure research of the unknown. In a strong art education, this starts at the very beginning. But as institutional education in other areas is organized to convey only known information and to perpetuate conventional habits, these are two pedagogies in fundamental conflict. Where, then, should the fight against illiteracy be placed? Should alphabetization be handled as a subject for training or as a tool for discovery?

The question may be too schematic. In art, pure discovery leads to amateurism, while pure training leads to empty professionalism—good preparation ultimately seeks a balance between them. The question does not concern which activity should be eliminated, but rather which one should inform the other. Those in favor of training often defend it with the need to supply good scaffolding for the student. Yet if one ultimately hopes that discovery will be the main purpose of a student's life, whether for self-realization or for collective enrichment, it is clear that the student should not just learn to build scaffolds.

We now find ourselves in an age when the amount of available knowledge far exceeds our capabilities for codification. The imbalance is such that we must speculate on whether the concept of restricted alphabetization based on the re-presentation of known things may be an unforgivable anachronism. We may have arrived at a point where we need an education that goes far beyond all this: one that first makes the subject aware of the personal need for literacy and then identifies the coding systems already in use, so that they may be used as a reference; one that proceeds to activate translation processes as a primary tool for entering new codes; one that, from the very beginning, fosters the ability to reorder knowledge, to make unexpected connections that present rather than re-present. In other words, we need a pedagogy that includes speculation, analysis, and subversion of conventions, one that addresses literacy in the same way any good art education addresses art. This means putting literacy into the context of art. By forcing art to focus on these things, in turn, the art empire itself will also be enriched.

1 This essay began as a paper presented at the 1st International Meeting on Education, Art and Functional Illiteracy, which took place in Rio de Janeiro, December 1–3, 2008. The meeting was sponsored by Daros Latin America and co-organized by Eugenio Valdés, Director of Casa Daros in Rio de Janeiro, and myself as Pedagogical Curator of the Iberê Camargo Foundation in Porto Alegre. After the meeting it was decided that we would pursue several objectives within a continuing project we named *Art-phabetization*: a) to study institutional dynamics in existing organizations like the Samba schools to fight illiteracy among their members; b) to blur the borderlines between schools and their neighborhoods and between schoolwork and leisure; c) to study the role of errors in the generation of metaphors and new knowledge; d) to create a literacy or alphabetization laboratory to explore methodologies to be tested in institutional settings; e) to study the possibility of the creation of mobile laboratories; f) to create a blog and an interactive databank of exercises and games that connects the laboratory with literacy teachers.

Jadwiga Maziarska

JADWIGA MAZIARSKA
(1913, SOSNOWIEC – 2003, KRAKOW)

A Polish painter and creator of objects and collages, and a pioneer of art informel in Poland. She mainly executed abstract compositions that experimented with texture, form, and color, developing a unique painterly language on the verge of realism and abstraction. Maziarska's text states that art is a process of discovering the secrets of reality and human existence, in which the artist, through her imagination and intuition, tries to grasp the invisible. The avant-garde traditions like Dadaism and Surrealism have shown art and life to be interlocked; the search for meaning in art is the search for meaning in existence.

Jadwiga Maziarska, "Notes," *Jadwiga Maziarska: Atlas of the Imaginary*, ed. B. Piwowarska, (Warsaw: Centre for Contemporary Art Ujazdowski Castle, 2009), 184–85.

NOTES (CA. 1966-1967)[1]

Whatever painters say about themselves, it strikes a discordant note with their painting. Every human being is filled with discord; the discrepancy between the picture and the artist's opinion is of great importance.

Frequently, in various circumstances, we tend to gaze at a specific piece of bark or a stone, at a specific part of a cloud. Hegel said: "The human being is constantly alert in his need for development in the presence of objects as they evoke a mystery which remains unknown to humans."

Contemporary art differs from that of the Surrealists; however, they were the first to pay attention to the internal space, which evokes a world unknown to us and of whose existence we all should be aware.

The Surrealists demonstrated that there was no dividing line between art and the mystery of human existence.

Contemporary art has little to do with the art of Dada, Surrealism or Futurism, today we focus on absorbing reality via the imagination.

An artist is an individual who looks for sense where it seems to be non-existent. Every work of art evokes a mystery that is hard to unravel. This secret is identified with the power and energy at the artist's disposal.

The truth about myself remains intangible to me; it is described in my paintings. If I found the truth, perhaps I would not feel the need to paint, as a world devoid of mystery would be devoid of sense.

The human calling is to discover life; we have the duty to surpass ourselves by means of intuition and spontaneity. All this, however, needs to be accompanied by strict attention and awareness.

The passion of doubt, the intellect and the subconscious are invested in a painting; their intensity affects the assessment of that painting. Art may become identical to life, while the meaning of life may depend on the results of artists' searches. The generation of post-WWII artists, plagued by shattered myths, expressed a peculiar desire to become deeply involved in the reality of life in the broadest sense of the meaning. The source of this desire appeared clear to me when I saw the Dada exhibition at the Musée d'art Moderne de Paris in 1966. By demonstrating an attitude of self-destruction (self-annihilation) and approving their own deaths, the Dadaists identified the reasons for their actions as being utterly unselfish. They sowed the seeds of Surrealism, which transformed human dreams into reality and brought them into the light of day. They showed that apparent coincidences conceal laws which combine us with the fundamentals of existence. It was they who noted that an artist was a mirror reflecting the universal, rather than a centre of things. Their attitude exuded a cathartic breath, an ecstasy and an epiphany of the sudden comprehension of the totality of existence. An artist becomes one who deciphers himself while his epiphany is genuine and unique; it is a transition of the sensible to the objective.

By laying various traps for oneself, an artist attempts to break through the rule of the inscrutable.... What is invisible to the human eye does not always indicate the unknowable. The almost blasphemous passion of an individual looking for a mystery takes humans closer to its revelation; it is the antithesis of passivity. Rationalizing what is irrational in its essence is a sign of our times.

Contemporary yearnings are rooted in Dada.

The affinity of say the neo-visualists does not occur via Cubism, which in retrospect looks like discovering a purely external reality with no prospect of embarking on another path but via Mondrian, whose universe approaches the world of crystals, minerals and plants.

The achievements of contemporary art are far more audacious, while the exhibitions are accompanied by a climate of much wider reception. However, the exhibitions by Dada artists in the Musée d'Art Moderne were as unforgettable as they were shocking. The modest works whose lives were to be prolonged in these distinguished halls were not the pulsating Dadaism which tended to seize the environment, but more like cave paintings from thousands of years ago in the world's great museums, shocking casings with a frozen breath. This is the defeat and the victory of Dada.

Edited by Barbara Piwowarska and Józef Chrobak

Translated by Marcin Wawrzyńczak and Ewa Dratwa

1 The notes come from the never published catalogue compiled by Józef Chrobak on the occasion of Jadwiga Maziarska being awarded the Jan Cybis Prize in 2001. Maziarska's original notes are now stored at MOCAK Archive, Krakow. – Ed.

CHAPTER

SUPEROBJECTS

XI

Les Levine

411

LES LEVINE
(B. 1935, DUBLIN)

An Irish-Canadian multimedia artist, a pioneer in video art, installation, and media practices. His essay "The Information Fall-Out" (1971) analyzes the status of art in a society dominated by the media. He posits a departure from aesthetic authority toward the production of information. He compares art actions to the fall-out of media events: spectacle, repetition, and strident communication become more important than the work's physical presence. Art emerges as a form of "social software," competing with television, advertising, and popular culture for attention and influence. Artists no longer create a work, they arrange information to model collective perceptions.

Les Levine, "The Information Fall-Out," Studio International 181, no. 934 (1971): 264–67.

THE INFORMATION FALL-OUT

Most of the works that are concerned with information are using media as a form of "evidence creating". The photographs or documents act pretty much in the way they are used in the courtroom. They are presented to make it absolutely clear that such and such a thing has occurred. They are not to be considered for their particular aesthetic quality. They're merely brought into the courtroom as a form of circumstantial evidence to prove that in fact a specific thing has occurred, and this is the way it looked when it did occur. The medium, in most of these works, is information.

The best informational works are those that abdicate completely any aesthetic authority, make no judgment about the kind of information, but merely present it as a logic vacuum. In a systematic society, when a situation has no logic (a logic vacuum), immediately logic rushes in to fill it. If something is not called by a particular name, immediately the information sources will put a name on it. Because we are a systemic society, we cannot live under circumstances that do not have a system. Therefore, we apply a system whether it be the wrong one or not. The importance of the artist maintaining the position which abdicates aesthetic position, or aesthetic authority, is that aesthetic authority is not "positive" to a socially supportive environment, because it generally tends to say simply, "You don't know what I'm doing. You don't understand this. If you could understand, you would be on the same intelligence level. I'm telling you this is something you should aspire to." If the artist abdicates aesthetic authority, he allows the work to be whatever the viewer wants it to be, to be a success or a failure on his level. And it doesn't matter whether it is a success or a failure, because the activity of the viewer dealing with it offers *him enough support anyway. The artist is now dealing with environmental energy.*

Television commercials are the real programming of television. The programmes are basically commercials for the network. A commercial that is short works better than one that is long. A commercial that is long is an apology. So the information is somewhat dissipated. One advertisement basically says, "We have a product and we want to sell it." The second advertisement says, "We have a product and we haven't sold it." The third says, "We have a product and we still haven't sold it." The fourth says, "We're going to keep at this until we sell it." And the fifth and sixth and so on, continually remind you of the previous advertisement rather than the product. People who advertise every day are telling you, "We advertise more": the idea, of course, being that if we advertise more, we have the money, we have the power. The everyday advertisers are not selling the product, they are selling themselves. A company that advertises once or twice is saying to the public that they need them as a customer, and a company that advertises a lot is saying, "We don't need you as a customer because we're very powerful".

The reason long television commercials don't work as well as short ones has to do with the nature of television. The viewer is watching the programme and if he is not getting information at a one-to-one ratio, he tends to go to sleep. In other words, as soon as he's got the information, and it is not immediately changed to another piece of information, it becomes softer and softer all the time until it gradually dulls in his mind. Whereas if the information is changed quickly, it acts more or less like a strobe light, which is constantly shaking him up all the time.

The idea that we have any choice whatsoever, in a completely technological environment, is pretty ridiculous; we only assume we make a choice. However, most of the choices that we make are merely selections taken out of a pre-coded number of choices that society has already made for us. The society is clearly *pre-choiced*. Relative to this idea, these selections have nothing to do with a moral or religious position. Previous to moral-ethical beliefs man believed that choices were quantitative. A farmer's crop was a good crop because it was a large crop, and a bad crop because it was small. Then with the advent of "religious teaching" it was made clear that it would be possible to consider something that was small as being good and something that was large as being bad: morality as it relates to choice. Now, continuing on this the idea of aesthetics as it relates to religion and morality, aesthetic activity, such as art making, then became a "moral activity". The idea of making good art became, in the religious sense, moral, and making bad art, in the religious sense, immoral. However, we now have passed to a state where choices are no longer relative to morality. The media and technology have made clear that everybody in a democratic society has a right to say for himself, "This is good or bad for me, and this is what I want, and this is what I don't want. What I want and what I don't want are decided by society anyway". Therefore it's no longer a moral issue. If you decide that it is a moral issue, then there are certain groups of people who are doing the right thing and there are certain people who are doing the wrong thing, relative to aesthetics. We have a society in which it is possible for everybody to make art. That fact is more interesting than any particular moral or aesthetic code that you might apply to art.

We have created a media society. Things are done for the effect that they will have in the media, rather than the effect they have on the environment. It's assumed that the effect in the media will automatically affect the socio-economic environment. Hence, the court trials of Abbie Hoffman[1] create an environmental theatrical work, which in effect is turned into a novel. So that the overall effect is that the government, the courtroom, the lawyers, the defendants, etc., are engaged in a piece of media theatre. This is what Jerry Rubin[2] calls the "Do It" generation. You do something because the doing of it will have information fall-out and burn-off, which then will be assessed logically by the society. The logic of the activity will be the fact that it has been done.

Then Charles Manson,[3] who so desperately wants to become part of the media environment, (allegedly) slaughters eight people. This dire destructive crime, which has various witchcraft overtones, is horrible in its scope. However, when we analyse it more closely, Manson very quickly becomes a superstar of the media. He becomes a charismatic character of unbelievably celebrated proportions; he is sought after by every newspaper and network in the country for interviews; he's on the front page of every newspaper and magazine; he's become a historical figure overnight. For Manson to "make it" as a rock-and-roll star was one way of leading him into the media, of receiving great adulation from the press, etc.

But then, deciding to kill all these people, in order to achieve fame, is one of the nightmares of the media generation. This negative action is another one of those "Do It" things. And it is even further extended when Richard Nixon,[4] who understands very clearly the enormous energy the activity has, no matter how dire it may be, decides it is necessary for him to plug into that energy (by saying that Manson is guilty), the same way a politician decides it's necessary to plug into the pollution problem, the war in Vietnam, urban renewal, or any other charismatic piece of energy in the media. Manson has taken media paranoia to the ultimate point of destruction. The outcome of the situation is: What are eight lives in order to make a "software superstar" of national proportions? Would a television network be prepared to sacrifice eight lives for a programme that would constantly get them, over a period of a year, sixty million viewers?

Relative to this, we have the movie *Woodstock* in which the people went to Woodstock to hear music and to be together. Actually they paid to participate in the production of a movie. The Woodstock Festival occurred solely to make a movie. The movie relates in the way the photographs, as evidence, relate in information art. The movie is merely evidence that this festival occurred.

Instead of using closed format approaches to writing scripts, which in some way will represent the cultural operative trust of society, we merely take the operative trust directly and use that as a working model of itself and present that as the work. We're looking at a direct piece of life, which has been presented as art. Instead of taking a work of art, which if it were translated would present an aspect of life or decode as a particular concern, we merely take the direct working situation and present it (documented) as the work. This is *Woodstock*, this is Manson, this is Hoffman, this is information art. Now we must achieve motivation retrospectively: *we look backward to see the effect of what we have done and that becomes our reason for doing it.*

Whatever anybody says in the media, always happens. If someone on television says the economy is in bad condition, the economy will be bad the moment after he has said it. Anything that stands out on the media as negative at a given moment will become positive in a very short time. The media accelerates its own information.

Through information processing, a negative logic occurs. What you attempt to give power will reject power; an attempt to detract power will immediately attract power, like a negative energy system. It is not possible to say something is bad (or good) because the viewers see that *you* are *telling* them that it's good (or bad). Therefore, they do not believe you. Trying to undermine something on television works in absolute reverse. For example, commercials to stop smoking tell us how dangerous it can be to our health, etc. They also remind us that this is a very enjoyable habit, and it would be nice to be smoking right now. When CBS[5] covers up Abbie Hoffman's face on television because he is wearing an American flag shirt, the viewers see that they are putting Hoffman down, and therefore automatically put him up higher than before.

Talking about a problem in the media is almost the same thing as solving the problem. People used to say "Everything will be okay, so long as we keep the dialogue going." This bred the mediocre intellectual who thought there was nothing more to do except be semantic about the problem, never actually considering what should be done. So that the consideration in itself became the problem, and the semantics with it became the problem, more than the real "problem".

Information, that is in the environment, always relates to other kinds of information. The Pollution Control Board virtually means that "x" number of people will get a job in the United States Government. Before that it was urban renewal. These things are supported by politicians because they provide a large amount of political patronage. Government sees art as a way to pretty up the environment.

The media refused to recognize any subtleties in art whatsoever because they transform art into information. In other words, Earth Art, Electronic Art, abstract art, Pop art and so on. The practitioners of these styles in art attack the media for being nothing more than commercial. It would be impossible for any style to exist as a real entity without the media. "Great American Art from 1940-1970": it was not that when the Museum said it was; it was that when the media had decided that that's what it was.

In information processing, there is always a key phrase that simplifies: Impressionism, out-of-focus images; Abstract Expressionism, slopping around in paint; Pop Art, big popular images that we consider banal; Earth Art, holes in the ground. Light Art is anything that has light bulbs; Electronic Art is anything that flashes electrically. While artists are appalled all the time by the way the media read art out, none of these movements would exist as realities to the general population without the media. I think it is clear that Ad Reinhardt[6] would not have been "Ad Reinhardt" without the media. The idea of the "black painting with nothing on it" (which is what most people in the media thought it was) as opposed to abstract painting, is the way the media established a man who abhorred the media.

"Great American Art from 1940-1970" was probably the last important show about hierarchical Western taste. It was the final stance in an approach to moralistic, aesthetic and ethical art. The sad part about that situation was a curator expressing a lack of support for the artistic environment, at a time when the artistic environment needs support more than ever. It is a position that says, "We will set up these idols at the cost of the rest of the art community, and who cares about the rest of the community if it's all crap anyway. Museums only want to show the good stuff." We have come to the point that showing the good stuff may in fact be good for only a small group of people and for a very large group of people it may act as a negative, non-supporting system. The "ideal" in a post-moral, post-conscious society is of little value.

Behaviours in our society occur because we have laws about them. The nature of the environment combined with the law clearly expresses what is possible and permissible within that environment. Whether we morally agree or disagree doesn't make too much difference.

The Museum of Modern Art's "Information": the style of the show was photographic, while at the same time there was no style. While there were some eighty artists in the show, there were no artists in the show: no one stood out any more than another. Every movement previous, such as Pop, Op, Colour Painting, always had its figures. In Pop, it would be Andy Warhol, Roy Lichtenstein, Oldenburg[7] and a few others. In colour painting, it would be Louis, Noland,[8] and on down the line. In "Information", it was clear that the only outstanding figure was the curator. The curator in this situation becomes the artist. We have a "Woodstock" situation at the Museum of Modern Art. All of these people are brought together to make this show under the authorship of the curator. The curator presents the media with a package.

The value of shows like this is that, because they are so open, they tend to have no taste or choice position. Now having no taste or choice position is valuable because it is a supportive position. It supports the socio-economics of the art community. So it is decided that, rather than make breakthroughs with artists who hit home runs, you give the overall scene a vehicle to work with, an open communication system. If you see a show with eighty or more people in it, all of the people dissipate into one person, the curator, and the people who are not in it stand out more than the people who are in it.

A careful selection was made so that none of the works would be outstanding. So none of the works could in fact actually exist as themselves, as personal elements belonging to a particular artist. The ideas were all interchangeable with any of the other ideas in the show. It is clear now that ideas are not the property of anybody.

If you present the media with a show which apparently has no particular artist, they will make one of the people involved "the artist". And seeing that none of the artists stand out any more than others, the person who becomes "the artist" is the curator. The curator has made an artistic breakthrough. The curator has not only gathered the information, he has also made information: an artistic system which is supportive to the members of that system equally, rather than a system which supports particular figures in it and downgrades others.

"Information" came at a time when the Art Workers' Coalition had its many fights with the Museum of Modern Art. You can't take energy away from a powerful system without giving that system a considerable amount of energy. The Art Workers' Coalition was constantly attacking the Museum of Modern Art. The Museum of Modern Art then puts on this giant "Information" show, which includes all of its enemies. It becomes more powerful than it ever was before. It gets rid of the idea that there are going to be any further personal breakthroughs in art. Because the idea of a personal breakthrough means that there is a particular set of facts or group of information or sensitivity to a situation which is particular to a specific person or group of people. However, it is impossible for any one person to have more facts than any other person now.

Shows of this type are presented as: This is the art of now. However, they are not the beginning of anything;

they are the end. They show very clearly what art has been like in the past. In presenting the "Information" show, the Museum made it virtually impossible for any artist of integrity to continue making pieces about information. Many people will say that the effect of this show was to de-mythologize art. I don't think they de-mythologize art. They put art in line with the social conditions.

There are two kinds of software; one, the very technical term which is something a computer programmer needs to know, and the other is social software, which refers to the kinds of information in the environment which make us behave the way we do. The media environment is telling your brain how to operate; it is telling your body how to operate; it is telling you how to behave, what to look like, what to desire, what to look at, what to care about, what not to care about, what to be politically in favour of, what morally would be wrong, what would taste good, what doesn't taste good. In an environment that is constantly telling its inhabitants all these things, there is no such thing as individualism or personal property. If things become important to the general environment, the general environment will own them, and the individual will not. So the idea that the collector owns the artist's work is merely a hangover from a period in history where everyone viewed everything as property. The artist's work, whether it is owned by a collector or a museum, is always his work; it always will be owned by him no matter who has it in their possession, To assume we are individuals is very much beside the point. Of course, one could say, "I want that automobile there in red, with white-walled tyres, and an air conditioner, etc". But you have to take into consideration that the company who makes that automobile has done market research to find out that someone who looks pretty much like you, who earns about the amount of money that you do, who wears the same clothes, who lives in the same kind of house, who has the number of children that you have, who is related to the number of people that you are, who vacations in the place that you vacation, who goes to see the movies that you go to, etc., will come in and say, "I want that car in this colour with white walls". Our culture gives people an illusion of choice.

This tendency to be constantly involved in the idea of individual choices stems from the sexual: we have a sort of crotch complex. We realize that everything about us, our minds and our bodies, is hooked into the environment and the only things left unhooked are our sex organs. It's unusual for people to engage in sexual activity that has never occurred in their software. People's sexual habits are not much different from their conversational habits. They sexualize in the same way they converse.

The desire to remain an individual in a society which is obviously not fostering individualism is sexual and biological; we say, "The society may influence my mind; it may govern my work patterns; it may govern what I wear; but it does not own my body". The body is the last stand for the individual in this technological society. The environment has laws pertaining to biology. It is not possible for biology to behave absolutely biologically. In most cases, this is against the law. The biological package must behave relative to the social conditions. Otherwise the social conditions will clamp down on the biological package.

We are not consciously controlling our lives; the technological environment, the structural environment, and the information environment are controlling us. When we act as individuals in this society, we act as negatives to the conditions of others. When we act as non-individuals, we act as supportive to others.

It is reasonable to say that the media have a divisive nature. While they have brought everybody in the world together, they have given everybody in the world an electronic neighbour. They have also separated people into factions, one group attacking another all the time. If you had a television that was hooked up to a computer in your own home, and you could tell the television what your problems were or what kind of thing you want to do, the television would go to the computer software and pick up all the various information that the computer knows about the problems and then come back saying, "Yes, this is what I think you should do and I think you are capable of doing it. If you need any help along the line, just let me know". Then the technology becomes a support system, rather than a device used to read-out. It becomes a system of information which is based on a biological model. This could be very supportive. You can't interact with a computer, unless you interact in a reasonably passive way.

Information has affected law. A smart lawyer realizes that evidence which is passed across an information retrieval system, such as television or newspaper, is just as valuable as evidence which is presented in court. So what is occurring in the courtroom now is a direct reflection of what occurs in the media. It is often possible to actually lose a case in a courtroom, but win it in the media. If it is won in the media, it will be reversed in the courtroom. There is no way of un-knowing information. In a society that is addicted to information, it is extremely dangerous not to put out information. In a society that demands to know everything, the man who remains quiet is guilty.

Now privacy is redundant; privacy only works in a society that is technically private. It is possible for the government to spy on a citizen at any time. It is possible for one firm to spy on another firm. If you live in a society that does not permit privacy, trying to be private is foolish. If you have sex in your living room, it shouldn't matter if everybody in the world can see you. Because if they wanted to, they could. Privacy becomes one-sided when you resist it. If you don't resist, then you become part of the working environment. The correct organic cell in the correct organic environment. You take the same attitude towards the government that they take towards you.

Now people say that computers are dehumanizing us; that there are too many machines. There are even people who blame the war in Vietnam on computers. Very few people have had any first hand use of computers as an information retrieval system, as a surrogate brain, as an outside intelligence support, as a form of artificial thinking. We must realize that if everybody has computers, then it becomes possible for everybody to talk to everybody else. If you have a Telex terminal and you want to say, "Screw you" on that terminal, everybody who owns a Telex terminal will get a print-out saying, "Screw you". So that while companies do have the possibility to control you, if you are hooked into them you have the possibility to control back. Once we all have technological access, then we can talk to one another. The computer is going to bring about a new era of primitivism in art. The computer will in fact be the new folk art.

In a city, where people have answering services, instead of talking to people directly, the technology talks to the technology. You phone a person, his answering service answers. You leave a message. He phones you back and your answering service answers. The technology is making the decision and the people are sitting about on the sidelines. One computer is talking to another computer. One telephone is talking to another telephone. One television is talking to another television. Humans are merely looking at it once in a while to see what the result of all this activity is and deciding what they should do with it.

Technology has had a greater effect on the cultural thrust than art. Technology has created technological man. It has created political change. It has created aesthetic change. It has created many levels of things that we thought art would. Probably the greatest reason why technology has taken over from art is because art was always technology anyway. The art of the cave painter was a technological art. It was an art of how to do it, how to image the society, how to present society with a working model of itself that would in fact be a "conceptual tool", a valuable and useful device for the shaping of that society. Now we are arriving back technologically to cave painting. We're now at a point where technology can present us with a working model of ourselves.

It is important that we expand the technological environment into a completely bio-technology environment so that we are interconnected very directly with the technology and that we can plug into any area of thinking to create a support system between one another. It is true that we are further apart ideologically than ever before in the world. It is also true that we are closer together than we have ever been.

Where does the art collector fit in? Apart from gathering objects to surround him, which give him a certain sense of place or personal environment, it's also true that collecting art has been a way of socially identifying oneself. The sophisticate now realizes that having a number of paintings on his wall is not going to increase his image to very many people. Buying works of art today would have little value or importance; everybody can buy everything anyway. There are no rich people, only middle-class people. The rich merely have more "middle class".

So the artist will have to create a personal publicity system for the collector. He will have to identify these people to the society. So he has to decide that these people will become media packages. He will package these people in such a manner that they will become information for society. The problem of collecting art objects is that the information reads out more about having money and power than it does about being aesthetically involved or concerned with art. Therefore, if one does have money and power, there is very little value in buying art because it's going to create bad information. Money and power represent personal politics at a time when everyone is trying to get to a broader inter-supportive system. The only step left now would be for the collector to become an artist. He must be directly involved in art production. He could do it by selecting various groups of art and showing them in a similar way to that in which the curator of the Museum of Modern Art put on the "Information" show, or he could begin to make art which expresses the kind of person that he is, in the kind of environment that he finds himself. Museums will probably undergo an enormously difficult period; it will become evident to them that there will be an enormous increased production from artists. And the collection of this production will cause real-estate problems, will cause economic problems, and will also cause political problems. What it will probably be important for museums to be doing within the next few years will be bringing in the various underprivileged social groups in our society. Presenting the museum as a community cultural laboratory rather than a place that sets up high standards and aesthetics.

The absurdity of formal art criticism is that it is pretty much umbilical to collecting. Formal art criticism must be judged as organized power. For all that formal art criticism hates commercialism, it always acts as a very straight commercial for the art it's talking about. In formal criticism when you say, "Something is good", you're saying, "buy it". When you say, "It is bad", you're saying, "Do not buy it". So formal art criticism will find itself with the same problem that the collector finds himself in. People do not want to be told constantly what their taste should be any more. Good taste, at this time, in technical democracy, ends up as nothing more than taste prejudice. Expressing aesthetic authority over another human being is arrogant.

The artist must, without question, abdicate. He must realize that his work must not contain authority. It must in fact have the capability to succeed or fail as the viewer wants it. Thereby being much more supportive to the viewer. It must, in fact, be completely devoid of logic. The logical vacuum must be there so that the viewer applies his own logic to it and the work in fact makes itself before the viewer's eyes. So that it becomes a direct reflection of the viewer's consciousness, logic, morals, and ethics. The work should act as a feedback mechanism to his own working model.

Once you have information about something, there is no need to do it. The one thing that so-called "Do It" activities, such as Woodstock, make absolutely clear, in information terms, is that you do it to get the information. That if you have the information, you don't do it because having the information means it's been done. So what we would have in art is a series of "doing it" that would create information. Television is pretty much like art in this situation. The only thing that occurs which is of interest to most people is commercials, sports events, and newscasts. We will have to get all the people watching television on television so that everyone's watching themselves and everyone else.

What we are seeing now is a series of works that are made for the reason that they can be turned into media. Art now reads out as social software: information. Once we know that the purpose is to influence the social software we can do away with art and start influencing the social software directly. Beyond that the artist will probably dissolve, cease to exist in our society as a separate heroic figure.

1 Abbot Howard „Abbie" Hoffman (1936-1989) – American political and social activist. – Ed.
2 Jerry Rubin (1938-1994) – American political and social activist. – Ed.
3 Charles Manson (1934-2017) – American criminal, leader of "The Family" cult who murdered several people in 1969. – Ed.
4 Richard Nixon (1913-1994) – the 37th president of the United States, serving from 1969 until his resignation in 1974. – Ed.
5 Columbia Broadcasting System – a radio and television station in the United States. – Ed.
6 Ad Reinhardt (1913-1967) – American painter and writer. – Ed.
7 Claes Oldenburg (1929-2022) – Swedish-American sculptor. – Ed.
8 Morris Louis Bernstein (1912--1962) – American painter; Kenneth Noland (1924-2010) – American painter and sculptor. – Ed.

LES LEVINE, *Game Room: A Tribute to the Great American Loser* © Les Levine, ARS 1977, cardboard, 76 × 101 cm, 1977

MINI-BASEBALL

Jerzy Janisch

JERZY JANISCH
(1901, HORODOK–1981, WROCLAW)

A Polish painter, printmaker, and scenographer associated with the Lviv avant-garde scene of the 1930s and the Artes group. His work melded an interest in modern art with reflection on the experience of the contemporary city. In an extract from his memoirs (1961–62), Janisch recalls his experience of aesthetic shock when confronted with the latest European art. It shows the process of shaping a "new way of seeing"—the departure from naive, provincial formulae of perception toward a visual consciousness rooted in modernity. Janisch describes pictures as signs of urban visual culture: Expressionism, abstract art, ornamentation, and perspective operate on an equal footing with parts of the day-to-day landscape.

Jerzy Janisch, *Wspomnienia, 1961–1962*, typescript, Department of Documents, National Museum in Wrocław, Artes Materials collection, from: Piotr Łukaszewicz, *Artes. Nowocześni plastycy lwowscy* (Wrocław: Ossolineum, 2023).

MEMORIES, 1961–1962 (EXTRACT)

A most ill-advised pavilion of the Secession, crowned with an openwork dome. Upon paying the entrance fee, I find myself before a wall hung with paintings born of an entirely different convention of beauty. This leaves me unsettled; as though my mind had gone blank. Across a vast expanse of pozzolana, a figure sketched fleetlingly in white flaunts an exaggerated clarity of eye and pupil—being, as it were, a paraphrase of Mediterranean drawing. Parallel to the upper edge of the picture is a Wandering Jew with his sack, suspended above the winter landscape of Vitebsk. Nearby: the wounds of German Expressionism, dealt in blood, by the slash of a knife. On the opposite side of a fictitious, yet profoundly real, abyss—an abyss unnoticed by the public—on whose very precipice a cypress or a laurel jutted from a vase, Western European painting spoke of the misery of the cocotte in Pascin,[1] a misery altogether different from that in Lautrec;[2] it spoke of Russian folk ornament transformed into a flat, hard abstraction bound by a heavy contour. Léger[3] was present with his buttery rolls, round and coated in a neutral colour, from which he fashioned bodies and thick fingers, setting them in contrast to a geometry in perspective, suspended within an ashen void. On the other side of this abyss, so near that by stepping closer I can perceive the very epidermis of the canvases—here, postwar painting, by mocking the hitherto valid laws of optics, had claimed for itself an infinite license.... Personally, I feel as if I have undergone an operation on my eye, which, after unavailing encounters with Tytus Czyżewski and Witkacy, has at last shed the innocence and naivety of its Galician gaze.... I am left to contemplate who I am, who we are, and what we are truly capable of.

Translated by Łukasz Mojsak

1 Jules Pascin (1885-1930) – Bulgarian painter who emigrated to Paris. – Ed.

2 Henri de Toulouse Lautrec (1864-1901) – French painter. – Ed.

3 Fernand Léger (1881-1955) – French painter. – Ed.

CHAPTER

OUT TOWN

XII

OF

Stanislav Kubicki

STANISLAV KUBICKI
(1889, ZEGRZE – 1942, WARSAW)

A painter, printmaker, poet, and art theorist with ties to the Polish and German avant-garde. He was a founding member of Bunt and of international artist networks, and an editor of *a bis z*, the journal of the Progressive Artists Group. He combined aspects of Expressionism with Constructivism, making forms of nature geometrical and seeing the organic world as a sphere of full-fledged subjecthood. He often depicted animals and plants in simplified, rhythmic structures, reflecting a utopian vision of harmony between humanity and nature. In his essay "Mankind's Relationship with Creation" (1931), he stood up against the anthropocentric tradition of the West, which justifies the exploitation of nature through a distinction between humanity and the rest of creation.

Stanislav Kubicki, "das verthältnis des menschen zur schöpfung," a bis z, no. 21 (1932): 81–84.

MANKIND'S RELATIONSHIP WITH CREATION

"Rule over the fish of the sea, and over the fowl of the heaven, and over every beast that moveth upon the earth."
(Genesis 1:28)

"The dread of you shall be upon every beast of the earth, and upon every fowl of the heaven, upon all that moveth on the earth, and upon all the fishes of the sea: into your hand are they delivered."
(Genesis 9:2)

No other commandment of Yahweh has been obeyed by man as literally and faithfully as this one. And this obedience is both touching and astonishing when one contrasts it with the commandment that one should love one's neighbor, which has been consistently and persistently disregarded for millennia. Thus, for centuries and centuries, mankind (Semites and Europeans in particular) has blindly passed by the rest of creation—plants and animals. The Christian conviction that only humans possess an immortal soul widened the gap between them and their brothers to an insurmountable degree. For even the Gospel, which was intended to be a supplement and perfection of the Old Testament, and of whose high ethics Christianity, which calls itself the religion of love, is so proud, did not feel moved to abolish or at least mitigate these passages of the old law. Other people think differently: the pariah greets every creature with the words: "I am you!" and the Buddhist prays daily: "May all people be free from pain today!" But these are people far beneath us! Beneath us: the inventors of gunpowder, the cannon, and poison gas! We pray: "Give us this day our daily bread!"

Even the latest discoveries of natural science have not changed mankind's relationship with animals and plants. It has indeed been recognized that humans came from the very same source from which all living things originate. The serum reaction has indeed proven that humans are close to and related to the higher ape species. Practitioners of animal and plant psychology publish experiments daily, showing that the so-called spiritual abilities and functions of humans differ from those of animals only in degree, but are essentially the same, etc., etc. However, all these and similar findings and experiences have not yet compelled any scholar to draw ethical conclusions from them. Because—apart from the fact that this is none of the scholars' business—it takes courage and love to draw these conclusions and even make a serious attempt to live by them. Among natural scientists and university professors, however, there is no one who loves creation for its own sake. Nor do they love it enough to forgo a (not even interesting) vivisection for the sake of a creature's pain. They all love nothing but their own work, their own theory, their own discovery, however small. The average person, however, lacks the courage to represent and realize their innermost convictions. Even unconditional, unbiased thinking frightens them, for they have a thousand social and economic considerations to take into account, a thousand inherited and imagined inhibitions.

When one considers how many good and noble animals have been sacrificed on the altar of science, how much pain has been cold-bloodedly and curiously observed and recorded, that loving animals are at every clumsy student's disposal, that every novice has to fail a dozen tortures before he succeeds in making an observation, the result of which, incidentally, has been known for decades—a person who has not acquired the brutality of a scientist is overcome by horror and a profound abhorrence of the whole study of nature. For all this torture brings humanity little benefit—mostly unjust advantage—it is simply abhorrent. Here is one example in a hundred from the beneficial application of science in medicine. A remedy used for stomach weakness and digestive disorders is prepared as follows: a strong and healthy dog is suspended from wide leather straps, its paws strapped to the ground. In this position, the animal must starve for several days. Then, the dog is presented with appetizing morsels that trigger a strong secretion from its gastric glands. To obtain this secretion, a metal cannula is inserted through its body into its stomach. The fluid that drips out is collected—ergo, the animal gives up its life. Since the secretion thus obtained is not pure enough, because food residues and juices have found their way into it, a "scholar" named Pavlov "invented" the following procedure: the dog, treated as described above, has its esophagus opened by an incision in its throat, so that the morsels it swallows do not enter its stomach but fall through the hole to the floor. The resulting remedy is pure—and expensive. It is of no use to mankind, 99 per cent of which consists of proletarians. But the millionaire who has ruined his stomach with caviar, oysters, champagne, and a crazy lifestyle is cured instead of being punished. The juices that his lazy body no longer wants to provide are stolen from the dog, a noble and good animal whose life is sacrificed for a man who is certainly unworthy of being saved. Only a fool would expect the inventor of such a remedy to show love for the creatures he tortures to death; he doesn't even feel anything for his solvent, stomach-sick patients.

He wants to earn money from his invention. That's the magic word: "earn"! They all want to make money: with their books, with their lectures, theories, medicines... just earn, capitalize on it.

This all-too-human greed is the greatest obstacle on the path to the love of creation. An obstacle so great and insurmountable that not even once every thousand years is someone born like Buddha, like Francis of Assisi, who casts aside all "possessions," whose love is then greater than all the universities, slaughterhouses, and canning factories in the world.

But the saddest thing is the knowledge that there are great, highly cultured peoples who have never killed or tortured an animal, and that for the sake of love; that there is Buddhism, a great and good religion, for which no sword has ever been raised and no blood has ever been shed—a religion for which the commandment of loving one's neighbor, extended to all living beings, is a matter of course and is practiced.

Our much-praised science has ultimately led to the very results that were discovered in Asia thousands of years ago, without torture or bloodshed. Essentially, this enormous detour, this vast amount of pain and suffering, was unnecessary, as for thousands of years we have only had to fight against our own stupidity, and we still do. But all this is a trifle compared to the countless murders and tortures that humans inflict on animals out of greed, speculation, and to satisfy their need for luxury. Most fur-bearing animals—millions upon millions annually—are hunted. Here, the animal is killed with a shot; it is not torture, but stupid, senseless murder. The prized Persian lamb fur, however, is obtained by torturing the pregnant ewe with beatings and chasing her back and forth until she sheds her still premature foal. The fur of these painfully stillborn lambs—dear ladies—is indeed the Persian variety! Approximately 10 million seals are killed each year. Since the fur could be damaged in the process, they are not killed, but rather the skin is removed from the living animal, which dies in the process. The elephant seal is extinct, except for the specimens at Hagenbeck and the Berlin Zoo. Ninety per cent of the fat harvested from these animals has been dumped into the sea so as to raise the price. The elephant of India and Africa will also soon disappear, to provide billiard balls, combs, and toothpicks. Hunters who could pay 1,000 marks for a permit, but who had a terrible respect for this noble animal and its fury, heroically attacked it with machine guns in the paradisiacal times before the World War. And this list of misdeeds could be continued indefinitely. Gentle souls have founded animal protection associations, created an animal protection law, and are demanding its further development. These half-measures are fundamentally ridiculous. Humans will always be cruel, will always exploit and lustfully torture animals, as long as they see them as their property, as long as they believe that God gave Adam all of creation as a gift. No animal protection legislation can remedy what humans are unwilling to do. The little bit of love we show our dog or our canary is irrelevant. Buddhism in Asia protects animals far better than our animal protection laws. Yet this religion has neither a police force nor any other means of power at its disposal. Here, as elsewhere, the same spectacle presents itself: the means employed by European states are either inadequate or wrong. We believe that we can accomplish everything through regulations and laws and do not consider that a law has no meaning and remains ineffective unless the spiritual transformation has first occurred in people themselves.

But there's something special about the love of creation. It's a secret that one can only experience for oneself. From a certain point of realization, love for creation grows like an avalanche, submerging all economic and social considerations, becoming like a frenzy and not resting until it can encompass the entire earth. It's like madness then; but I confess that a madman like Francis of Assisi is infinitely dear and close to me. The mere thought that such a person once lived is comforting.

I believe it makes no sense to make any demands on people based on the above. The fundamental experience is pure, private, but all other demands lead to an expanded animal protection association. And it's inconceivable that in one of our capitalist countries, the animal protection association should prevail over the slaughterhouses and canning factories of the entrepreneurs.

Translated by Marcin Wawrzyńczak

Joseph Beuys

451

JOSEPH BEUYS
(1921, KREFELD – 1986, DÜSSELDORF)

A German artist, teacher, and art theorist, a central figure in the European avant-garde. He combined performative actions, symbolic gestures, theory of sculpture, and political involvement, developing a concept of the social sculpture, by which every person has the creative potential to transform society. In his manifesto "I am Searching for Field Character" (1973), he formulates a utopian, radically political vision of art as a revolutionary and evolutionary force. He posits expanding the concept of art into every creative activity, as focused on building a future social order, conceived as a holistic work of art. From this approach, ecology is an integral spiritual-material dimension of the development of humanity and the planet.

Joseph Beuys, "I am Searching for Field Character" (1973), in *Energy Plan for the Western Man: Joseph Beuys in America*, ed. Carin Kuoni (New York: Four Walls Eight Windows, 1990), 21–23.

I AM SEARCHING FOR FIELD CHARACTER

Only on condition of a radical widening of definition will it be possible for art and activities related to art to provide evidence that art is now the only evolutionary-revolutionary power. Only art is capable of dismantling the repressive effects of a senile social system that continues to totter along the deathline: to dismantle in order to build A SOCIAL ORGANISM AS A WORK OF ART.

This most modern art discipline—Social Sculpture/Social Architecture—will only reach fruition when every living person becomes a creator, a sculptor or architect of the social organism. Only then would the insistence on participation of the action art of Fluxus and Happening be fulfilled: only then would democracy be fully realized. Only a conception of art revolutionized to this degree can turn into a politically productive force, coursing through each person and shaping history,

But all this, and much that is as yet unexplored, has first to form part of our consciousness: insight is needed into objective connections. We must probe (theory of knowledge) the moment of origin of free individual productive potency (creativity). We then reach the threshold where the human being experiences himself primarily as a spiritual being, where his supreme achievements (work of art), his active thinking, his active feeling, his active will, and their higher forms, can be apprehended as sculptural generative means, corresponding to the exploded concepts of sculpture divided into its elements—indefinite—movement —definite (see theory of sculpture), and are then recognized as flowing in the direction that is shaping the content of the world right through into the future.

This is the concept of art that carries within itself not only the revolutionizing of the historic bourgeois concept of knowledge (materialism, positivism), but also of religious activity.

EVERY HUMAN BEING IS AN ARTIST who—from his state of freedom—the position of freedom that he experiences at first hand—learns to determine the other positions in the TOTAL ARTWORK OF THE FUTURE SOCIAL ORDER. Self-determination and participation in the cultural sphere (freedom); in the structuring of laws (democracy); and in the sphere of economics (socialism). Self-administration and decentralization (threefold structure) occurs: FREE DEMOCRATIC SOCIALISM.

THE FIFTH INTERNATIONAL is born

Communication occurs in reciprocity: it must never be a one-way flow from the teacher to the taught. The teacher takes equally from the taught. So oscillates—at all times and everywhere, in any conceivable internal and external circumstance, between all degrees of ability, in the work place, institutions, the street, work circles, research groups, schools—the master/pupil, transmitter/receiver, relationship. The ways of achieving this are manifold, corresponding to the varying gifts of individuals and groups. THE ORGANIZATION FOR DIRECT DEMOCRACY THROUGH REFERENDUM is one such group. It seeks to launch many similar work groups or information centres, and strives towards worldwide cooperation.

JOSEPH BEUYS, *What Is to Be Done? 1984*,
printing ink on paper,
102 × 68.4 cm, 1980

"WHAT IS TO BE DONE?"

EXHIBITIONS. TALKS.

1984

PUBLIC DEBATES.

ALTERNATIVE TECHNOLOGY VERSUS NUCLEAR POWER.

179 Canongate 9 am–8 pm, every day 18th August–6 September 1980.

with the support of the Scottish Arts Council, Joseph Beuys & Edinburgh Festival Society

CHAPTER

XIII

NIGHT SHIFT

Libuše Jarcovjáková

LIBUŠE JARCOVJÁKOVÁ
(B. 1952, PRAGUE)

A Czech documentary photographer known for her raw, personal photographs of minorities, underground communities, and night life in communist Czechoslovakia in the 1970s and '80s. Her work, often in black and white, documents intimate moments from her own life and her friends'. In her highly personal text "Photography? It's Love!", the artist describes her unusual relationship with photography, not just as a form of art and emotional expression, but also as a way of experiencing life. Working in photography, she created a space and tools to transform her experiences into messages. Jarcovjáková describes the process of picture-taking as a daily fascination with transient images.

Libuše Jarcovjáková, “Photography? It’s love!” in *Libuše Jarcovjáková*, ed. Lucie Černá, (Prague: National Gallery in Prague, 2025), 23–24.

PHOTOGRAPHY? IT’S LOVE!

If only it were possible to take photographs without cameras, to absorb the image, and let it expand inside yourself in a curious photographic emulsion full of silver, and then, just to the sound of the beating pulse you hear in your ears, to welcome it into the world beneath a red-orange light. I know very well that feeling that you simply must capture something, that you can't let it get away. The sudden burst of the flesh, so similar to the impulse of sexual arousal. Everything inside you stiffens, your ligaments tighten up like iron bars. You’re short of breath, and now, exactly now is that fraction of a second that you need to preserve forever... forever? After all, we’re working with such a fragile, vulnerable medium. Where will all these celebrated works of today be in a couple of decades? This causes me to reflect that the reason I love photography is precisely for those hundredths of seconds when it happens... when something happens.

I associate the first photograph that ever fascinated me with a dramatic sense of fear: “When we come across one of them we’ll take no notice of him, so he doesn’t seize us...” I can no longer remember exactly what kind of apparition my sentence related to, I know I was browsing through a book that my uncle brought back from Africa and the photographs in it terrified me—the natives could snatch us all and take us away with them! At the same time I yearned for that kind of adventure. I've always yearned for adventure. Naturally, those photographs were black-and-white, just like in my childhood picture book, I think it was *The Songs of Josef Mánes*. Recently I found a copy of this book again and I realised that I know the illustrations in it almost by heart.

In a certain way, photography was a kind of gesture of defiance for me. Both my parents were painters, both immersed in their own thing. I needed to go my own way. To have my own space to create images. To have my own tool I used to transform feelings and thoughts from the present into messages. What kind of messages? Messages about eternity? About infinity? About light, droplets, leaves, movements of wings, fleeting smiles, and sleepless nights? Ultimately they were mostly messages about my own existence, about where I was, the life I was living and with whom, the time when all this was taking place. I was fascinated by the time-lag, the waiting for the image. The interim period between the moment when you click the shutter and the moment the image started to appear in the developer was magical. Just the word CLICK! I clicked something and now this something, somewhere, is waiting for its moment, when it'll either arrive and mean something, or arrive and mean nothing. Or when it will be definitively destroyed: by vandalism, through negligence I might overexpose the film or even lose it, I might leave it on a train, in a pub, wherever. Where are those images in the meantime?

I was always an insatiable viewer, I watched and watched. At how raindrops turn into bubbles, I read whole stories in crumbling facades, I discovered faces, contorted dwarves, and strange animals in the cracks in the pavement. I tried to extract from paintings, photographs, and illustrations what wasn't and couldn't be there. Like the pack of "nudie cards" that I spread out on layers of cardboard, only to eventually discover that these voluptuous young ladies could be seen only from a frontal view, that the cards weren't two-sided and that I simply wouldn't get to see their arses. I wanted to impose some greater magic and space onto these two-dimensional reproductions of the world. And at the same time I was fascinated by nakedness, there was something improper about it. For me, nakedness wasn't something I associated with sex. For a long time the latter, if I remember rightly, was something I had little interest in. But that white body, that luminous, even radiant naked body took my breath away every time. The first time in the back yard in Uherský Brod, with my great-grandmother in a short skirt. We went on a walk all the way out back to the barn, and it didn't turn out too well. I couldn't walk very well yet, and she was really old by then. I was told to turn my back, and I heard a trickle of piss hitting the ground. Of course I turned round, and probably gave a shriek of horror. Ever since then, that huge, smooth white orb beneath the embroidered miniskirt has remained a fixture in my personal picture gallery.

Translated by Elizabet Kovačeva

Karol Hiller

KAROL HILLER
(1891, ŁÓDŹ – 1939, LASY LUĆMIERSKIE)

A Polish painter, printmaker, and art theorist, connected to the avant-garde of the 1920s and '30s, he studied in Kyiv, Moscow, and Paris, contributing to the Łódź arts scene gathered around the a.r. group. His *Heliographic Compositions* and journalism are a major link in the Polish Constructivist chain. In the text "New Seeing" (1934), Hiller analyzes the evolution of visual perception in the modern world, determined by industrial development. He points to the influence of photography, cinema, and transportation on reducing perceptual distance and creating a "psychovisual aura" that accompanies a picture. He also emphasizes the role of the proletariat in the development of new art. He combines formal analysis with a conviction about the social role of art: visual perception emerges as a dynamic process, historically determined and partly created by the viewer.

Karol Hiller, "Nowe widzenie," *Forma*, no. 2 (1934): 3-8, in: *Karol Hiller 1891-1939. Nowe widzenie: malarstwo, heliografika, rysunek, grafika*, eds. Janina Ładnowska, Zenobia Karnicka (Łódź: Muzeum Sztuki w Łodzi, 2002), 61–65.

NEW SEEING

When in 1907 Cubism signaled the coming of a world war, art seemed to have been slightly ahead of life. But that always tends to happen, even when it happens only seemingly but we have no links to confirm the connection. Lack of these links usually results in the improper use of the method employed in the process of interrogating a given phenomenon.

Art is, beyond a doubt, a function of social life. But if we were to apply the dialectic method, entirely adequate for the examination of sociological affairs, to the field of art, particularly that created in the last quarter-century, it would have yielded little past a simple statement of fact. It would have given us the claim that Picasso is a vehicle for middle-class ideology, but little insight into his painting. Without penetrating deep into the subject matter, without understanding of the specific character of art's inherent properties, we will always be doomed to drawing, by way of analogy, from those areas of knowledge and life that we know best. Such an approach, however, often results in experts in one field becoming wholly backward in another only because they failed to probe the matter deeply enough. This mistake most often befalls social activists, which is a shame as the harm that results from it tends to spiral, especially when such views become entrenched among groups. To reiterate—the error lies in the sociologist or the dialectically-inclined activist stopping his inquiry after only scratching the surface of external changes in art, and not knowing how to analyze form itself, i.e. how to apply his trustworthy method at a point where going forward would propel him toward uncovering the most important attributes of a barely perceptible truth. It is paramount that he knows how to do just that.

Dialectics is a method best suited to analyzing phenomena in a state of flux. For such inquiries to yield results abiding by the principles of scientific objectivity, all the attendant premises and circumstances must be thoroughly examined. In essence, a method of inquiry presuming that all things are fluid cannot be expected to find much purchase in capitalism, because the worldviews of the owning classes have spawned virtues that are enduring and static in nature, and it should come as no surprise to see the interests of these classes unfolding along similar lines. Preserving the status quo, meanwhile, grows more difficult with each day, as it finds itself assailed by not only developments in economic theory, but the entirety of modern art and literature as well. Most interesting to us, however, are the changes in the minds of people far removed from theoretical positions of culture. The kaleidoscope nature of events after the war necessarily prompted ardent criticism against any stabilizing idea and fostered conditions that encouraged using dialectics in every area of modern life. Reawakened skepticism toward established, purportedly unshakeable truths, and the shift in the perception of time and space introduced by advances in science and technology, profoundly affected the subject that interests us the most—the formation of visual sentiments in postwar society.

The formal differences in modern art reflect the differences in society, and the still-raging economic crisis has only emphasized them further. Few today would undertake to argue in defense of art's total autonomy from society, but its inherent social value too often remains uninterrogated, while we tend to lose sight of the community on whose behalf we take on the task. Before engaging in a review of modern art, we must first settle all the necessary questions pertaining to our own position in the social structure, as only then, by dissecting relevant delights and phobias, will we be able to reach substantial conclusions. We are free, however, to divulge those sympathies for all things artistic and use them to perform a preliminary selection on the entirety of phenomena making up life and art. The results will lay us completely bare, as the process will likely leave us with all things constant, traditional, epigonic on the one hand, and their antitheses on the other. We are aware that the true state of affairs is somewhat different, as every point in time is necessarily accompanied by its attendant cause and effect, meaning that it cannot exist without the presence of a series of indirect phenomena. This, however, does in no way lessen our affinity for everything oriented toward tomorrow and for the role that the proletariat will play as the instrument of building that tomorrow in the area of visual culture.

Meanwhile, drawing on what we already know, we may try to draft horoscopes for the future, or at least try to divine the direction that the visual imagination of future art audiences will move in. That, however, requires an additional caveat—because we will be trying to explain the emergence of modern art forms, much of our attention will necessarily be directed at the cultural consumer, unwaveringly embedded in the present.

Few of us have any idea of how profoundly our perception of space and time changed within the formation of visual representations. Photography, the cinema, the car, and the airplane have thoroughly upended our past contemplative attitudes toward images of memory, captured in moments of stillness. Due to the surfeit of visual stimuli that we are inundated with nowadays, the images in our minds often form as dense visuals, their essence close to what we would once consider a vision. By using shortcuts, clarity of vision, and immediate elimination of insignificant forms, we arrive at conceptual constructs, the essence of which testifies to the acquisition of entirely new knowledge about things. We declare that these conceptual complexes are persistently accompanied by a sort of psychovisual aura, which does not decamp from our minds even when we decide to direct our attention at one of the objects making up that particular nexus. Not only that, it allows the reversal of the direction that sensations radiate in—from the aura of the object toward the object itself—while granting it certain autonomous properties.

Our relationship with our surroundings has been imbued with a range of new sensibilities, which, however, we ought to strip of any veneer of wonder. It is high time we illuminate the sphere of sensation and inspiration with the light of understanding for those creative states that, until recently, most artists tended to leave fallow, believing them realms of chance and irresponsible frolics of intuition. This jealously guarded preserve of inspiration, believed for the past two centuries to be taboo to protect it against incursions of unwanted thoughts, must surely have had a mechanism in place that artists accustomed to deterministically awaiting the coming of the muse would never figure out. Although many find it convenient, it should be somewhat shocking that this old wives' tale about intellectual effort ultimately being detrimental to artists could survive well into the twentieth century. After all, the essence of art was defined as the creation of the very properties of deliberate beauty long before positivism came around.

We do not want to cast any doubts on the existence of inspiration; instead, having probed the nature of this essentially physical force, we seek ways to handle the wilfulness of its oft-humiliating impact. That is what is required mainly by the painter's new vision of modern reality if his work is ever to contend with the facts that have long been a part of our collective psyche. By simultaneously coupling a variety of phenomena within a single conceptual plane, the act of seeing has been somewhat corrupted, the change plainly visible when we juxtapose current and past practices of seeing. The process in question involves one particular genre of the psychovisual aura that this aggregate emanates taking over as the overarching impulse organizing the linkage of its individual parts, replacing in this capacity the logical connection of objects organized according to the properties of the forms. It is a very peculiar shift, one that requires a certain state of inspiration as a constant, both in the implementation of seeing in the visual arts as well as in the ordinary construction of artistic vision, and which results in the establishment of lasting emotional contact with reality, propelled by all the resources involved in its interrogation, from purely physiological sensations all the way up to the final results of its speculative examination. This increased sensory receptivity reveals a great intellectual hunger among the masses, the individuality and persistence of their reactions undeniably indicating the advent of a new cultural era. Am I speaking about the proletariat again? Of course I am.

Day after day, we witness the rising wave of hunger for life in whatever form. Those who suffer it will never lack appetite and succumb to melancholy. The capacity of their stomachs and hearts is so great as to easily devour whatever comes their way. We may interpret this escalating process of consumption however we will, but the period is inevitable. What we do know, however, is that it shall pass. We are even ready to make some predictions as to the changes in the realm of painting that will follow, as the conditions that will invite them are already present among the masses of enlightened and proletarized middle class. The continuity of culture, sustained by even the thinnest of threads, is a deeply entrenched notion and it is only up to us not to lose the ability to identify its manifestations among the surfeit of eclecticism, which itself is symptomatic of those delirious periods that usually give rise to new social organisms. And thus we are left again with a test of man's deeds and abilities, dictated by the conditions of his existence, and emphasize that we allow ourselves these digressions only to help shield ourselves from the consequences of a strictly formalist approach to art, which tends to push the artist to the fringes of both life and art.

Art expresses the potential inherent in the strength of that hunger through intensified activity, revealed to not only nature, but man, too. Attempts to revise his relationship with his surroundings take place, aimed at establishing contact with the intended recipient of the sensations. Alongside the probing of nature, inquiries are being made into the sources of the artist's creative work, in order to learn more about the viewer's reconstructive apparatus. In other words, the question of the viewer becomes relevant again.

Could this contact with surroundings have been established without sensation being a decisive factor? Never. And that is where the essence of this quintessentially social character of modern art lies; conceivable only though the spirit of human collaboration, modern art exposes art for art's sake as a petty cliché driven by unambiguous indifference toward the affairs of modern society. Simultaneously, this factor plays a key part in the emergence of new forms of modern art. To understand the prominent role played in the process by emotion, we must first realize how profoundly it affects and shapes the aforementioned psychovisual aura of visual sensations. The question of emotion, however, diverges somewhat from lyricism as inclination, meaning that the concept covers a significantly broader pool of emotional knowledge, obtained by tirelessly tilling the creative undersoil. This is rather a mode of perception, founded upon specific truths of things that we, and our antecedents, decided to discard. At this point, however, it is important to assert that all these snippets of flashing thoughts are directed by forces which, as ever before, have been invariably coloring all our actions—forces we know as sympathy, indifference, and hostility. The slight overintellectualization of modern art stemmed either from ignorance or insufficient appreciation of those unseen forces, hence forms created without the involvement of this process could not be reconstructed by the process within the mind of the viewer; at best, spawned by indifference, they return to the same indifference in the end. In any event, we always ought to remain aware of the subordinate position of the intellect, its unbalanced servility, worked out in the course of its long service with man, and the role that is has heretofore been playing—that of a fixative for matters much more ethereal.

Consequently, the development of painterly knowledge results in a shift from description of external properties of objects toward the discovery of methods of expressing emotions that they imply and without which any knowledge of objects we have cannot be considered complete. This, in turn, expands the field for the study of the magic of objects, whose centuries-long existence is no less real than the realness of objects around us. The difference lies in the public's sensitivity toward their allure, as the hesitation itself is directly linked with the activity of society in general.

Within this field, we are left to our own observations. While knowledge of ethnography may be helpful here, many-volumed treatises on the history of art, encyclopedic in their detailed descriptions, dates, and dry facts, will be of no use. Similar expertise could be provided only by a painter capable of retracing the history of those unseen linkages that bind art to a given period. I dedicate this field to the painter, because I cannot fathom that retracing being performed without in-depth knowledge of even the most arcane aspects of painting. Much of what we know on the subject has been worked out by painters throughout the years, but due to their aversion to writing, entire sections of the visual culture of the past remain unavailable to the broader public and unassimilated into mainstream knowledge. With such access, we would have a much clearer picture of a given era, derived from specific properties of shapes, colors, and contours, revealing propensities deeper and more entrenched than the thought processes accompanying the development of specific social views. These are much more enduring proclivities, which penetrate deep below the threshold of conscious human judgment, and have little attachment to borders, nations, and races. I am referring here to qualities similar to Ozenfant's[1] tropisms. They allow us to reach all the way back to the eldest formations of the human psyche, stemming exclusively from the physical properties of earthly existence, from the essence of light, and the structure of the human eye. These properties could be considered permanent, enduring, if it were not for the human psyche, the biggest unknown, raising so much resistance. In any case, the pragmatism of our history has ultimately had so little impact on these primal psychological reactions to colors and figures that they have to be taken into account during all inquiries into the emergence of *universalist* elements in art.

Understandably, these are the elements that art ought to cultivate if it is to prevail in a society bent on worshipping that which binds rather than that which divides. It is hard to predict whether art will evolve toward a more global character, gradually merging all tendencies and forms, but we should emphasize, without passing final judgment, that the formation of universalist elements may ultimately become a permanent link between the arts of different nations. They facilitate the establishment of direct contact between art and its audiences, by exploiting that deep, primal knowledge of things that all humans share. One of the greatest achievements of Surrealism is its contribution to this cause and its realization.

At first glance, it would seem that any knowledge a graphologist may glean about the character of a person whose handwriting he analyzes would necessarily have to be less comprehensive than the insight produced by the study of the much richer pool of attributes offered by a work of art. If that is not so, we know why. To date, we have failed to properly appreciate the sheer, direct force of visual suggestion in painting, because we have for far too long relied on literature for suggestions. We know very little about the deeper reactions of sensitive viewers to the configuration of visual elements as a whole, because our entire knowledge about the painterly form was limited to just the harmonious shaping of the *surface* of the painting. We were satisfied with creating beautiful things, pleasantly irritating the external layer of our eyes and providing the viewers with ever new sensory pleasures from discovering new material states, for a world that we were happy with. The role of that art and its position within the social structure seem to raise no obvious doubts.

We believe that the contemporary condition of the visual arts ought to find expression in the amplification of the dynamic content of the forms involved, because in view of the profound potential of this general yearning it may not exactly be viable to encourage taking particular joy in having well-established, average qualities. These premises align completely with the factual state of things in Surrealism, which seeks to reintroduce to modern art, despite recent assertions to the contrary, not only a more *augmented expression* of forms, but also a more *substantial repository* of themes to draw on. By no means does its initial irrealism lessen or assuage modern art's attitude toward life, as that irrealism only expresses the negative view of only certain forms of life rather than of life in general. Comparing photomontages compiled during the Dada period and those created later is incredibly illuminating in this respect. Back then, the ubiquitous apotheosis of nonsense—later on, the obstinate pursuit of the lawlessness of the privileged in the name of the new order of nonsense. Literature played a considerable part, but we must not forget that the visual source material was provided primarily by the naturalism of photography. The dynamic of the photomontage stemmed almost entirely from the ability to contrast cognitive facts, and only to a very small extent was a competent artist capable of backing this dynamic with a more meaningful expression of the black-and-white qualities of art.

The clear influence of photomontage on early Surrealist works was likely motivated more by the similarity of the attitudes toward reality held by the artists than any similarity of used forms. Nevertheless, as was the case with photomontage, their greatest strength lay not in purity of form. Surrealism approached this supremacy of the visual gradually, by purging realistic and narrative content in favor of abstract forms, but used differently than ever before. One way or another, this particular evolution, from its very beginning, unfolded under the auspices of framing the work of art as deliberate documentation of the period's prevailing mode of expression, alongside a fundamental shift in the view of the role of abstract forms. In the past, objectless art sought to free itself from the burden of naturalistic shapes in order to expose and visualize the relationships underpinning pure structure. This pure structure was supposed to offer to the viewer a picture composed of a congruous assemblage of forms, which, in turn, also made up the structure. And so we see that the narcissism of the conceptual-slash-visual loop precludes it from making contact with reality at any point in its trajectory, thus condemning visual arts to an existence beyond time and place. This purely speculative, suicidal, and asocial position of this art could never last, if only because of the further formal development of abstract forms which, initially used for other purposes, began appearing to the artist not only as intermediate links, but also as ideographic symbols, replete with expression and meaning. The broken bridge between art on the one hand and nature and man on the other was rebuilt, prompting the continuing regeneration and enrichment of abstraction by way of introducing new forms drawn from the limitless bounty of nature. This development process began essentially when artists, alongside the simplest forms and geometric relationships, began introducing strokes with curved lines, surrounding the normal elements of vital shapes. We could argue here that the contact with reality was only incidental, but only if we knew nothing about the essence of similar instances. We know that they are usually born of necessity, but the credit for the evolution they tend to prompt is rarely theirs alone. Here, the necessity was the desire for an art armed with the means to more strongly express the will to pursue new values of living.

If we circle back to the question of fluidity of phenomena and the changes that they had to elicit in the formation of sensations, we do it only to explain that the continued evolution of the art of painting is a question of the further development of abstract forms. This results not only from the formal consequences of paintings itself, but also the methods of recording contemporary visual phenomena. The fluidity of things had to redirect our attention toward certain laws according to which these changes unfold. We penetrate ever deeper toward the center of these phenomena and dissect their essence, expressed here in the immutability of the governing functions. In the evolution of painting, this path has been marked by the shift from plain naturalist recreation of entire objects toward condensing their form into their e s s e n t i a l v e s t i g e s.

The economy produced by the description of superficial shape further intensified the potential of the visual fluid, spread by condensed shapes, resulting in another leap in the evolution of art—the transition from material to p s y c h o l o g i c a l s u b j e c t m a t t e r.

Were this art not rooted in the persistent mutability of life and the distillation of its specific premises, declared in the form of painting subject matter, this final stage of the evolution involving the rendition of emotional states would quickly exhaust the soil it was rooted in and eventually produce oversubjective results. Assuming that art as a whole has overarching objectives, then contemporary painting strives, as we already mentioned, to establish direct contact with the viewer by exploring the breadth of his visual perception resources. By providing itself with uninterrupted nourishment, drawn from the common experience of life, Surrealism seeks to protect itself from the consequences of the quite recent speculative efforts which, on account of the obfuscation of the provenance of specific geometric shapes, had to base their actions solely on the implication of logical relationships. These relationships, meanwhile, transposed onto painting, lose their most important asset—their objectivity and clarity, because the perception of visual stimuli cannot take place without specific perceptual knowledge, which enables certain abstract forms to appear as rudimentary versions of specific shapes and imply entirely unintended emotions.

The task of modern art is to map out these unseen linkages and springs in order to both eliminate inadvertent action and move the breadth of direct suggestions to reinforce certain directions that perception can unfold in. The rationalist character of this inquiry, irrespective of the emotional circumstances, provides this process with the ability to successfully penetrate the creative and reconstructive undersoil which, without the stability offered by certain axioms, would quickly succumb to disorientation.

Although some recent geometric abstraction offerings prompted confusion in the viewers, many artists see this somewhat intimate art as something of a trusty compass. The openness exhibited by contemporary artists toward the abundance of available forms of life has much in common with the inner peace typical of a man who trusts his direction and the knowledge acquired in the course of prior service. This cause of self-discipline is further assisted by the subject matter picked by the painter. This deliberate effort to narrow down the intended conglomerate of forms is also intended to amplify the impact of individual shapes, because their inherent implication is further amplified by the overall suggestion of the picture and vice versa. With the subject matter, the painter calls the viewer to witness the paths he took and the means he employed, pre-empting the viewer's need for a pared down assortment of impressions. If we tap into the singularity of these impressions, their speculative-slash-visionary unity in multiplicity and condensed expression, then we will understand that new emotions can be realized solely through forms that, by amplifying the potential for action, only abstract art is capable of producing.

Translated by Jan Szelągiewicz

1 Amedée Ozenfant (1886-1966)– French painter.

Jerzy Lewczyński

485

JERZY LEWCZYŃSKI
(1924, TOMASZÓW LUBELSKI – 2014, GLIWICE)
A Polish photographer, theorist, and creator of "the archaeology of photography," who documented traces of the past and researched memory and identity through pictures. He gained fame and recognition through his photography series combining a documentary approach, experimentation, and reflection on the role of the medium of photography. Lewczyński defines the archaeology of photography as research to uncover and comment on the past through photographs, which provide visual contact with old strata of culture. He treats photography as a testimony of past events, and the light captured by the negative is a key witness.

Jerzy Lewczyński, *Archeologia fotografii* (Katowice: Górnośląskie Centrum Kultury "Pusta 4," 1997), 5.

THE ARCHAEOLOGY OF PHOTOGRAPHY

The archaeology of photography is the term I use for activities aiming to discover, research, and observe events, facts, and situations that happened long ago, in the past of photography.

Photographs provide a continuity of visual contact with the past, creating an opportunity to amplify the effects of past culture and creativity on our time.

This transmission through time is the main theme of various photographic discoveries. Perhaps all our present-day audiovisual activities are just an initial phase before we can capture life in its time and form in the future!

The impossibility of knowing the Unknown forces us to settle for better or poorer approximations of the truth. This pulsation is the essence of many archaeological studies; its rhythm recalls breathing, or the beating of the heart.

Another aim of the archaeology of photography is searching for witnesses of bygone events! In photography, one such witness is light. Light, which stimulated technological processes to capture reality and which carved what was once a universal presence into the negative! The negative is thus a trace of "that" light and is, therefore, an authentic witness of past events. This observation of light on the negative can lead to fascinating discoveries and reveal the secret of the sculpture of the negative!

A discovery:

The Orthodox cemetery in Sosnowiec. A monument bearing a sculpture of a woman in a long dress, stepping into the past and closing the door behind her.

I have photographed this monument several times, trying to grasp the meaning of the mystery in this sculpture. Only after twenty years did I discover the past. The woman was the wife of Brandenburg, the Prussian director of the Katarzyna Factory. Born in Yalta as a Russian aristocrat. During World War I, she died of a heart attack, after being arrested for helping the first Russian prisoners of war. The husband commissioned a monument in Dresden. A few years later, he perished during the revolutionary uprisings in Sosnowiec.

These scraps of the past are only approximations. Photographs of a woman in Caucasian national garb and another showing the subject's full figure in a long, flowing dress.

Here, photography led to the past being revealed!

Translated by Soren Gauger

Mladen Stilinović

491

MLADEN STILINOVIĆ
(1947, BELGRADE – 2016, PULA)

A conceptual artist, a leading representative of the Yugoslav Nova Umjetnička Praksa (New Art Practices), working in Zagreb. He paused his formal education as a teenager, and went on gaining knowledge through avant-garde cinema, literature, poetry, and exchanges with his contemporaries on the arts scene. In "The Praise of Laziness" he posits that true art requires laziness, a passivity and freedom from the pressures of work and production. Eastern artists had fewer means than their western counterparts, which meant they could focus on creativity and laziness. In the West, Stilinović thought, artists were consumed by the system, causing them to lose contact with what the author believed to be true art.

Mladen Stilinović, "The Praise of Laziness," in *Art Always Has Its Consequences: Artists' Texts from Croatia, Hungary, Poland, Serbia, 1947–2009*, eds: Dóra Hegyi, Zsuzsa László. Emese Süvecz (Berlin: tranzit.hu, Sternberg Press, 2011), 147–48.

THE PRAISE OF LAZINESS

As an artist, I learned from both East (socialism) and West (capitalism). Of course, now when the borders and political systems have changed, such an experience will be no longer possible. But what I have learned from that dialogue stays with me. My observation and knowlesge of Western art has lately led me to a conclusion that art cannot exists any more in the West. This is not to say that there isn't any. Why cannot art exist any more in the West? The answer is simple. Artists in the West are not lazy. Artists from the East are lazy; whether they will stay lazy now when they are no longer Eastern artists, remains to be seen.

Laziness is the absence of movement and thought, dumb time – total amnesia. It is also indifference, staring at nothing, non-activity, impotence. It is sheer stupidity, a time of pain, futile concentration. Those virtues of laziness are important factors in art. Knowing about laziness is not enough, it must be practiced and perfected.

Artists in the West are not lazy and therefore not artists but rather producers of something... Their involvement with matters of no importance, such as production, promotion, gallery system, museum system, competition system (who is first), their preoccupation with objects, all that drives them away from laziness, from art. Just as money is paper, so is a gallery a room.

Artists from the East were lazy and poor because the entire system of insignificant factors did not exist. Therefore they had time enough to concentrate on art and laziness. Even when they did produce art, they knew it was in vain, it was nothing.

Artists from the West could learn about laziness, but they didn't. Two major 20th-century artists treated the question of laziness, in both practical and theoretical terms: Duchamp and Malevich.

Duchamp never really discussed laziness, but rather indifference and non-work. When asked by Pierre Cabanne[1] what had brought him most pleasure in life, Duchamp said, "First, having been lucky. Because basically I've never worked for a living. I consider working for a living slightly imbecilic from an economic point of view. I hope that some day we'll be able to live without being obliged to work. Thanks to my luck, I was able to manage without getting wet."

Malevich wrote a text entitled "Laziness – the real truth of mankind" (1921). In it he criticized capitalism, because it enabled only a small number of capitalists to be lazy, but also socialism because the entire movement was based on work instead of laziness. To quote: "People are scared of laziness and persecute those who accept it, and it always happens because no one realizes laziness is the truth; it has been branded as the mother of all vices, but it is in fact the mother of life. Socialism brings liberation in the unconscious, it scorns laziness without realizing it was laziness that gave birth to it; in his folly, the son scorns his mother as a mother of all vices and would not remove the brand; in this brief note I want to remove the brand of shame from laziness and to pronounce it not the mother of all vices, but the mother of perfection."

Finally, to be lazy and conclude: there is no art without laziness.

WORK IS A DISEASE
– KARL MARX
Mladen Stilinović

WORK IS A SHAME
Vlado Martek

1 Pierre Cabanne (1921-2004) – French art historian. – Ed.

MLADEN STILINOVIĆ, *Rad*,
photographic paper, 9 × 13 cm, 1980

THE PRAISE OF LAZINESS

As an artist, I learned from both East (socialism) and West (capitalism). Of course, now when the borders and political systems have changed, such an experience will be no longer possible. But what I have learned from that dialogue, stays with me. My observation and knowlesge of Western art has lately led me to a conclusion that art cannot exists any more in the West. This is not to say that there isn't any. Why cannot art exist any more in the West? The answer is simple. Artists in the West are not lazy. Artists from the East are lazy; whether they will stay lazy now when they are no longer Eastern artists, remains to be seen.

Laziness is the absence of movement and thought, dumb time - total amnesia. It is also indifference, staring at nothing, non-activity, impotence. It is sheer stupidity, a time of pain, futile concentration. Those virtues of laziness are important factors in art. Knowing about laziness is not enough, it must be practiced and perfected.

Artists in the West are not lazy and therefore not artists but rather producers of something..... Their involvment with matters of no importance, such as production, promotion, gallery system, museum system, competition system (who is first), their preoccupation with objects, all that drives them away form laziness, from art. Just as money is paper, so is a gallery a room.

Artists from the East were lazy and poor because the entire sistem of insignificant factors did not exist. Therefore they had time enough to concetrate on art and laziness. Even when thay did produce art, they knew it was in vain, it was nothing.

Artists from the West could learn about laziness, but they didn't. Two major 20th centery artists treated the question of laziness, in both practical and theoretical terms: Duchamp and Malevich.

Duchamp never really discussed laziness, but rather indifference and non-work. When asked by Pierre Cabanne what had brought him most pleasure in life, Duchamp said: "First, having been lucky. Because basically I've never worked for a living. I consider working for a living slightly imbecilic from an economic point of view. I hope that some day we'll be able to live without being obliged to work. Thanks to my luck, I was able to manage without getting wet".

Malevich wrote a text entitled "Laziness - the real truth of mankind" (1921). In it he criticized capitalism because it enabled only a small number of capitalists to be lazy, butalso socialism because the entire movement was based on work instead of laziness. To quote: "People are scared of laziness and persecute those who accept it, and it always happens because no one realizes laziness is the truth; it has bees branded as the mother of all vices, but it is in fact the mother of life. Socialism brings liberation in the unconscious, it scorns laziness without realizing it was laziness that gave birth to it; in his folly, the son scorns his mother as a mother of all vices and would not remove the brand; in this brief note I want to remove the brand of shame from laziness and to pronounce it not the mother of all vices, but the mother of perfection".

Finally, to be lazy and conclude: there is no art without laziness.

WORK IS A DISEASE - KARL MARX
Mladen Stilinović

WORK IS A SHAME
Vlado Martek

Mladen Stilinović

Cezary Bodzianowski

CEZARY BODZIANOWSKI
(B.1968, SZCZECIN)

A leading exponent of performance art in Poland, whose practice is based on subtle, often ephemeral interventions in social reality, much like conceptual gestures. His works, rooted in Dadaism and the performance art of the 1960s, explore the limits of art's visibility, questioning the institutional framework of the perception and reception of a message in art. Bodzianowski's brief text shows the artist to be inextricably bound with art, whose work is both a process of self-exploration and self-destruction in a creative act. This is a reflection on the line between the individual and the work; the artist loses themselves in the art, becoming an integral, almost impersonal part of it.

Cezary Bodzianowski, a text to accompany the exhibition *Herbalife* (2023) at the Foksal Gallery Foundation in Warsaw.

[UNTITLED]
The artist, in creating art,
involuntarily becomes the essence of art itself,
drawing from it and from himself,
pursuing it and himself,
escaping from it and from himself
by creating with his whole self
until he dissolves into
the boundless ocean of art.

2023

EMPLOYEES THE IN ŁÓDŹ

OF
MUZEUM SZTUKI

EMPLOYEES OF THE MUZEUM SZTUKI IN ŁÓDŹ (OCTOBER 2025)

DIRECTOR
DANIEL MUZYCZUK

DEPUTY DIRECTOR FOR PROMOTION AND DISSEMINATION
LESZEK KARCZEWSKI

CHIEF ACCOUNTANT
KATARZYNA HODYNIUK

CONTROL MANAGEMENT OFFICER
ANDŻELIKA BAUER

HEAD OF THE HERBST PALACE MUSEUM
MAGDALENA MICHALSKA-SZAŁACKA

ASSISTANT TO THE DIRECTOR
FRANCISZEK SMORĘDA

OFFICE
JOANNA BRZESKA
DOROTA PLESIAK (DEPARTMENT HEAD)
MARZENA SZYBKA

DEPARTMENT OF MODERN ART
JAKUB GAWKOWSKI (DEPARTMENT HEAD)
JULIANNA GOŹDZIK
KATARZYNA RÓŻNIAK-SZABELSKA

DEPARTMENT OF THE MODERN ART COLLECTION
WIESŁAW ŁUCZAJ (DEPARTMENT HEAD)
ANNA PACYNIAK
PAWEŁ POLIT
PAWEŁ SOSNOWSKI
BOGUMIŁA TERZYJSKA

HISTORICAL ART DEPARTMENT OF THE HERBST PALACE MUSEUM
JOANNA CIEMIŃSKA
KATARZYNA KOŃCZAL (HISTORICAL ART AND EDUCATION)
MARIA MILANOWSKA
TOMASZ HELBIK (EDUCATION)
JOANNA JAŚKIEWICZ (EDUKACJA)
TATIANA SZYMAŃSKA (EDUCATION)
DOROTA WITUŁA (COMMUNICATION)

MUSEUM RESEARCH CENTER
WANDA JANAKIEWICZ
NATALIA SŁABOŃ (DEPARTMENT HEAD)

DEPARTMENT OF MAIN INVENTORY
KATARZYNA MRÓZ (DEPARTMENT HEAD)
MONIKA TROSZCZYŃSKA-ANTOSIK

DEPARTMENT OF PRESERVATION OF THE COLLECTION
ANITA ANDRZEJCZAK
KATARZYNA FORYSIAK
NAOKO KAMOJI
MAŁGORZATA KOWALSKA
TATIANA MATWIJ (DEPARTMENT HEAD)
EWELINA PAWLAK

DEPARTMENT OF EDUCATION
WIKTORIA HŁADKO
ADAM OLCZAK-LIPMAN
AGATA RYNKOWSKA
MAŁGORZATA STASIAK (DEPARTMENT HEAD)
MAŁGORZATA WIKTORKO
MARTA WLAZEŁ
PAWEŁ WOJDA

LIBRARY AND DEPARTMENT OF SCIENTIFIC DOCUMENTATION
ANETA BŁASZCZYK-SMOLEC (DEPARTMENT HEAD)
MACIEJ CHOLEWIŃSKI
MONIKA CYWIŃSKA-PRYT
AGATA MENDRYCHOWSKA
BARBARA MOKRZYCKA
MARTA PIERZCHAŁA
MILENA ROMANOWSKA
MARTA SKŁODOWSKA
MARCIN STASIEWICZ

DEPARTMENT OF EXHIBITIONS AND PUBLICATIONS
MARTYNA DEC
AGATA DZIRBA
ANNA PALUSIŃSKA
MIŁA POPOWSKA
EWELINA STRYNOWICZ
MONIKA WESOŁOWSKA (DEPARTMENT HEAD)
IZABELA WOJTYCZKA

DEPARTMENT OF COMMUNICATION
ANNA AUGUSTYN KAMIŃSKA
KLAUDIA BORZĘCKA
NATALIA KRÓLIKOWSKA (DEPARTMENT HEAD)
KINGA ŚWITONIAK

DEPARTMENT OF MARKETING
MONIKA AUGUSTYNIAK-DUMAŁA
NATALIA BIELECKA
BEATA PLAJZER
JAKUB SZYMAŃSKI
ANGELINA WIELICZKO-SKINDER (DEPARTMENT HEAD)

ACCOUNTANTS
ANNA MODLIŃSKA
AGNIESZKA PAWLAK
MONIKA PAWLICKA (DEPARTMENT HEAD)
BOGUMIŁA RUTKOWSKA

FUNDS
EMILIA ANTOSZ

LEGAL ADVISOR
MONIKA SOŁTYSZEWSKA

DEPARTMENT OF PERSONNEL
PAULINA CZESTKOWSKA
ANETA SATUR-KURCZAK (DEPARTMENT HEAD)

INVESTMENT AND INTERNAL CONTROL SPECIALIST
IWONA KRUPA

DEPARTMENT FOR ADMINISTRATION AND MANAGEMENT
IWONA AUGUSTYNIAK
WOJCIECH CIESIELSKI
ŁUKASZ JANICKI
ANNA MÓWIŃSKA (DEPARTMENT HEAD)
KONRAD PIANOWSKI
MAGDALENA PIETRZAK
ALEKSANDRA SCHIEWE
JOLANTA TRELA

DEPARTMENT FOR ADMINISTRATION AND MANAGEMENT OF THE HERBST PALACE MUSEUM
SŁAWOMIR BŁASZCZYK
MONIKA ERTEL
MARZENA JĘDRZEJCZAK
ANDRZEJ KACPRZAK
REGINA KMIECIŃSKA
JOWITA KORCZ
IWONA KOTKOWSKA-FURMANIAK
LUCYNA KROLL
MONIKA KUŹBIŃSKA-DAWID
ADAM MĄKA
KINGA MICHAŁOWSKA
IZABELA PIOTROWSKA-ŻMURKOW
PATRYCJA PLASZCZYK
URSZULA SAWOŚCIAN
AGATA SMACZNA
WIOLETTA SOBOLEWSKA
TOMASZ STAWIŃSKI

MAŁGORZATA SZEFLER-
-MILCZAREK
(DEPARTMENT HEAD)
MAŁGORZATA WITEK
SYLWESTER WROŃSKI

SAFETY, HYGIENE
AND FIRE REGULATIONS
RADOSŁAW RUTKOWSKI

TECHNICAL BRIGADE
ZBIGNIEW DWORAK
KRZYSZTOF FRANCEK
MARIUSZ KRĘŻEL
MAREK KUBACKI
ADAM MAJ
DARIUSZ MIKOŁAJCZYK
IRENEUSZ SZYMAREK
DARIUSZ ŚMIECHURA
MACIEJ WIĘCŁAWSKI

VISITOR SERVICES
MIROSŁAW BĄK
KATARZYNA
CHAŁACZKIEWICZ-MOSKWA
MAGDALENA FILIŃSKA
TOMASZ JAGODZIŃSKI
KRZYSZTOF KALINOWSKI
KLARA KAWECKA
BEATA KAŹMIERCZAK
SYLWIA KAŹMIERCZAK
IWONA KĘCIK-BASTA
HALINA KOWALCZYK
ANETA MAJ
MARIUSZ MAJ
MARZENA MAŃSKA
DAMIAN MICHNIK
ANNA NASTAROWICZ
AGNIESZKA PODEDWORNA
MAŁGORZATA
PODKOWA-STASIŃSKA
ANNA RABIEGA
RENATA RAJEWSKA
JOANNA RASZ
MONIKA RATAJCZYK
MICHAŁ SKUNKA
ALEKSANDRA
SZERSZYŃSKA
WERONIKA SZMAJA
ANNA WARZYŃSKA
MAGDALENA WENERSKA
ANNA WESOŁOWSKA
MAGDALENA WESOŁOWSKA
IZABELA WESOŁOWSKA
GRZEGORZ WOŹNIAK
AGNIESZKA WÓJTOWICZ-
-SKUNKA
NATALIIA YURCHENKO

PROTECTION
OF CLASSIFIED
INFORMATION
DARIUSZ MAJCHRZAK

Publication accompanying
the exhibition
*Ways of Seeing. Collection of
Muzeum Sztuki in Łódź*

Muzeum Sztuki w Łodzi
ms²
ul. Ogrodowa 19
91–065 Łódź
opening: October 17, 2025

CURATORS
Jakub Gawkowski
Daniel Muzyczuk
Paweł Polit
Katarzyna Różniak-
-Szabelska
Franciszek Smoręda

ARCHITECTURE
Maciej Siuda Pracownia
(Adrianna Gruszka,
Maciej Siuda)

GRAPHIC DESIGN
Kaja Kusztra

EXHIBITION
COORDINATION
Martyna Dec
Ewelina Strynowicz

EDITORIAL COORDINATION
Agata Dzirba
Matylda Makowska
Izabela Wojtyczka

MUSEUM RESEARCH
CENTER
Wanda Janakiewicz
Natalia Słaboń

EDUCATION
Wiktoria Hładko
Adam Olczak-Lipman
Agata Rynkowska
Małgorzata Stasiak
Małgorzata Wiktorko
Marta Wlazeł

COMMUNICATION
Anna Augustyn Kamińska
Klaudia Borzęcka
Natalia Królikowska
Kinga Świtoniak

CONSERVATION
Anita Andrzejczak
Katarzyna Forysiak
Naoko Kamoji
Małgorzata Kowalska
Tatiana Matwij
Ewelina Pawlak

MUSEUM COLLECTION
STORAGE
Paweł Sosnowski
Bogumiła Terzyjska

MARKETING
Natalia Bielecka
Angelina
Wieliczko-Skinder

INSTALLATION TEAM
Zbigniew Dworak
Krzysztof Francek
Łukasz Janicki
Mariusz Krężel
Marek Kubacki
Adam Maj
Mariusz Maj
Adam Mąka
Damian Michnik
Dariusz Mikołajczyk
Konrad Pianowski
Michał Skunka
Tomasz Stawiński
Ireneusz Szymarek
Dariusz Śmiechura
Maciej Więcławski

Instytucja Kultury Samorządu Województwa Łódzkiego współprowadzona przez Ministra Kultury i Dziedzictwa Narodowego

patronaty honorowe

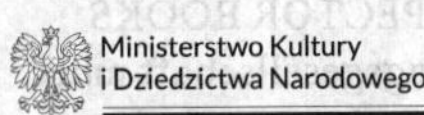

mecenas wystawy

partnerzy

INSTYTUT ADAMA MICKIEWICZA

patronaty medialne

SZUM

DailyArt MAGAZINE

Ways Of Seeing. Collection of Muzeum Sztuki in Łódź. Reader

EDITORS
Daniel Muzyczuk
Natalia Słaboń

TRANSLATION
Jennifer Croft
Soren Gauger
Katarzyna Gucio
Jerzy Jarniewicz
Łukasz Mojsak
Josef Schreiner
Jan Szelągiewicz
Marcin Wawrzyńczak
& Ewa Dratwa

COPY-EDITING AND PROOFREADING
Nicholas Hodge

EDITORIAL COORDINATION
Agata Dzirba
Matylda Makowska
Izabela Wojtyczka

PHOTOGRAPHS
Department of Scientific Documentation, Muzeum Sztuki in Łódź

GRAPHIC DESIGN, TYPESETTING AND IMAGES EDITING
Kaja Kusztra

PRINTED BY:
Drukmania s.c.

PUBLISHED BY:

ms
Muzeum Sztuki

Muzeum Sztuki w Łodzi
ul. Więckowskiego 36
90–734 Łódź
msl.org.pl

SPECTOR BOOKS
Verlagsgesellschaft mbH
Harkortstraße 10
04107 Leipzig
www.spectorbooks.com

DISTRIBUTION:

GERMANY, AUSTRIA:
GVA, Gemeinsame Verlagsauslieferung
Göttingen GmbH&Co. KG,
www.gva-verlage.de

SWITZERLAND:
AVA Verlagsauslieferung AG,
www.ava.ch

FRANCE, BELGIUM:
Interart Paris,
www.interart.fr

UK:
Central Books Ltd,
www.centralbooks.com

USA, CANADA, CENTRAL
AND SOUTH AMERICA, AFRICA:
ARTBOOK/ D.A.P.,
www.artbook.com

JAPAN:
twelvebooks,
www.twelve-books.com

SOUTH KOREA:
The Book Society,
www.thebooksociety.org

AUSTRALIA, NEW ZEALAND:
Perimeter Distribution,
www.perimeterdistribution.com

First edition: 2025

Printed in the EU

Spector Books ISBN
978-3-95905-935-0
Muzeum Sztuki in Łódź ISBN
978-83-66696-65-5